Also by Ze'ev Chafets

DOUBLE VISION

HEROES AND HUSTLERS, HARD HATS AND HOLY MEN

MEMBERS OF THE TRIBE

DEVIL'S NIGHT:
And Other True
Tales of Detroit

DEVIL'S NIGHT:

And Other True
Tales of Detroit

ZE'EV CHAFETS

Random House New York

Grateful acknowledgment is made to the following for permission to reprint
previously published material:

THE DETROIT NEWS: Excerpts from a column by Chuck Moss, September 20, 1989;
excerpts from an interview between the editorial board of *The Detroit News* and
Mayor Young, October 19, 1989; excerpts from an article by Chauncey Bailey,
November 11, 1989. Copyright © 1989 *The Detroit News.* Reprinted by
permission of *The Detroit News,* a Gannett Newspaper.
JOBETE MUSIC CO., INC.: Excerpt from "Dancing in the Street" by Marvin Gaye,
William Stevenson, and Ivy Hunter. Copyright © 1964 Jobete Music Co., Inc.,
and Stone Agate Music. Published by Jobete Music Co., Inc./Stone Agate Music.
Reprinted by permission.
DUDLEY RANDALL: Excerpt from "Detroit Renaissance" from *A Litany of Friends*
by Dudley Randall. Copyright © 1981 by Dudley Randall. Reprinted by
permission of Dudley Randall.
THE RICHMOND ORGANIZATION: Excerpt from "We Shall Overcome" by Zilphia
Horton, Frank Hamilton, Guy Carawan, and Pete Seeger. Copyright © 1960
(renewed) by The Richmond Organization. Copyright © 1963 by Ludlow Music,
Inc., New York, N.Y. Reprinted by permission.

Library of Congress Cataloging-in-Publication Data

Chafets, Ze'ev.
Devil's night: and other true tales of Detroit/by Ze'ev Chafets.
p. cm.
ISBN 0-394-58525-9
1. Detroit (Mich.)—Race relations.   2. Detroit (Mich.)—Social conditions.   I.
Title.
F574.D49N4333 1990
305.8'96073077434—dc20   90-8275

Manufactured in the United States of America
24689753
First Edition

BOOK DESIGN BY LILLY LANGOTSKY

FOR KIM WESTON, WHO WANTS TO SAVE THE WORLD.

Personal Note

This book was written in Detroit, where I lived during the last half of 1988 and, again, for several months of 1989. It is a personal account, based on people I met, things I saw and events in which I participated.

During the course of my stay in Detroit, I interviewed hundreds of people. In most cases it was impractical to use a tape recorder. I took notes or, on some occasions, reconstructed conversations from memory. Thus, the quotes in this book are not, for the most part, stenographic reproductions; some have been edited for length, others are close approximations. In every case, however, they are accurate reflections of what people actually said.

This book could not have been written without the help of a great many people. Foremost among them are two good friends: Arthur

Samuelson, who provided encouragement and expert advice at a critical juncture, and Gary Baumgarten, one of America's finest reporters, who gave me my first lessons on the city of Detroit. I would also like to thank Joseph Colten, Doug Ross, Beatrice Buck, Bob Berg, Chauncey Bailey, David Lawrence, Max Silk, Gary Miller, Cassandra Smith-Gray, Gerald Clark, Fred Williams, Dave Scott, Doron Levine, Steve Franklin, Sue Smock, Irving Bluestone, Nimrod Rosenthal, Bill McGraw, Linda Jones and Janis Goldstein for their generous assistance. I would also like to thank the many Detroiters and suburbanites who shared their insights about their city and their lives. All of them made a contribution to my understanding of Detroit, but, naturally, none is responsible for the finished product.

I want to thank my agent, Esther Newberg of ICM, who helped save this project at a very difficult juncture. And I particularly want to thank David Rosenthal, my editor at Random House, who believed in this book and made it possible.

Contents

DEVIL'S NIGHT:
And Other True Tales of Detroit

Introduction:
DEVIL'S NIGHT

It was in the fall of 1986 that I first saw the devil on the streets of Detroit.

We were introduced by a friend who works for a local radio station. "Spend the evening before Halloween with me and I'll show you something you've never seen before," he promised. "People try to burn down their own neighborhoods. They call it Devil's Night."

I vaguely remembered Devil's Night. When I was a kid growing up in Pontiac, a grimy industrial clone of Detroit ten miles north of the city, it had been a time of harmless pranks—window soaping, doorbell ringing and rolls of toilet paper in the neighbors' trees. But it had been twenty years since I lived there, and a lot of things had changed. One of them was Devil's Night.

Three years earlier, in 1983, for reasons no one understands,

America's sixth largest city suddenly erupted into flame. Houses, abandoned buildings, even unused factories burned to the ground in an orgy of arson that lasted for seventy-two hours. When it was over the papers reported more than eight hundred fires. Smoke hung over the city for days.

What at first appeared to be a bizarre outburst turned into an annual tradition. By 1986, Devil's Night had become a prelude to Halloween in Detroit in the way that Mardi Gras precedes Lent in New Orleans, or the Rose Bowl parade ushers in the New Year in Pasadena.

Even my friend's dramatic description did not prepare me for what I saw that night. From early evening, fires flared throughout the city. The scent of burning wood in the crisp Michigan autumn evening filled me with an incongruous nostalgia for the homecoming rallies I once attended at the University of Michigan. On the streets of Detroit I could sense the same rush of energy, the same sense of excitement that always accompanies nocturnal action. Police helicopters circled overhead and fire trucks, sirens blaring, raced from one conflagration to another. Cops guarded the firemen as they fought the flames. It was only when I saw the faces of the neighborhood people, mostly older blacks with long coats over their bathrobes, standing grimly on their porches, armed with shotguns and garden hoses, protecting their property, that I realized that this was no homecoming rally; on Devil's Night, they use homes for kindling.

At each fire there were crowds of onlookers. Some were black neighborhood kids in stocking caps and high school jackets. Others were white adults—professional fire fighters from surrounding townships on a busman's holiday and civilian thrill seekers from the suburbs, many of them on their one annual trip into the city. The crowds were augmented by people who had come from all over the United States, Europe and the Far East to participate in Devil's Night, the fire buff's Superbowl.

My friend's car was equipped with a police-band radio, and as he drove from fire to fire he gradually became the leader of a motorcade. At every stop, people gawked at the flames and passed around bottles of whiskey and thermos caps of steaming coffee. The suburbanites talked with bittersweet nostalgia about their old neighborhoods in Detroit, pointed to childhood sites now sunk into decrepitude and shook their heads. The message was tacit but unmistakable—Look at what *they're* doing to *our* city.

The biggest blaze of the evening was in a lumberyard. As fire fighters worked to put it out, a television crew from Tokyo suddenly appeared. The cameraman and reporter jabbered excitedly in Japanese and broken English, trying to find someone who could explain what was happening. They interviewed a man from Dallas, "Ah come up here every year," the Texan said happily. "There's nothing like it. Ah never miss a one."

Detroit that night seemed like some grotesque urban horror film. At the lumberyard, a patrol of Guardian Angels, pasty-faced kids in berets and sweatshirts, happened by. They had come down from Grand Rapids, two hours away, to help the fire fighting effort. The white spectators cheered them, and some of the blacks booed. The Angels took a break, watching the flames shoot into the dark night as they munched on candy bars.

At every stop there were rumors and speculation. Someone who had just come from dinner at the Summit, a posh restaurant atop the downtown Renaissance Center, said that suburbanite patrons were cheering the fires as they dined alongside revolving glass walls. A fat man with a droopy mustache claimed that a family was trapped inside a burning house on the east side, and led a party of sightseers off to look for them. A debate broke out about who was setting the fires—teenage hoodlums, wealthy slumlords after insurance money, feuding neighbors trying to settle old scores. The spectators swapped tales of previous Devil's Nights and watched the fire fighters' work with practiced eyes.

The fires raged on and on, more than two hundred that night (and, I later learned, almost four hundred in the three-day Halloween period). Detroit is a city of one- and two-story homes, most of them built on narrow lots. During the past thirty years, the city has lost almost half its population, and there are entire blocks where all but one or two of the houses are boarded up and vacant. Some parts of the city look like pasture land. Flames raced through the brush and into abandoned wood buildings. The gawkers cheered the firemen and jostled one another happily. Devil's Night 1986 was judged a resounding success.

At dawn, on the way home, I asked the reporter what it was all about. "Fuck if I know," he said in a weary tone. "Frustration, anger, boredom. I only work here. I stopped trying to figure out this city a long time ago."

So had I. In 1967 I moved to Israel, and in the intervening years I had rarely thought about Detroit at all. I knew in general terms that the auto industry was in bad shape; that the 1967 riot had sent whites fleeing to the suburbs in droves; that the city was now mostly black, and had a black mayor, Coleman Young; and that the national press referred to it as "Murder Capital, USA." Beyond that, Detroit held little interest for me.

But the fires of Devil's Night sparked my curiosity. Approaching forty, I found myself unexpectedly drawn to my old hometown, a place that had gone in one generation from a wealthy white industrial giant to a poverty-stricken black metropolis. I resolved that night to come back to the city, and to write about it.

For me, this was the closing of a circle. As a small boy I had always been fascinated by black people. In the gray monotony of a Michigan car-town they seemed like vivid, foreign strangers. I can still remember my earliest glimpses of the black section of town, ripe with intimations of exotic vitality and mystery.

There was one intersection in particular, Bagley and Wesson, known as The Corner, that captured my imagination. It was nothing special—a few country-looking stores, a small hotel, LaRoaches Tea Room, the Big Six Republican Club pool hall—but whenever I passed it I longed to leave the safety of my parents' Chevrolet and find out what was going on. I wanted to taste the food at LaRoaches, hear the musical banter of the poolroom, touch the dark flesh of the laughing women who stood on the street in front of the shabby hotel. I wanted to peek into people's homes and lives, find out why they were different from me, so different that they inhabited a separate world of their own.

Of course I never did, at least not then. The Corner had a fearsome reputation—Pontiac people claimed with perverse pride that it had once been listed by *Time* magazine as the most dangerous intersection in America—and I was afraid. Besides, I was too young to go wandering around strange neighborhoods, black or white, by myself.

And so, like other white kids drawn to the black world, I found safe substitutes. I listened to radio stations out of Detroit and learned the names of esoteric r&b artists, traded Ted Williams for Willie Mays even up, and practiced a loose-limbed ghetto strut in the mirror behind my bedroom door.

Then, when I was thirteen, something happened that gave a new dimension to my feeling about blacks. That year, my grandfather Max was beaten to death.

Max Chafets left Russia to escape the Czar's army and wound up first in Windsor, Canada, and then in Detroit. He was a gentle little socialist who raised three children, read the Yiddish papers every day and rooted for the good guys when he watched wrestling on television. For years he made a modest living with a small mom-and-pop store in a black neighborhood. When he opened the store he knew nothing about blacks, and unlike me, he was never fascinated by them. But he did care about people, and sometimes he had nightmares about the Ku Klux Klan chasing and hurting the children who bought Popsicles and Maryjanes in his store.

Max's daughter, Ruth, married a man named Jack Fine, who had his own grocery on the corner of Linwood and Grand, a neighborhood that went from Jewish to black in the mid-1950s. When Max retired, and sold his little store, he went to work part-time for his son-in-law. On Saturday mornings, when Jack went to the Eastern Market to buy produce, Max would take over, humming Yiddish melodies to himself as he stood behind the counter, next to the cash register.

On one of those Saturday mornings, only a few days after my grandfather celebrated his seventieth birthday, two black men entered the store. They pulled guns and demanded money. Max gave it to them. Then, for some reason, one of them pistol-whipped him. An hour later, he died in the emergency room of Detroit's Receiving Hospital.

My grandfather's death traumatized our family. For a full year afterward, my father and uncle got up at daybreak to say the prayer for the dead in synagogue. They mourned in the traditional way, refusing to go out for pleasure, or even to watch television. I recall that year as a harsh, painful time, made worse by my private sense of guilt.

Beyond a generalized liberalism, my parents had no special feelings about blacks. It was I who filled the house with the sounds of Ray Charles and Bo Diddley, insisted on being Elgin Baylor in neighborhood pickup games, demanded to be driven, time and again, past The Corner, for yet another glimpse of the exotic black world. And now two black killers had beaten my grandfather to death. For a time I was full of fear and bitterness and a strange sense of complicity. I had wanted to know the dark secrets of the ghetto; now they had invaded my own family in a way I hadn't imagined.

At about this time I met Charles. I was shooting baskets with some friends at a nearby playground when he turned up. For a while he stood silently and watched. My friends and I were all white, and pretty good, but from time to time we heard him emit a contemptuous snort.

The game ended, and playground court etiquette demanded that we allow him to pick a team for the next one. He was five-nine or so, broad across the shoulders but thin and very dark. His hair was cut close to his skull, his nose was narrow and flared sharply at the nostrils, and he had thin, cruel lips. There was something regal and fierce-looking about him, like the leader of a slave rebellion. I guessed he was a year or two older than us, probably fifteen or so.

Somebody tossed the ball to Charles and for a moment he stood there fondling it. Then, with the quickest move I had even seen, he faked his head upward, took several powerful dribbles to the basket, flew into the air and dunked the ball. No one had ever come close to dunking in one of our games, and we stood there frozen in amazement.

Charles chose me as one of his teammates, and we stayed on the court for the rest of the afternoon, unbeatable. I remember playing harder that day than I had ever played before, and once or twice I made a move or hit a shot that elicited his approval. But it wasn't until I had a rebound snatched out of my hands that he seemed to really notice me. "Man, you gotta use your 'bows," he said angrily. "You can't 'bound unless you use your 'bows." That was the first, but by no means last, admonition I heard from Charles; typically, it was sound advice.

That day was the beginning of a friendship that lasted for many years and ended badly. It was a friendship made up of mutual envy and curiosity, boyhood competitiveness and more than a little hero worship on my part. For in a town of runners and jumpers, Charles could leap higher and sprint faster than anyone else. He could also dance cooler, talk sweeter, fight tougher and make love to more girls than anyone I had ever met. Naturally, I hoped that some of these attributes would rub off on me.

Although we were friends, the balance of power between us was clear: I was Tom Sawyer to Charles's Huck Finn. He accepted his role of mentor naturally and with grace, and imparted wisdom with generosity. Once, when some bigger kids tried to coerce me into "loaning" them my lunch money, Charles found out and forced me to fight one of them. "You can't let nobody hold your money but you," he said, a sound fiscal principle that remained with me long after the swelling on the side of my face receded. After the fight, Charles inspected the damage with dispassion. "You ain't always gonna have Daddy and Mommy to give you bread, gray boy," he said. "You gotta learn not to let people take anything away from you."

Some of Charles's other advice was more gentle. It was he who taught me the secrets of teenage sex. "If you want to get some, you gotta ask for it," he instructed me. He also provided me with an infallible guide for knowing if "it" would be forthcoming. "When you dance with a girl, put your hand on her ass," he told me. "If she doesn't move it, she's gonna give you some." Twenty-five years later, that remains the single most reliable piece of sex education I ever received.

Charles and I shared a mutual curiosity about each other's world. He came to my house often and, to my mystification, enjoyed talking to my parents. In these discussions he assumed an adult attitude, casting me in the role of small companion. "This young man been neglectin' his studies," he would say avuncularly, although Charles himself was scarcely a paragon of scholarship. Still, he had his pretensions. On one occasion, he borrowed a paperback copy of the dialogues of Plato from our library, and carried it around in his back pocket for weeks. This brush with philosophy led to an incident at school, where Charles was a grade ahead of me. One day in the lunchroom a white teacher, spying the book, asked about it.

"Plato," said Charles. "He's my man. That Greek was a stone genius."

"And which is your favorite dialogue?" asked the teacher with heavy sarcasm. "'The Republic,' no doubt."

Charles looked at the teacher with contempt. "Man, Plato was a Democrat up to his nose," he said. Several teachers' pet types laughed, and for a brief moment my hero appeared ridiculous.

I hated the teacher, who was no Aquinas himself, for the putdown, but Charles took it with good nature. "Lot of white people think they smarter than they are," he explained, and proved it by slashing all four of the teacher's tires.

In the end, though, I was far more interested in Charles's world than he was in mine, and he became my guide to its mysteries. He taught me black English, although he wouldn't let me speak it. When I lapsed into the dialect he was both amused and offended. "Don't be talkin' like no splib, gray boy," he would say. "It make you sound common. You don't hear me tryin' to sound like no Jew, now, do you?" He was right, of course; Charles had perfect pitch for the resonances of his culture.

I doubt if he thought it *was* a culture; at least he never would have used such a big word. But hanging around his tiny house in the projects, I learned about extended families, the harsh limitations of poverty (which he insisted on calling "proverty," although he knew better), the solace of church and the self-hating color caste system among blacks, long before these things became the subjects of Black Studies courses and *Time* magazine essays.

Still, this knowledge was the by-product of a boyhood friendship. I was no teenage anthropologist, and mostly I concentrated on having a good time. Charles took me to breakfast dances at the Pontiac Armory and sock hops at the Colored Elks. We played ball together; listened to B. B. King, Nolan Strong and the Drifters on his mother's phonograph; sat in the park outside the recreation center and flirted with the neighborhood girls. And, on one memorable day, when I was sixteen, Charles took me to The Corner for the first time, to shoot pool in the Big Six Republican Club.

Even as a teenager, Charles was treated with respect by the men and boys who hung around The Corner, the basketball courts and the other places we frequented. In the beginning, my presence there aroused curiosity, but Charles defused it, saying that we were "goin' for cousins," or introduced me as his "play brother." After a while people came to take me for granted. A few of them became friends.

Jesse Stephen, the preacher's son, invited me to his father's church, where I first heard live gospel music. It was Jesse who taught me to replace my *American Bandstand* clap with the sanctified slap, and also once processed my hair. Ralph Grandberry, an overweight pool hustler with an artistic touch, helped me forge my first fake ID, which we used to buy and drain a fifth of Peppermint Schnapps. And Roy Ray Jones, an incipient radical who later became one of the first American deserters in Vietnam, gave me a recording of Malcolm X's "Message to the Grass Roots."

Roy Ray notwithstanding, politics played a very minor role for Charles and his friends. It was the height of the civil rights movement but we rarely discussed segregation or the Freedom Riders. When Martin Luther King came to Detroit for a march, in the summer of 1963, I couldn't convince Charles to attend. "I ain't left nothin' in Alabama," he said, dismissing the matter. I went alone, and was thrilled by the moral seriousness of the event.

A few months later, John F. Kennedy was assassinated. We heard the news over the high school PA system. As we filed solemnly out of the building, the Pontiac attitude was verbalized by a skinny friend of ours named Jewel. "Um, um, um," he intoned. "Shot that motherfucker in the ass. No school on Monday. Um, um, um."

Charles eventually dropped out of high school. I graduated, and he came to the ceremony, inordinately proud of an accomplishment I took for granted. As a gift, he invited me to LaRoaches Tea Room, where he presided over dinner with the pickish good manners of a rich uncle.

After graduation I attended the University of Michigan. Charles got drafted, an event he called "going to the war," although he wound up at a fort in Kentucky. For more than a year we lost touch with one another, and I missed him. In his honor I wrote a whimsical paper for a philosophy class: "Plato, Republican or Democrat?" More than once I successfully applied his courtship techniques to Big Ten coeds. And one evening, at a bull session dominated by a black power bully who was trying to impress my date, I cut off his harangue with a "Get your face out of my face," that came right off The Corner and won me a respectful double take.

Then, one day, Charles turned up unexpectedly at my small apartment in Ann Arbor. He was accompanied by an extremely pregnant girlfriend, and informed me that he had dropped an engine block on a racist corporal and was on the run. Since my place was too small for all of us, I gave him my keys and told him to stay as long as he wanted. It never occurred to me that I might be harboring a fugitive, and it wouldn't have mattered if it had. Charles and I had been play brothers a long time.

After a couple of days, Charles stopped answering the phone when I called. I went to look for him, and found he had gone, taking a television set, radio and my only suit with him. I was puzzled but nothing more, figuring that he must have had a good reason. But a week later I still hadn't heard from him, and it began to dawn on me that I had, in the current phrase, been ripped off.

I called Charles's mother in Pontiac, and she gave me the address and phone number of a flophouse in Detroit's Twelfth Street ghetto, where he was hiding out. I called, but he refused to come to the phone. I called again and again, but there was no answer.

I really didn't care much about the suit and the appliances, but I was devastated by the idea that Charles had stolen from me. If he had asked, I would have gladly sold the stuff myself to give him money. I had long since stopped thinking of Charles as specifically black, but I regarded his betrayal in racial terms. I saw it as a message that, despite our long friendship, I was still one of *them,* a rich white kid, fair game.

There was only one way to prove otherwise. Late on a rainy Saturday night I drove an hour from Ann Arbor to the flophouse on Twelfth Street. I walked into the lobby and asked the rheumy-looking desk clerk for Charles's room number. The clerk gave me the number but looked alarmed. "No trouble now," he said, and for the first time I considered that there might be.

If there was, I had no doubt about how it would end. Charles was one of the most fearsome street fighters I had ever seen. Once I watched while he beat four white high school football players into bloody submission, cracking one over the head with a brick for good measure. "Don't fight to fight, fight to kill," was his dictum on the subject. I knew that if he felt like it, he could easily toss me out the window.

Still, I went up and knocked on the door. It was instinct, not bravery, that propelled me up the stairs. Even after he took my stuff, I couldn't believe that Charles would do me any physical harm.

"Charles," I hollered through the wooden door. "Let me in."

There were muffled sounds, and I hollered again, banging on the door. Afer a long moment it opened and he stood there, shirtless and barefoot, wearing only a pair of shorts. The pregnant girlfriend lay in silence on the bed.

"You took my things," I said, hoping he'd deny it, or explain. Instead he looked at me steadily for a while. Finally he reached into his wallet, which he called his "secretariat," and produced two pawn tickets, which he handed over.

"I can't believe this," I said, unwilling to let it go. "If you needed money, all you had to do was ask. You stole from me, man. You're a fucking thief."

For a second I thought I had gone too far, but then tears welled up in Charles's eyes. It was like seeing Superman cry, and I covered my astonishment with anger. "Why?" I demanded. "Why in hell did you have to steal from me? I would have given you anything you wanted, don't you know that?"

"I didn't want to ask," he said. "I didn't know how to ask for any help." Tears rolled down his cheeks, but I was dry-eyed. My best friend had let me down, but he had also let me off the hook. I didn't have to care about his problems anymore.

We stood facing one another in silence. "Don't tell your mother," he said finally.

"My mother couldn't care less," I lied.

Charles said nothing. Then, from the corner of the room, the pregnant girlfriend spoke for the first time. "He's desperate," she said. "Can't you see that he's desperate?"

I looked at him hard and I saw that it was true; Charles, the baddest young blood on The Corner, was terrified. Standing there facing him, I sensed a subtle but unmistakable shift in the balance of our relationship. Charles was no longer a charismatic idol; he was just a young black man on the run, and he knew that when they found him he was going to catch hell. I belonged to the class of white people who would soon be running his life—federal agents and lawyers, judges and wardens. Mixed with my anger and sorrow, I felt a guilty, undeniable surge of power.

I turned to go, and remembered that there were only two pawn tickets. "How about the suit?" I asked.

"I wanna keep it, wear it to church tomorrow," said Charles.

"Man, I can't let you keep it, you know that," I said. "I learned that from you." He nodded at the justice of the remark, opened the closet and handed me the neatly pressed suit. I was on my way out the door when the girlfriend spoke again.

"Don't seem like you learned a thing," she said in a quiet, venomous voice. "Seems like you didn't learn one damn thing."

When I got back to Ann Arbor, I told several white classmates about my encounter with Charles. Their attitude was unsympathetic; what did I expect from a black kid from the projects? It was 1966, and they were University of Michigan liberals. None was ill-mannered enough to blame Charles himself. Instead they talked about his socioeconomic background and the forces of racism that made such behavior inevitable.

At first I resisted this analysis. Charles was my friend, not some case study. I thought of him at my bar mitzvah, tipsy on champagne, proudly wishing a long-practiced "mazel tov" to my parents; gently wiping the blood off my face after forcing me to fight the kid who tried to take my lunch money; lying next to me on the grass near the basketball court, singing snatches of Drifters songs and talking dreamily about what life would be like when we grew up. I knew Charles; I knew him well enough to blame him, personally, for betraying our friendship and his own nature.

And yet, despite this knowledge, I gradually came to see what happened in the same impersonal way my classmates did. What *can* you expect? I asked myself. It's not his fault, it's the way society made him. It was the easiest way of understanding what had happened, a thought that helped me forgive Charles and dismiss him from my life.

I didn't see Charles again after that night. A few months later I moved to Israel. I was able to take only a few things with me from The Corner: a dozen gospel albums, my Malcolm X recording, and some memories. Occasionally something from the old days would pop up. I was in the Israeli army, for example, when I read in the paper that Roy Ray was now living in Sweden. But after a while the records became scratched, and my memories faded. Detroit, The Corner, Charles—it was all part of another life. Until Devil's Night, 1986.

Chapter One

"WHITE PEOPLE DON'T KNOW A GODDAMNED THING"

I flew into Detroit in early July 1988. From the air the urban sprawl seemed as intricate and harmonious as a Persian carpet. The sun glinted off the Detroit River, which separates the city from Canada, and winked back from the tops of skyscrapers in the compact business district. At thirty thousand feet there was no hint that many of the tall buildings were empty, the streets deserted and the little houses full of people divided by fierce tribal rivalries.

As the plane flew over the city I could see the wide boulevards that fan out, like the fingers of a hand, from the city's riverfront center. I picked out Jefferson Avenue, which runs parallel to the river past the Chrysler factory out to the WASP stronghold of Grosse Pointe; Gratiot (the name an homage to Detroit's origins as a French trading post, but pronounced locally as "Grashit"), leading to the

Polish and Italian suburbs of the northeast; Michigan Avenue, which passes Tiger Stadium on its way west to the Ford plants and the Arab and redneck enclave of Dearborn; and, bisecting the city, the grandest boulevard of them all, Woodward Avenue, heading due north past the mile roads—Six, Seven—all the way out to the city's border, Eight Mile Road.

The geography of Detroit has not changed since my childhood. It is the demography that is different. In 1960, there were 1,670,000 people in the city, about 70 percent of them white. Poles and Italians lived in neat little boxlike homes along quiet streets on the east side. Jews and WASPs inhabited more substantial brick houses on the other side of Woodward Avenue. Blacks, who made up less than a third of the population, were crowded mostly into small neighborhoods downtown, near the river.

Detroit in those days was less a big city than a federation of ethnic villages bound together by auto plants, a place with more basements and bowling alleys than any other metropolis in the country. The only hint of sophistication was downtown. Woodward Avenue was lined with impressive mock gothic churches, an art museum and library, fine shops and grand theaters. At the heart of the hub were skyscrapers, citadels of commerce, where the paperwork for the Motor City of the world was signed and filed. Detroiters felt an awe and affection for their downtown that was unmatched in other, more urban cities.

The touchstone was Hudson's Department Store, a block-wide emporium that was the site of an annual winter pilgrimage for the city's children. Every year in December our mothers took us to the toy department, where we sat on Santa's knee (a pleasure only slightly diminished by my yearly admission that I was Jewish, and didn't really want anything for Christmas). Ask any white Detroiter over forty about his childhood, and he is likely to mention Hudson's.

Later, as teenagers, we spent Christmas week downtown at the

Fox Theater, watching the Motown Revue (Marvin Gaye, Little Stevie Wonder, the Supremes, the Miracles, the Marvellettes, the Temptations and a movie for two bucks). In the summer we cheered Al Kaline and the rest of the Tigers from seventy-five-cent bleacher seats and ate chili dogs at the Lafayette Coney Island. In those days Detroit seemed like a model American community, an impression confirmed by *Look* magazine in 1962 when it dubbed it "a city on the go."

Indeed, Detroit in the early sixties was what Los Angeles has since become—a place where poor people came to fulfill the American dream. Blacks and whites from the South, immigrants from southern and eastern Europe all came to work in the auto factories, where even an illiterate could find a steady, good-paying job and hope for something better for his children.

Like all dream cities, Detroit was not without a violent underside. In 1925, racial animosity boiled over when a black physician, Ossian Sweet, bought a home in a white neighborhood on the east side. An ugly crowd formed outside the house, and Sweet, along with some relatives and friends, barricaded himself inside. During the course of the incident, gunshots were fired from the house, and a white man was killed. Sweet and his friends were tried for murder, defended by Clarence Darrow, and after a second trial (in the first, the jury came to no decision) Sweet was acquitted.

Again in 1943, racial tensions spilled over into a riot, in which thirty-four people were killed and the army was called in to restore order. Nor was all the violence racially motivated; throughout the twenties and thirties, the auto unions fought bloody, occasionally fatal battles with company goons.

Still, people in Detroit tended to view these incidents as the unfortunate but necessary growing pains of an industrial giant. And, following World War II, in which Detroit became the Arsenal of Democracy, they seemed more and more a thing of the past. A year after the war, *Detroit Free Press* editorial director Malcolm W. Bingay described his city this way:

> The world is filled with talk of new ideals of government and business. And the thoughtless, as they prattle of such things, do not seem to realize that even these, like the motorcar, were born in Detroit.
>
> The whole modern philosophy of higher wages and shorter hours was born in Detroit, born in high vision and common sense ... Detroit has always led the world in high wages for its workmen.
>
> For years Detroit has been the talk of the world. European writers on our civilization have even coined the word "Detroitism," meaning the industrial age. From all parts of the globe, men have come to our doors to gain knowledge and inspiration. Detroit has been hailed as Detroit the Dynamic; Detroit the Wonder City.

In 1961, the Wonder City got a boy wonder for mayor, a thirty-three-year-old Irish lawyer named Jerome P. Cavanaugh, who bucked the Democratic establishment to win election. In office, Cavanaugh set about forming alliances with Walter Reuther's UAW, appointed a progressive chief of police, and brought blacks into municipal government. When Martin Luther King came to town in 1963, at the invitation of Reverend C. L. Franklin (Aretha's father), he was warmly welcomed by a city that regarded itself as the avant-garde of American liberalism.

In those days, everything seemed to be going in that direction. The vicious oligarchs of the auto industry had been replaced by brilliant technocrats who believed in computers and cooperation. One, Robert McNamara, was secretary of defense. Another, George Romney, widely considered a genius because he had concocted a way to save time by playing golf with three balls instead of one, was governor. On the labor side, Reuther and his followers were fast becoming partners, not adversaries, in the automotive dream.

The Cavanaugh administration epitomized the city's glowing image. The mayor was considered one of the brightest young stars in America, a politician with the perfect Kennedy-era blend of old-fashioned blarny and state-of-the-art technocracy. In 1965, at a national mayors' conference, he stunned his colleagues by unveiling a new system in which computers would constantly monitor developments on every block of the city, allowing experts to intervene at the first sign of economic or social dislocation.

The bubble burst on the twenty-third of July, 1967. A police raid on an after-hours club on Twelfth Street, in the heart of the black ghetto, erupted into rioting. Forty-three people were killed in the streets of Detroit—most of them blacks shot by police or National Guard. Whole neighborhoods were looted and torched. Cavanaugh's computers could do nothing to restore order. When the cops and National Guard failed to end the insurrection, President Johnson sent in 4,700 troops from the elite 82nd and 101st Airborne Divisions. Twice before, in 1863 and 1943, federal forces had been dispatched to put down racial disturbances in Detroit; their 1967 deployment made Detroit the only U.S. city in history to be occupied three times by the American army.

The Detroit riot was the worst of fifty-nine racial disturbances across the country in 1967; indeed, in terms of property damage and lives lost it was the worst in the twentieth century, and its impact on the city was dramatic. For Sale signs sprung up in every white neighborhood, seemingly in front of every house. There had always been a lot of vacant land outside the city, and Detroit's suburbs had been expanding slowly since the fifties; now developers threw up houses, schools and shopping malls beyond Eight Mile Road. Some people were so panicked that they spent the winter of 1967–68 sleeping on their relatives' couches, or shivered in half-completed tract homes. The riot touched off an exodus that left Detroit with a black majority within five years.

It also broke the spirit of Jerry Cavanaugh, who had left office in 1966 and run, unsuccessfully, for the Senate. His computers and good intentions had been useless in understanding the passions and grievances of the ghetto, just as McNamara's had proven worthless in deciphering the realities of Southeast Asia. In the mayoralty election of 1969, a moderate black candidate, Richard Austin, was narrowly defeated by Roman Gribbs, a former sheriff. But it was a last gasp; four years later, the now mostly black city elected its first black mayor, Coleman Young.

In the aftermath of the riot, Detroit became the national capital of disingenuous surprise. People suddenly discovered what should have been obvious—that beyond the glittering downtown, the leafy neighborhoods, the whirring computers, there was another city: poor, black and angry.

For years, Detroit's growing black population had been dealt with through repression and neglect. The police department recruited southern cops who knew how to deal with Negroes; blacks took a risk just walking down Woodward Avenue. There was no place for their children on Santa's knee at Hudson's, which only employed light-skinned sales personnel (paper bag brown was the darkest permissible hue). Residential segregation and urban renewal, which plowed down the old Black Bottom ghetto without replacing it, caused extreme crowding. It was only through the smoke of burning buildings that these things became visible.

A committee, New Detroit, was established, ostensibly to "attack and overcome the root causes of racial and social disorder." In fact, the committee, whose members included Detroit's business and industrial leaders, produced the rhetorical cover that enabled many of them to get themselves and their businesses out of town. A few whites did invest in the city. Henry Ford II helped finance the Renaissance Center, a gleaming white elephant of offices and stores, along the river. Suburban multimillionaires Max Fisher and Alfred Taubman put money into high-priced condos on the riverfront. But most of the city's merchants and financiers had no intention of leaving their money in Detroit, where any damn thing could touch off another riot. Besides, they argued, the money was already in the suburbs, and business is business.

Detroit's shift from a prosperous white city to a poor black one was extraordinarily fast; within six years of the riot, it had a black majority and a black administration. And the change was far more complete than in other major American cities. Chicago maintained stable white ethnic neighborhoods and a vital business district; Washington, D.C., remained anchored by the federal government, which provided jobs; in Atlanta, mayors from the civil rights movement built economic and political alliances with white suburbia.

But in Detroit, events conspired to leave the city uniquely impoverished, abandoned and militant. The bottom fell out of the auto industry, causing mass unemployment. The abundance of land beyond the municipal boundaries enabled surburbanites to create an alternative downtown in the suburb of Southfield. And the new mayor, Coleman Young, elected in 1973, did not come from the Southern Christian Leadership Conference. He was a militant former union man who consolidated power by adopting a confrontational policy toward the city's suburban neighbors.

For the two and a half million whites who lived in America's most segregated suburbs, Detroit became The Corner writ large—an alien, threatening wreck, a place to drive through, if at all, with the windows rolled up and the doors securely locked. Whites not only left the city physically, they abandoned it emotionally as well.

When I told suburban friends that I planned to live and work in Detroit they reacted with disbelief and alarm. Some suggested a bodyguard, others a pistol. Most, however, simply warned me that I would probably not survive six months as a white man in the Murder Capital of America.

I was not unaffected by their warnings. I had no Charles to vouch for me, and in the preceding twenty years I had lost whatever street smarts I once had. My first trips into the city were jumpy affairs, spent mostly looking out the window of my car; in a way, I was back in my parents' Chevy, watching the action, afraid to come too close.

This was not simple paranoia—Detroit today is genuinely a fearsome-looking place. Many of its neighborhoods appear to be the victims of a sadistic aerial bombardment—houses burned and vacant, buildings twisted and crumbling, whole city blocks overrun with weeds and the carcasses of discarded automobiles. Shopping streets are depressing avenues—banks converted into Fundamentalist churches, party stores with bars and boards on their windows and, here and there, a barbecue joint or saloon. The decay is everywhere, but it is especially noticeable on the east side, which has lost roughly half its residents in the past thirty years—the most extreme depopulation of any urban area in America.

Worst of all is downtown. Several of the landmarks on Woodward Ave. remain, and in the past few years there have been several grandiose building projects, but they can't obscure the fact that downtown Detroit is now pretty much empty. Hudson's stands deserted, and there isn't a single department store left in town. Entire skyscrapers—hotels, office buildings and apartment houses—are vacant and decaying.

During what should be rush hour, reporters from the *Free Press* play a macabre game, called King of the Corner. The object is to stand at a downtown intersection and look all four ways. If you can't see a single human being in any direction, you are King of the Corner. Every morning anoints its own royalty. Detroit, America's sixth largest city, is the only metropolis in the country where you can walk a downtown block during business hours without passing a living soul.

Suburban whites are dismayed by the physical degeneration of what was once their city, but they are truly terrified by its racial composition and the physical threat they associate with blacks, who constitute between 70 and 80 percent of the population. Some whites, mostly elderly, still live in the extremities of the city, and municipal employees are required to reside there by law (although a good many have fictitious addresses). But in most parts of town, most of the time, Detroit is as black as Nairobi.

The white abandonment of Detroit, coupled with the collapse of the auto economy, has left the city with a diminished tax base and a set of horrific social problems. Among the nation's major cities, Detroit was at or near the top in unemployment, per capita poverty, and infant mortality throughout the eighties.

The city is an impoverished island surrounded by prosperous suburbs, and almost nothing connects them. The Detroit area has virtually no mass transport, due mainly to the unwillingness of
suburbanites to make their communities accessible to blacks. A few
cultural institutions, such as the symphony and the art museum,
have remained in town, but they are patronized mostly by whites.
So are the Detroit Tigers and Red Wings (the Pistons and Lions play
in the suburbs). Detroit and its satellite towns share a water system,
two newspapers, and broadcasting facilities. The place where black
and white Detroit come most intimately together is on the airwaves,
where radio talk shows offer a steady diet of racially loaded charge
and countercharge.

Most of all, the city and suburbs are separated by a cultural and
emotional gap as wide as any that divides hostile nations. The suburbs purr with the contented sounds of post-Reagan America while
the city teeters on the brink of separatism and seethes with the
resentments of postcolonial Africa.

Twenty years in the Middle East had given me a good eye for
tribal animosity, and in Detroit, even during my first days there, I
recognized it. Strangely, it didn't seem personal. The local disposi-
tion is mild, even friendly. A great many people, black and white,
were born in the South, and it shows in their manners. Strangers nod
to one another on the street and make small talk in elevators. Standing next to one another at public urinals, men smile and say "How
y'doin?" Black and white Detroiters rarely meet, but when they
do—at work, in suburban shopping malls or at other neutral sites—
it is not at all unusual for them to get along amicably.

In fact, the tribal rivalries, fears and hatred in Detroit tend to be
collective and abstract. Each side has an orthodox, almost ritual
explanation for what has happened to the city they once shared and
no longer do, and, not surprisingly, each side blames the other.

Shortly after coming to the city I was introduced to Tom De Lisle,
an engaging man in his early forties who grew up in Detroit and, in
the seventies, served as spokesman for the city's last white mayor,

Roman Gribbs. Although he now lives in the suburbs, he still works in town, as a producer for WDIV, the NBC television affiliate. It was from him that I first heard the white version of what went wrong.

"This is the place where the wheels came off the wagon of Western civilization," he told me in a voice that mixed sadness with anger. "This town has become unlivable. What I want to know is, where's the outrage? There is no outrage here. This is a town that is down for the count—and maybe already being carried out of the ring. You'd think there would be an outcry, or at least some sympathy for the victim. Detroit is as helpless and hopeless a place as any in America.

"Believe me, this town is a goddamned disaster area; it just exists from day to day. I've lived in New York and L.A., but the difference is that here, there's no way to get out. Detroit is one big prison with Eight Mile as the gate."

Tom De Lisle is not unaware of the conditions that brought the city to its present state. "It was never easy to be a black in Detroit," he conceded. "Blacks felt—rightly—victimized. There were always racist cops. But the riot never stopped in Detroit. Both the criminals and the cops understood that it was a whole new ball game. In the seventies, it was like a gang war between the blacks and the cops— and the blacks won."

The flight to the suburbs—by both whites and middle-class blacks—was, in De Lisle's view, a simple desire to escape the endemic violence of the city. "In metropolitan Detroit today, fear is the most pervasive single factor," he said. "When I worked for the mayor, almost every member of his staff suffered a major crime. One night someone pumped three shots through my window for no reason. One of the mayor's secretaries was brutally raped. In the City-County Building. During working hours.

"My grandparents lived on East Grand Boulevard," he continued. "Somebody stole their air conditioner right out of the wall. My grandmother used to look out the back window to tell my grandfather when it was safe to get his car out of the garage. There are thousands of stories like that. And when people report them to the cops, the cops say 'Move.'

"Everything goes back to the racial situation. Detroit has been the first major American city to cope with going from white to black. And whites left. That's the American way—people have a right to move in, or move out. There's evidence to point out that white people who moved had something to fear. Who wants to put their kids in a situation where they are likely to be crime victims? That's as basic as life gets.

"If I were mayor, I'd declare Detroit a disaster area," he said. "It desperately needs national assistance. But Coleman Young has no compassion. He says, 'Things have never been better.' What a goddamned lie! The bottom line is, Detroit is an orphaned city. There's no sense that anyone cares. What's happening here is the death of a city."

In the following months I heard this view repeated a hundred times. It is a constant refrain—blacks, especially black violence, drove people out of their homes and their city. This is the white way to look at it; but Arthur Johnson reminded me that there is another perspective as well.

Johnson, president of the Detroit chapter of the NAACP and a vice-president of Wayne State University, is a scholarly-looking man with thick glasses and a white beard. He leads an organization that for many years symbolized moderation and interracial cooperation. But when we met in his office on the campus of Wayne State, he sounded anything but moderate on the subject of his white neighbors.

"Blacks in Atlanta feel their city is loved," he said. "Here, white people are proud to say, 'I haven't been downtown in ten years.' We know we're not loved. We know our city has been scarred by the media on an unprecedented scale. I attribute this to the fact that we have a black majority and black leadership. Detroit has unjustly come to represent the worst in America. If they make that stick, it's possible to justify our neglect and separation."

Johnson, who serves as one of Detroit's four police commissioners, is not naive about the city's problems. But in his view, they spring not from black incompetence, or violence, but from white hostility.

"Whites don't know a goddamned thing about what's gone wrong here. They say, 'Detroit had this, Detroit had that. . . . But economic power is still in the hands of whites. It's apartheid. They rape the city, and then they come and say, 'Look what these niggers did to the city,' as if they were guiltless. Then they go out and vote for Ronald Reagan. I look at white working-class people talking about taxes are too high and I don't know them. I just don't know them at all."

De Lisle spoke about the death of a city; but to Arthur Johnson and the rest of Detroit's black intelligentsia, something is being born in Detroit—a new, black metropolis.

"Detroit has helped nurture a new black mentality," Johnson said, pounding his desk for emphasis. "More than any other city, blacks here make an issue of where you live. If you're with us, you'll find a place in the city."

Whites often say, in their own defense, that many middle-class blacks also leave the city at the first opportunity. I mentioned this to Johnson, but he waved it away. "The majority of the black middle class is here. We are engaged in the most determined, feverish effort to save Detroit. Why? Because Detroit is special. It's the first major city in the United States to have taken on the symbols of a black city. It has elected a strong, powerful black mayor, powerful in both his personality and his office. Detroit, more than anywhere else, has gathered power and put it in black hands."

My own instincts and experience told me that each man was, in his own way, right. It was hard to deny the harsh portrait of the city painted by Tom De Lisle. Judged by the standards of the white middle class, Detroit is an urban nightmare, a place that offers neither safety nor prosperity to its citizens. The American part of me sympathized with this view; after all, my own grandfather was murdered there, and my relatives moved to the suburbs.

At the same time, I was intrigued by Arthur Johnson's concept of Detroit as a developing black polis in the American heartland. He sees it as more than simply another city; it is, to him, an island of black self-determination in a sea of white racism and hostility.

My Israeli side responded to this notion. Israel, like Detroit, is a place where people with a history of persecution and dependence finally gave up on the dream of assimilation, and chose to try, for the first time, to rule themselves. Both are rough, somewhat crude places; both feel embattled and rejected (Detroit by whites, Israel by American Jews who have remained in the United States); and both have learned hard lessons about the limitations of going it alone.

From time to time, American friends, looking at the hard economic conditions and precarious security of Israel, have asked me why I would choose to live there. The answer is simple enough: Israel, for all its faults, is home. It is a place governed by people like me, a place where I feel secure and self-assured about being a Jew. It may not be much by the standards of Scarsdale or West Bloomfield, but it's all mine.

Talking to Arthur Johnson, it occurred to me for the first time that this is what Detroit represents for blacks. I was fascinated by the parallel, and challenged (as he meant me to be) by his assertion that white people don't know a goddamned thing about Detroit. "Don't believe what you read in the papers," he told me. "If you want to know what this city is all about, go out and see it for yourself."

Chapter Two

COWBOYS AND INDIANS

What you read in the papers about Detroit is not inviting. The two dailies, the *News* and the *Free Press*, relentlessly chronicle the events in America's most violent city. Shortly after I arrived in town, they published the FBI's crime statistics for 1987, a compilation that showed Detroit once again leading the nation's major cities in homicide.

According to the FBI, there were 686 homicides in Detroit in 1987—almost 63 per 100,000. (Since then, the rate has declined slightly, and Washington has become the nation's leader.) Atlanta, second among major cities, averaged 48 per 100,000. Highland Park, a tiny enclave entirely surrounded by Detroit, led all cities, large and small, with a murder rate even higher than the Motor City's. And Pontiac, my old hometown, had the highest number of rapes per capita in the United States.

The papers also published charts showing Detroit's homicide rate over the previous eight years. During that time, the city averaged 47 per 100,000—almost 50 percent more than second-place Dallas.

Since I was about to embark on a long journey into the city, I viewed these numbers with more than passing alarm. The one reassuring note was the contention of some law enforcement officials that most of the murders were underworld or family-related. I had no gang connections, and (as far as I knew) no outraged relatives, so I felt relatively safe—until Tom Delisle explained the local accounting system.

"Back in the early seventies, when I worked for Mayor Gribbs," he told me, "we had more meetings on how to get rid of the Murder City tag than how to stop the murders. In those days, the big PR thing was, 'It's an in-family problem; it's not generally dangerous.' I was there when that bullshit was invented. To this day, people still quote it; it's a real pacifier."

According to current Detroit police statistics, approximately half of all murder victims knew their killers; but even if this is the case, there is still plenty of random slaughter. While I was there I heard reports of women caught in the cross fire of rival drug gangs, little girls raped walking to school in the morning, kids assaulted on their way to evening church services, teenage boys shot and killed on buses or at the movies and tiny children struck by bullets from careless drive-by gunmen. These stories carried a clear message: The police had lost control of the city.

I asked a reporter who spends a lot of time in Detroit if things were really as dangerous as they seemed in the media. "Are you kidding?" he said. "They're worse." And he took me to meet John Aboud.

Aboud and his two brothers own and operate a small grocery store, the Tailwind Party Store, on the lower east side, in one of the city's toughest neighborhoods. Aboud was born in Detroit, in 1956; his parents, Iraqi Christians known as Chaldeans, came to the city from a village not too far from Baghdad.

The Detroit area has the largest Arab population in the United States, estimated at anywhere from 80,000 to 250,000. Since 1967, Syrians, Palestinians and, especially, Chaldeans (who often do not consider themselves Arabs but are generally regarded as members of the Arab community by outsiders) have replaced the Jews and other white ethnics as the city's shopkeepers.

It was a transition I had seen in my own family. After my grandfather was murdered in 1960, my uncle Jack reopened the store. Going in every morning was painful, especially for my aunt Ruth, who was never able to see a new customer without wondering 'Is he the one?' But they were working people, the store was their livelihood, and so they stayed on.

Despite my grandfather's death, Jack and Ruth did their best to maintain good customer relations. They supplied local softball teams with soft drinks, donated turkeys to church suppers and gave after-school jobs to their customers' kids. They probably weren't beloved figures—white grocers in black neighborhoods seldom are. But they were friendly and fair and they had a loyal, mostly black, clientele.

Early on a Sunday morning in July 1967, Jack got a call from a customer. "You better get down here," the man said. "All hell's breaking loose." By the time he arrived, the store had been looted. "They took everything except some 'yortzeit' candles and a few boxes of matzohs," he said. Within a few hours, Jack Fine was out of business.

There was no point in trying to reopen the store; the 1967 riot made it clear that white merchants were no longer welcome in Detroit. Jack offered the place to a young black man named Donny who had worked for him as a teenager. He asked only a few thousand dollars for the building and whatever goodwill he had accumulated over the years. Jack promised to work with Donny for six months, until he learned the business. He made the offer because he liked Donny, and because he had nothing better to do.

Donny wanted to buy the store, but he had no cash. Jack and Ruth went to the Urban League and explained the situation. Officials there listened unsympathetically. They had no money to loan, no help to give. "If you want to sell your business to this young man, why don't you loan him the money to buy it," they said.

Jack Fine sold the store to a Syrian family that promptly installed bulletproof glass and put weapons behind the counter, and the same process repeated itself all over town. Today, roughly 70 percent of the neighborhood grocery stores in Detroit are owned by Arab-Americans and Chaldeans.

These merchants, known locally as A-rabs, are enormously unpopular in the black community. Their control of the city's petty commerce is a rebuke to blacks, who have been unable or unwilling to set up their own stores. It is generally believed that the Arabs came to America with large sums of money, but this isn't true. Most of them arrived with very little, worked like demons to save money and, after the 1967 riot, bought businesses at fire sale rates.

Even today it costs only $60,000 to open a grocery store in Detroit—not an astronomical sum by any means. Many blacks say that it is hard for them to borrow that much from banks or other financial institutions. Arabs, with their tradition of family solidarity, don't have a similar credit problem; well-established relatives usually help new arrivals to go into business on their own.

Relations between blacks and Arabs are often tense. "They exploit us," said Robert Walls, a senior official in the city's Neighborhood Services Department. We were sitting in his office one day with his boss, Cassandra Smith-Gray, and George Gaines, the deputy director of public health, talking about the lack of black commerce in the city. When the subject of Arab merchants arose, the conversation turned angry.

"Let me tell you about overcharging," said Gaines. "They operate on pure greed."

"It is greed," said Smith-Gray. "And it's the way they act toward us. You can go into some stores where kids have to walk with their hands at their sides"—presumably an antishoplifting measure.

"Or, only one child at a time is allowed in," Gaines added. "If there's another riot in Detroit, it will be against the Chaldeans."

No one challenged the prediction. "They came here with assumptions about blacks," said Smith-Gray angrily. "I have been here since 1754. How dare they make assumptions about me? Their stores smell, too. I don't like 'em. That's my right. . . ."

But like all the coins in Detroit, this one has another side. Since 1960, roughly one hundred Arab and Chaldean merchants have been murdered in their stores. Six of them were related to John Aboud.

In April, Aboud, a man in his early thirties with hard brown eyes, a soft voice and a weight lifter's torso, attended a mass commemorating the fallen shopkeepers at the Chaldean Mother of God Cathedral. There were speeches about gun control and prayers for the souls of the departed. A special booklet, with pictures of more than forty slain merchants, was distributed. Many were wedding photos of young men dressed in frilly shirts and tuxedos, sporting tentative mustaches and blow-dried haircuts.

Johnny Aziz's picture was not in the book. A second cousin of Aboud's, he was murdered coming out of his store not long after the memorial mass. Someone ambushed him in his parking lot, stole his cash and left twenty-two bullet holes in his body.

"Johnny was a weight lifter," said Aboud. "He walked into the emergency room himself. He died there. His older brother was shot and stabbed this year, too, on Christmas Eve." Aboud's voice choked with emotion, and he ran a callused hand over his face. "You may not believe this, but right now my family is involved in three separate murder trials."

Family is the most important thing in John Aboud's life. He and his brothers had just bought a second store, in the suburbs, and they split the work, each putting in about one hundred hours a week. "Nobody does anything out of the family," he said. "We are all in partnership or no one is. One pocket, one heart." Aboud is still single, but he hopes to get married soon. In the meantime he works and saves for his nieces and nephews, and to build something for his unborn children and grandchildren.

"I haven't had a day off in two years, and I haven't wanted one," he said. "Why do I do it? To please my family."

The members of Aboud's family take care of one another. Every night at 10:45, just before closing time, Aboud's father calls. He always has the same message—"Watch yourself," a Chaldean warning. At precisely eleven, the brothers take their money home. "We have the same ritual every night," Aboud told me in a matter-of-fact tone. "Just before going out we say, 'Eyes open,' and then the lead man goes out with a weapon and scans the street. If things are clear, the others follow with drawn weapons. There's no talking—it's done that way. You get careless, you get burned."

His cousin Johnny was murdered because he didn't take precautions. "Johnny was a good kid, a gem," said Aboud. "He was closing the store by himself, at two in the morning. He didn't have help and he was scared. Four days before he was killed, he asked us to find someone to help him close." He shook his head. Detroit after dark is no place for a single man to be with a bag full of money.

In their years at the Tailwind, the Aboud brothers have never been held up—a record that Aboud attributes to the family's honest business practices and its militance. "When we caught shoplifters we never used to call the cops," said Aboud, preferring the past tense. "We took care of things in our own way. If somebody killed my brother, I'd get even, that's the type of family we are. People who think we're crazy are right—we are crazy. But we don't look for trouble. We've got a friendly store. Come over any night and you'll see."

The following Friday I took him up on his offer. After all the horror stories I had heard, I was surprised by the relaxed atmosphere in the Tailwind. Customers, mostly black, bantered with Aboud and his brother Mike, exchanging neighborhood gossip. John Aboud flirted amiably with several of the young women and they flirted back. Over the cash register there were snapshots of kids from the block.

After each customer left, Aboud provided me with a thumbnail biography. Some were solid working people, but many were drug addicts or dealers, teenage mothers and ex-cons. Each story was told in a flat, nonjudgmental way. Aboud is a merchant, not a missionary, and he accepts the foibles and weaknesses of human nature philosophically.

Aboud's tolerance has not impaired his vigilance, however, and the Tailwind's security system could be fairly characterized as forbidding. The front door has a permanent squeak, to let the brothers know when someone comes in. They work behind a thick shield of bullet-resistant glass (Aboud told me that when they come out from behind it, they wear bulletproof vests) and on the shelf behind the counter there was a small arsenal: a .44 Magnum, a 9-millimeter pistol, and a couple of AR 15 semiautomatic assault rifles—tools of the shopkeeper's trade in Detroit.

In addition to the guns, Aboud spends hours keeping himself in fighting trim. "I know karate and I do body building," he said. "I do these things to protect my store. You have to act like it's a war zone. A stranger walks in, you have to stand up straight and not turn your back. You can't show an ounce of fear. If you do, they'll eat you up, you'll be a meal. The main thing is respect."

Friday nights are especially busy at the Tailwind, and John Aboud and Mike waited on a steady stream of customers buying bread and lunch meat, beer, soft drinks and other weekend staples. During the week, when things are quieter, they go downstairs into the basement and take target practice in a makeshift pistol range. Their current target was the face of Mike Ditka on a Lite Beer poster. They had nothing against the Chicago Bears coach; the targets change with the posters.

"When my brother was eighteen he got his first Magnum," said John, in a tone that some people use referring to their first bicycle. "Know what he did? He shot out the furnace." Aboud laughed, a soft, melodic sound.

The basement serves a less sporting purpose, too; it is where the brothers take shoplifters. "We handcuff them to this," he said, pointing to a metal post. Legend has it that years ago, on the other side of the room, on a chain-link leash, was the family Doberman, Taza ("tender" in Chaldean Arabic). When extended, the leash let Taza come within inches of the genitals of the defendant. After a few charges, thieves usually got the point. "At the end of the evening we come down, beat their ass and send them home," said Aboud.

One of Aboud's hobbies is monitoring the police radio. That night we heard a weekend crackle of announcements—shootings, break-ins and other assorted crimes and misdemeanors. Aboud didn't seem to be listening, but suddenly he held up his hand for silence. Together we heard the report of a holdup at a nearby grocery store.

Aboud responded like a Chaldean minuteman. He dashed from behind the counter, jumped into a van parked outside and headed for the scene of the crime. As we raced through the ruined streets of the east side it crossed my mind that if anything happened, my friends in Tel Aviv would never believe that I was killed trying to protect an Arab grocer.

To my profound relief, it proved to be a false alarm. Aboud turned the van in the direction of the Tailwind and drove with adrenaline-fueled speed back toward the store. We hadn't gone more than a few blocks before spotting an agitated crowd of kids on the front lawn of a ramshackle house.

Aboud pulled over. As we got out, we saw a fourteen-year-old boy lying on the grass, oozing blood from a knife wound in his chest. A friend held his head in his arms and moaned softly, "Don't die, Matthew, don't die now baby," but the stabbed boy didn't respond. Neighbors on either side of the house stood on their porches and watched the scene with dismay. In the distance, we heard the sound of an ambulance siren. Within a minute or so it arrived, and the stretcher bearers took the boy away. "God damn this city sometimes," Aboud said.

When we returned to the store, John told his brother Mike and their helper, Danny Boy, about the incident.

"This isn't even a jungle, it's barbaric," said Mike, shaking his head sadly. He studied criminal law at Wayne State University and is considered the bleeding heart of the family. Less physically prepossessing than his older brother, he has a gentle face and a courteous manner. It isn't easy to picture him shooting a Magnum or cuffing a shoplifter to a post. But on the lower east side, people do what they need to do.

"Yeah, it's rough down here all right," said Danny Boy, a pimply, pudgy white teenager who lives in the neighborhood. He took out a Samurai switchblade and pounded it in his palm, looking at Aboud, his macho role model, for approval.

"Still, I ain't never had no trouble," he continued. "People don't mess with me. One reason is, I can talk like a white guy or a black guy." He demonstrated his black accent, which sounded the same as his white one, with an added "man" here and there.

"No trouble? How about the bullets they shot into your living room?" Aboud reminded him. Danny Boy shrugged. "That was only some stray shots," he said. "Hell, it was no big deal."

Danny Boy is a Catholic, and he was anxious to talk about a parochial school that had closed, a church that had shut down, people who had moved away. "This used to be a real fine parish," he said. "We had parks, a movie house, it was nice. You could walk around and nobody would bother you. It was great."

"Can you remember all that?" I asked.

"Naw, not really, but my dad told me about it, about the way it was," he said. At sixteen, Danny Boy already had a vicarious case of the white man's malady, nostalgia.

The Abouds are less emotional. They live in the suburbs; to them, Detroit is a place to make money. This has given them a certain detachment regarding the city and the complaints of the blacks against their fellow Middle Eastern merchants.

"Go around and see other stores, a lot of them are filthy," said Mike. "They treat their customers bad, call them 'nigger' and 'bitch.' That's not right. A man may be a crackhead or a stone killer, but you should be respectful. He may not have as much as you, but he's still a man. At least he's a man."

"That's right," said John. "If we ever sell this store, I'll always come back to visit these guys. People come in here in their party times, their sad times. You see people in their moods."

"Somebody said that if there is another riot in Detroit, it will be against the Chaldeans," I said.

John Aboud thought about that for a moment. "A riot against us?" he said pensively. "Well, it'll be a good war. They'll be going up against some good warriors. Nobody's taking anything from my family."

In John Aboud's defense strategy, the police play virtually no role. Coleman Young's first priority as mayor had been to tame the city's racist, violent police department. Nowadays, Detroit has the country's most integrated force: more than half of its senior officers are black. But some people feel that the department has gone too far in a dovish direction.

Not surprisingly, chief William Hart disagrees. Hart is a quiet man in late middle age who collects police caps from around the world and runs his department according to the liberal principles of his boss, the mayor. "This is a gentle police force," he told me when we met at his office, a spacious room decorated with plaques and awards from community groups, police pennants and bric-a-brac bestowed by visiting law enforcement delegations. "We are public servants. We can't enforce the law by being unlawful. It just don't happen here."

When William Hart joined the police, in the fifties, he was one of only a handful of black cops, whose duties consisted of helping to patrol black neighborhoods. When he was named chief by Coleman Young, the appointment took everyone, including him, by surprise.

"I can remember when they made Hart chief of police," said Fred Williams, the police spokesman. Williams, like Hart, is a black cop; they used to be partners. "After the ceremony we came to my place and talked, and I said, 'Man, do you realize that you are the chief of po-lice?' And Hart said, 'It's no big thing.'"

"Then the next day I got a call to come to his office. I walked in and he was sitting behind that big desk, and he looked at me and said, 'Fred, do you realize that I am the chief of all this here crap?' It took him that long for it to sink in."

Hart's critics say it hasn't sunk in yet. His gentle approach to law enforcement seems oddly inappropriate in the nation's most lethal city; sometimes, it appears to border on impotence. "In this city, a lot of times cops just walk away from trouble," a white crime reporter told me. "I've seen cops on duty drive right past drug deals. People who call 911 have to lie and say there's a man with a gun outside to get a patrol car to come. For cops in this department, the emphasis isn't on busting criminals, it's on not screwing up."

During my travels around town I met a pharmacist who owned a drugstore on the west side, near the University of Detroit. Inside, behind bulletproof glass, the druggist filled Medicaid prescriptions; outside, in the parking lot, pushers ran an alternative apothecary. Some of their merchandise came from the druggist's own stock— people would sell the pills they had just received to the pushers, who resold them for a tidy profit. Tough young men loitered in front of the place, drug deals were made in the open, and occasionally shots were fired.

All this action proved bad for business. The druggist called the cops dozens of times, but nothing happened. And so he sold the store and moved to the suburbs.

Chief Hart knew about this case. "We've been over there time and time again," he said. "We arrest these people but they beat us back to the parking lot. Usually they don't even go to trial. Dope is a big problem. If we locked up every dealer in town, it would be going full blast again in five days. It's that lucrative."

Guns are another problem. Everybody has them, from shopkeepers like John Aboud to the young criminals who drive around town in late-model Mercedes with Uzis under the seat. Even members of the clergy carry guns. A couple of years ago, a busload of nineteen Baptist ministers decided to cross the Ambassador Bridge for a Canadian excursion. Border guards searched them—and uncovered nineteen pistols.

My only personal brush with the law came when a suburban visitor had the hubcaps stolen off his new Cadillac while we were downtown eating. A few blocks from the scene of the crime we spotted a cop. "Officer," said the visitor, "I've just had my hubcaps stolen. Should I report it or something?"

The cop looked at him as if he had just driven into town from Mars. "Report it?" he said. "Are you kidding? You ought to be grateful that they didn't take the car."

My friend, who was raised in Detroit and now lives in a town where hubcap theft is considered a major crime, was obviously upset by the cop's reaction. I told him not be be naive—there isn't a big city in the country where the police investigate petty larceny. "I know that," he said. "And I don't care about the hubcaps; they're insured. What got me is the policeman's attitude. He seemed so damn proud of the crime in this city."

Chief Hart knew all about the prevalent feeling that the police are too soft, but for him sensitive law enforcement is a matter of ideology. Like the mayor, he sees Detroit as a postcolonial city, liberated from oppressive white police occupation; to him, gentle law enforcement is an expression of black home rule.

"I'd hate to turn the clock back to when we kicked ass and took names," Hart said. "It's unconstitutional and it leads to false imprisonment. Besides, you just can't do that with the kind of officers we have. We recruit out of the neighborhoods. It's hard to practice brutality and then go home and live among the same people. This city is just one big ghetto, all the way out to Eight Mile Road."

As we talked it became clear that Chief Hart had an answer for every question, a reasoned explanation for every grievance. He blamed the media for sensationalizing crime, the courts for handing down lenient sentences, the county for not providing enough jail cells, and most important, parents for not controlling their children. "We're hired to arrest criminals, not raise people's kids," he said.

Like the police chiefs of other big cities, Hart's biggest problem was the spread of crack. Drugs, particularly cocaine, were a hot topic in Detroit while I was there. During my stay, a young drug lord, "Maserati Rick" Carter, was murdered in his hospital bed by a rival gang, and his friends treated the city to one of the gaudiest funerals since Prohibition. Sixteen Cadillacs ferried mourners to the cemetery, where they saw Rick buried in a casket made out of a Mercedes—headlights, grill and all.

In the city, where cheap cocaine is sold more or less openly in houses and on street corners, blacks talked of it like a biblical plague. In the suburbs, it aroused less alarm than fascination. There was something about the word "crack," redolent with the hard city sounds of cracking bullets and cracking bones, that tickled the suburban ear. And since more than one of these discussions took place with an expensive vial of white powder on the coffee table, calling it "crack" put some distance between upscale consumers and the dope-crazed blacks below Eight Mile Road. But whatever it was called, people talked about it constantly; there was an aura of glamour surrounding it that all the disapproving social commentators on *Nightline* couldn't dispel.

The drug dealers I met in Detroit were anything but glamorous. One of them, a young white man in a Detroit Tigers warm-up jacket and a blank expression associated with drug-fried brains, was introduced to me by Aboud. "You want to know about drugs, he'll tell you all about drugs," said Aboud. "The man is an expert, the hard way."

"That's right, the hard way," agreed the young man, who told me with a look of cunning invention that his name was John Doe.

"I was born right here on this street," he said in black-inflected English. "When I got eighteen I began to deal drugs, cocaine. Opportunity knocked. I used it, too, I ain't gonna lie, but mostly I was just selling it.

"One day, last year, I was ridin' around in my father's Tempo and someone came up and shot it thirty-four times. I ducked. I didn't get hit; it's amazing. The insurance company said, 'What are you, *Miami Vice?*' That's when I decided to quit."

At the high point of his career, as a teenage pusher, Mr. Doe worked as a salesman in a local crack house that cleared three thousand dollars a day. His cut was a salary of seven hundred dollars a week—good money for a near-illiterate kid, although the hours were arduous.

"I worked between five and seven days straight," he said. "Twenty-four hours a day. People would come to the door with their spoon and their money. I'd take the money, fill up the spoon and pass it back.

"I sold on the street, too," he continued. "See, the police didn't expect a white dude to be sellin'. But I got out. I didn't dig the pressure, y'know? Today I make a hundred and fifty dollars a week as a busboy. But the guy I was working for, he killed a guy who was like his brother. It's a bad business."

John Doe was shot at thirty-four times and survived. Jacqueline Wilson was shot only once, and didn't. She was killed coming out of a grocery store on Woodward Avenue, where she had gone to buy cigarettes. Two rival drug gangs happened to be staging a shootout in front of the store, and she got caught in the cross fire.

Normally this kind of murder doesn't arouse much interest in Highland Park, a 2.2-square-mile urban enclave surrounded by Detroit. Highland Park is the headquarters for the Chrysler Corporation, and two generations ago it was a model of urban progress, with the country's first freeway and one of its first junior colleges. Academics, mid-level auto executives and businesspeople lived in large, comfortable brick homes and shopped in smart shops along Woodward Avenue, which bisects the tiny town.

Today, Highland Park is a smaller, meaner version of Detroit. Hookers and drug dealers ply their trade on its main streets, and homicide is more common there than anyplace else in the United States. But Jacqueline Wilson's murder was not a common killing. She was the daughter of the late singer Jackie Wilson, and her death received extensive local and even national publicity. The mayor wanted action, the chief of public safety demanded action, and the case wound up on the desk of Jim Francisco.

Francisco took their calls seated, feet on the desk, in his dingy office in the Highland Park police station annex. A powerfully built man dressed in jeans, a sweatshirt and a Crimson Tide baseball cap, he answered each call with "Francisco, Morality," in the slight southern drawl of Detroit's working-class whites. He chomped a wad of gum vigorously as he listened, occasionally making polite responses to a superior's questions. From time to time, he ran his massive hand over the pistol in the shoulder holster he wore.

Each conversation ended with Francisco's earnest assurance that he and his men were working on the case. But despite the pressure, he wasn't at all sure that they could deliver. It was, after all, a random killing with no motive and no witnesses. "We'll probably never solve the motherfucker," said Francisco of Morality, cheerfully.

Jim Francisco is a man who loves his work, which is chasing bad guys through some of the most dangerous streets in America. "Working here is like playing cowboys and Indians with real Indians," he told me.

It was a Francisco thing to say, tough and funny and tinged with bravado. He exudes competence and courage, the kind of cop that other cops refer to as a "legend in his own time," and his exploits provide a seemingly endless supply of station house anecdotes. In the Highland Park police station, which resembles a fortress, and on the streets of the tiny town, which is often compared by its residents to a battlefield, Jim Francisco is the perfect platoon commander.

A few days after the Wilson murder, Francisco got a break: an informer turned in the name and address of the killer. The cops decided to raid his home, which was in Detroit, less than a mile from the police station. On a Friday afternoon, Francisco gathered his troops—a dozen officers, six white, six black, each outfitted in assault overalls, combat boots, bulletproof vests and riot helmets, armed with a variety of very powerful weapons.

Officer Larry Robinson was not dressed for the occasion. A stoic black veteran, he wore a civil-service-blue short-sleeve shirt and black slacks. Robinson looked at eager young cops and sighed. "I'm near retirement and I don't really like to do this anymore," he said. "But I've gotta think about the rookies, help them save *their* ass. And I'll tell you something else. I've done this before, plenty of times, but when I hit the corner and pull out my gun, it's no longer routine. The adrenaline flows, I guarantee you that."

Although the raid was scheduled for 2:00 P.M., it was postponed again and again. At a desk, a young officer pecked at a typewriter with leaden fingers. The tension in the room rose and fell as deadlines neared and were deferred. Because the suspect's home was in Detroit, the city police had to be involved, and there were problems coordinating the raid. Finally Robinson picked up the phone impatiently. "Okay," he said, "I'm gonna call the thirteenth precinct, get me some menfolks and we gonna bust."

Apparently the call worked, because within a few minutes the Highland Park strike force was gathered in the parking lot, making last-minute checks of their weapons. The plan was simple. They would surround the house, and Francisco would lead a group of officers through the front door. They had no idea what to expect once they got inside, nor did they know how many guns they were likely to encounter. The uncertainty led to some gallows humor as the cops crowded into two vans. Francisco, who wanted to drive by the house before going in, sped on ahead.

Half a mile from the station house, on Woodward Avenue, the vans came to a screeching halt. Three black men were spread-eagled, facedown, on the pavement, and Francisco stood over them with a gun. The other cops leaped out and drew their guns, too.

"What's your name, sir?" Francisco drawled, addressing one of the prone men.

"Lucky," he said.

"Well, Mr. Lucky, you got some ID?" The man handed Francisco his wallet. "Thank you, sir," he said. "And you other gentlemen, please bear with us." If there was irony in the remark, it wasn't apparent from his courteous tone.

Francisco had stopped their car on instinct—he thought one of them might be their man—but their IDs checked out. The three suspects rose and dusted themselves off. Although police vans blocked two lanes of traffic and there were a dozen cops in riot gear milling around, pedestrians and cars passed without more than a glance. "It's a pretty common sight down here," explained a huge black cop named Caldwell.

The raid itself was an anticlimax: There was no car parked in front of the suspect's house. Francisco decided to try again later that night. On the way to the station Robinson was in a foul mood—the new hour was certain to screw up his weekend—and he grumbled about the false alarm on Woodward Avenue. "Some people think all blacks look alike," he said. "Please. The guy we want has close-cropped hair. That guy on the street had long hair. Now, *we* can't grow hair overnight. I mean, please."

There was nothing personal in Robinson's remark, though. I recognized the tone from my army days, the sound of a man who just felt like bitching. In Detroit today, tough white cops like Jim Francisco could not survive if they were even suspected of racism.

That night at eleven, Francisco's task force regrouped. Before going out, they sat around a television set and heard a news report about two Detroit police officers who had been accused of raping a woman. This was greeted by hoots of disbelief. "There's enough women chasing cops, they don't have to rape anybody," one officer said, and the others voiced their agreement.

Woodward Avenue was twitching with weekend nightlife when the cops headed out. Once again I rode with Robinson. "The man that shot Jackie's daughter is going to get some justice tonight," he said, his good spirits restored.

I mentioned to Robinson that it seemed strange that a murderer would simply go home and continue with business as usual, but he told me that it happens all the time. "These punks think that they're above the law, just like Richard M. Nixon," he said. "Nobody will tell anything, that's what they think. We dealing here with the Richard M. Nixon of northwest Detroit."

Despite Robinson's prediction, Jacqueline Wilson's killer did not get any justice that night; he still wasn't home. A dozen disgruntled cops, weekend plans shot to hell, drove back to the station to get into civilian clothes. Robinson, adrenaline pumping, decided to cruise for a while. Within minutes, we heard a radio report of gunfire outside a motel. When we arrived, a crowd of people were hanging around the parking lot, but there was no sign of any shooting.

"Just hookers," said Robinson, disappointed. "I would venture to say that if someone was chasing someone with a gun, these people wouldn't be out here sunning themselves at midnight." He nodded to several of the women as he drove slowly through the lot; Highland Park is a small town, and the police and street people know one another. "Just a bunch of little Richard Nixons," Robinson grumbled as he headed in.

The Highland Park police never caught up with their suspect. They didn't have to—he caught up with them. A couple of weeks after the abortive raids, he walked in off the street. Although the police had what they considered an ironclad case, he was released on a fifty-thousand-dollar bond—five thousand in cash.

On the day that the suspected killer was released on bond, I went to see Jacqueline Wilson's mother, Frieda. She was living in a flophouse motel, across the street from the store where her daughter was killed. The first thing she said to me was that she was glad her husband, Jackie, wasn't alive to hear about the murder.

"Happy Jackie Wilson," Frantic Ernie Durham, the rhyming disc jockey, used to call him, but it was a misnomer. Wilson had the best voice and the worst luck in Detroit show business. Berry Gordy wrote some of his first hits—"Reet Petite" and "Lonely Teardrops"—but Wilson never rode the Motown bandwagon. He was locked, instead, into a recording contract with Brunswick Records, which had no idea of what to do with his remarkable gifts. Wilson could have been bigger than Marvin Gaye or Smokey Robinson; instead, he wound up entangled in grotesque musical arrangements full of florid strings and peppy white background singers. He recorded songs that Eddie Fisher would have rejected, including a never-to-be-forgotten rendition of "My Yiddishe Mama."

As a stage performer, Jackie Wilson was in a class with James Brown, far grittier than the choreographed and coiffured teenagers at Motown. His sweet-and-sour good looks and prizefighter grace inspired frenzy in his audiences, and passion in women. One, a fan, shot and almost killed him. Another, a neighborhood girl named Frieda, married him.

Frieda and Jackie met when he was nine and she was ten. They wed as teenagers, in 1951. Together they had four children, Jacqueline, Sandy, Anthony and Jackie Jr., and they lost others—Frieda was pregnant fifteen times.

"Jackie believed in keeping me barefoot and pregnant," she said. "And not just me. I don't know how many other children he had. Women always liked Jack, even churchwomen. And he wasn't the kind of man to say no."

In 1965, Frieda and Jackie Wilson were divorced. Ten years later, during an oldies show in Cherry Hill, New Jersey, the singer collapsed onstage from a heart attack. He lingered on in a coma for years, his money tied up in legal tangles, until he finally died in 1984.

But even before his stroke, the streets of Detroit began to claim Jackie Wilson's children. Jackie Jr. was shot and killed at the age of sixteen in circumstances that his mother did not want to discuss. Sandy died, of "unknown causes," at twenty-three. And, in the summer of 1988, Jacqueline Wilson was gunned down.

The music community was shocked by the news, and saddened; many remembered Jacqueline as a little girl, backstage at her father's shows. Berry Gordy sent money to bury her. The Four Tops dispatched a telegram. And Frieda Wilson, a prematurely old woman in a red ski cap, tattered overcoat and torn plastic shoes, went back to her rented room at the sleazy motel across the street from the party store and cried for days.

Once, when the money was good, Frieda Wilson lived like a celebrity. She had a big home and a fancy car. Her children were educated at exclusive Catholic academies, and she traveled in Detroit's show business circles. In those days, she was an envied woman. But no one envies her anymore. Three of her children are dead, and she shares a room with a dying old man in a wheelchair, whom she nurses. There is only one window in the room, boarded up because of the gunfire of drug dealers in the parking lot. Frieda cooks on a Bunsen burner and cleans her dishes in the bathroom sink.

"The income tax people took my house," she said, sitting on an unmade bed. "And Jack's estate is still all tied up, because of all these women and children he had." Frieda Wilson picked up a picture of her dead daughter and stared at it. "When Jackie Jr. was killed, Jack couldn't even come to the funeral. He just locked himself up in his room and wouldn't come out. He wanted to see pictures of his son in the casket. He was very, very close with his kids; he was a family person. And now look what's happened. . . ."

Frieda Wilson has been battered by circumstances and she knows it. At times she seems confused and helpless. But occasionally she summons the strength to pull herself together, and you catch a glimpse of her as an articulate, ambitious young woman who dreamed the Detroit show business dream, a dream so powerful that it could, for a moment, dispel the gloom of the present.

"You know, Jack's songs are starting to sell again in England," she said. A few months before, "Reet Petite," written by a man who has been as lucky as Jackie Wilson was unlucky, hit the charts in Great Britain, and a generation of young kids there were thrilled by the great singer's voice. "Maybe they'll be some money from that," she said wistfully. If there is, it's safe to say that Berry Gordy will get his share. Frieda will get hers—maybe.

"And you know, the people from *Entertainment Tonight* were here," she said. "They visited Jack's grave. After he died, we reburied him next to his mother. I told you, he was a family person. And we're negotiating with ABC about a miniseries. . . ."

Loud laughter from the pimps and dealers in the parking lot wafted through the open door. Frieda looked once more at her daughter's picture. "Maybe something good will come of all this," she said, and then she began to cry again.

Jacqueline Wilson was murdered because she got caught in the cross fire of an unsuccessful drug transaction. Much of the violent crime in Detroit is drug related, and there is little the cops can do about it. Crack is sold openly; police say that there is simply no way to arrest everyone. The main thrust of enforcement is to keep the supply to a minimum. No one believes that it can be dried up altogether.

From time to time, the cops stage raids on known crack houses, which are nothing more than apartments or homes from which drugs are sold. Locating them is as easy as finding stockbrokers on Wall Street, but busting them can be dangerous—most pushers are armed and ready to fight.

Not long after the search for Jacqueline Wilson's killer, Jim Francisco gathered his troops for a raid on a crack pad. Robinson was off that night, but half a dozen others were there, including Caldwell, the massive, bearded black undercover cop. The raiding party also had one woman, a thin redhead with a southern twang. Francisco took the wheel of the van, and the raiders climbed in the back. They were in good spirits that night, buoyed by the prospect of action, and as the van turned onto Woodward Avenue, they began to sing— "Roll 'em, roll 'em, roll 'em," to the tune of the theme song from *Rawhide*. They sounded like a high school football team on the way to a big game.

The singing stopped when we pulled up in front of a seedy apartment building on a side street. Without a word the cops jumped out of the van and raced into the building. Caldwell carried a battering ram, and the policewoman held a shotgun in both hands. A couple of people stepped aside to let them pass as they ran up the two flights, stopped in front of a door, hollered "Police, open up!" and, without waiting for a response, bashed in the door and flooded into the apartment.

Inside they found a very frightened black woman of twenty, dressed in a flimsy nightie and holding an infant. They were alone. One of the cops looked in a nightstand drawer and found several packages of cocaine.

"That's my boyfriend's," the woman said, crying. "He's not here. I don't know where he stay. We don't even get along that good— he's just the baby's father, that's all." The policewoman sat on the bed and talked gently to her while the others continued their search. Under the bed they found a police scanner, a pager and a loaded carbine. "I don't know nothin' about all that stuff," the young mother protested. "It belongs to my boyfriend. I ain't mixed up in nothin'. . . ."

The small apartment was neat and clean. A high school equivalency diploma hung on a wall, next to a shelf of stuffed animals. Record albums were stacked near an expensive stereo. The cops, respectful of neatness, searched gently, replacing things as they went along.

The baby, dressed in pink-and-white pajamas, began to cry. "He had a shot today, that's why he don't feel good," his mother explained.

"Yeah," said the policewoman empathetically. "Those shots make me feverish, too." She gently undid the baby's diaper, looking for hidden drugs.

The police stacked the carbine and the cocaine on a counter, next to a box of Oh So Nice Baby Wipes, and began to make a list of the seized material. By this time the young woman had calmed down and was watching the search without apparent emotion. Her composure irked the policewoman. "If we bust you again, we'll take your baby and get it a good home," she threatened. "Not no crack house." The mother nodded, but said nothing. Now that she knew she was not going to be arrested, she was simply waiting for the police to complete their business and leave.

As they carried out the search, I could hear people scurrying through the halls. The building is a maze of crack houses, and many of the tenants were quietly leaving with their inventory. Francisco, who had no warrant for any other apartment, seemed unconcerned. This wasn't his first visit to the building, and it wouldn't be his last.

The task force gathered up the drugs and weapons, put them in bags, and trooped down the stairs. Francisco, pistol in hand, potbelly drooping over his jeans, Crimson Tide baseball cap set back on his head, swaggered down the hallway, just to make sure the neighbors knew who had been there. In the stairwell he met a tall, thin black man with a heavily bandaged hand and the look of someone caught in the act.

"Excuse me sir," said Francisco, his mouth working on a large wad of gum. "I can't help but notice that you have been wounded." The man nodded in guarded affirmation. Francisco waited. "I got shot," the man finally said.

"May I ask you a personal question?" said Francisco in an intimate tone. "Was the shooting by any chance, ah, drug related?"

"Naw, man, it was a family situation," said the thin man.

"I'm glad to hear that, sir. It's a pleasure to meet a family man in a place like this," said Francisco of Morality, and walked down the stairs, pistol in hand, whistling the theme song to *Rawhide*.

It was around this time that I decided to move into the city. I had been living in West Bloomfield, commuting every day across the Eight Mile border, then retreating behind it every night. But this was an inconvenient arrangement and, more to the point, I found myself increasingly comfortable in Detroit.

The time I spent on the city streets, my evenings with the cops or hanging around the Tailwind and various other neighborhood spots, had convinced me that Detroit's reputation as a violent city was well deserved. It was possible, I knew, to get caught in cross fire, like

Jacqueline Wilson, or stabbed or mugged. But strangely, I didn't feel any real sense of personal danger, certainly nothing that justified the dire warnings of my suburban friends. Years in the Middle East had given me good antennae for hostility, and the truth is, I didn't feel any. When I went into a bar or a club where there were no other whites, which was pretty often, I got some wondering looks. If I was taking notes, people sometimes clammed up. But that was all.

My decision to move into the city was made easier by the fact that, during the course of interviewing people, I had become friendly with a number of black Detroiters. They rarely admonished me for living in the suburbs—to them it seemed natural—but the time I spent with them made Detroit seem a less alien place.

Many of my new acquaintances had little experience with books and authors; most of the younger ones had known very few whites. But they surprised me with their willingness to speak openly about their lives and their city. Clearly they enjoyed the chance to educate an interested foreigner. "I know you've never eaten any of this," a woman would say, handing me a plate of collard greens. "I know you've never heard anything like this," a man would tell me, putting on a Little Milton tape. Any evidence that I understood black culture was greeted with good-natured surprise. Once, at a party, I astonished a room full of people by dancing without breaking an ankle.

As time went by, and people became more relaxed around me, I heard a great deal of candid black talk. Detroiters constantly discussed race, often, I suspected, with the intention of shocking me.

"If you want to write about us," a playwright told me one night at a party, "you've got to realize that we come in four types—Afro-Americans, blacks, colored folks and niggers."

"What's the distinction?" I asked.

"Well, take vacations," she said. "An Afro-American goes to the Bahamas. A black goes to Harlem. Colored folks load their kids in the car and go down south to visit their kinfolks." She paused, forcing my hand. "And what about niggers?" I finally asked. "Niggers don't go on vacation—they wait for you to go on vacation," she whooped, and the others laughed loudly.

On another occasion, a group of people were discussing a media controversy that had erupted around the question of why blacks excel in sports. Several experts had been roundly criticized as racists for suggesting that black anatomy is better suited for some kinds of athletic activities. My hosts, however, happily asserted that the experts were right.

"Do you really think that blacks are built differently than whites?" I asked.

"Sure," said a woman. "We've got bigger butts and thinner legs."

"That's considered racist," I pointed out, but she didn't agree. "All you got to do is look at us," she said.

From time to time, the tables were turned and I became the subject of other people's scrutiny. Despite the fact that race is a constant topic among Detroiters, there is a surprising confusion about who is what.

One night in the 606 Club, a sort of black Cheers located downtown, a man who had obviously had a couple of drinks approached me at the bar. "Excuse me, brother, but are you a white man or a light-skinned colored man?" he asked.

"What do you think?" I asked him.

The man looked at me closely, and then ran his fingers over my scalp. "You got nappy hair," he said. "I guess you one of us." Satisfied, he returned to his seat and announced in a loud voice that I was, indeed, a light-skinned black. Apparently several other patrons had been wondering, because they looked at me, nodded in satisfaction and smiled.

The incident at the 606 brought back memories of a childhood friend, Jesse Stephen. Jesse was a preacher's son, and one day he told me that Jews aren't white, but red. "Noah had three sons," he intoned, borrowing his father's sermonic cadence. "Ham, who was black, Japheth, who was white, and Shem, who was red. The Jews are Shemites."

For years I considered this a personal eccentricity of Jesse's, but in Detroit I learned that it is a widespread article of faith. People were constantly telling me that I was "almost white" and they would buttress this belief by pointing out that I had "bad hair" and swarthy skin. "I know plenty of black people lighter than you," a woman told me, "and they don't go around pretending to be white." (There was another side to this coin, too. Many people I met believed that Jews are the chosen people. "Do I look chosen to you?" I once asked a churchwoman who scrutinized me and said, "I never said God made the right choice.")

Not only Jews fail to qualify in Detroit as whites. During my visit I got into an argument with a very sophisticated city official who tried to convince me that all Arabs are black because they come from Asia and North Africa. She believed this despite the evidence of her own eyes—most of Detroit's Arabs are unquestionably not black-skinned. But it soon emerged that we were talking about different things. "To me," she said, "a white man is somebody like George Bush."

The longer I stayed in Detroit, the more accustomed I became to the local habit of immediately classifying everyone by color; and I also began to see the world through the race-conditioned eyes of the people I met. Once, watching *Nightline*, I asked a friend what she thought about the discussion, which had to do with the economy. "You notice that there are never any black people on these interview programs," she said. "They don't think our opinions matter, or that we even have any opinions." Of course she was right; and from then on I watched American television with a new sensibility.

Constant daily contact with black people was enlightening; and it was also reassuring. I began to think about moving into town, and one day, in the midst of a discussion about the violence on the streets of Detroit, I surprised myself by asking a black auto executive if he thought it would be safe. "Nobody's totally safe here," he said. "But you won't be in any special danger because you're white. And one thing's for sure, it's a hell of a lot more interesting than in Bloomfield Hills."

And so I left the suburbs and moved into Detroit. At first, I rented a room from a black woman who lived on the east side, not far from downtown. Later, feeling more independent, I moved into one of Detroit's few high-rise apartment buildings, a short walk from City Hall and the river. The manager proudly pointed out the building's security features, which included a special service: residents returning at night could call ahead, and an armed guard would escort them from the parking lot into the lobby.

I never used the service, because I didn't feel threatened. But from time to time I got intimations of danger. One of them arrived at my apartment in the person of Floyd.

Floyd was a young man with a passive ferocity and yellow, malign eyes that peered out of a hard dark skull. When he walked into my living room, in the midst of a small cocktail party, he suddenly made some comfortable people very nervous.

Floyd was brought by Gerald, a heavyset black man who lives in the Brewster projects. We met in the course of my research; Gerald was trying, unsuccessfully, to promote music concerts at one of the downtown theaters, and I went to talk to him about the difficulties faced by a small entrepreneur. We soon discovered that we shared a love of fifties rhythm and blues, and struck up a friendship.

An inveterate do-gooder, Gerald met Floyd in the projects shortly after Floyd had been released from Jackson Penitentiary, at the end of a six-year term for armed robbery, and decided to rehabilitate him. "You got to learn how to interface with white people," he told Floyd, and brought him to the party.

Actually we were an integrated group that evening, but to Floyd, one of ten children born to an unwed mother, the blacks must have seemed as white as the whites. All the guests were middle-class and well educated. They sipped white wine and looked out at the city through wide glass windows and tried to act like they weren't scared stiff of Floyd. He drank a gin and orange juice and looked at his red tennis shoes. After a few moments he took them off and stretched out, uninvited, on the couch. Everyone pretended not to notice.

"Feel good layin' back," said Floyd sociably. "Up to Jackson, they ain't got no soft mattress." A halfhearted chuckle went up, and I thought, How in the hell do I get him out of here?

Gerald believed that it would be therapeutic for Floyd to talk about his past. "I come from Memphis," Floyd said. "Got some bad motherfuckers down there. Got some up here, too. Met some bad motherfuckers up to Jackson." The guests waited, but Floyd had summarized his biography to his own satisfaction.

A lady asked about his brothers and sisters. "I got seven brothers. Six of 'em been to Jackson, same as me," said Floyd, the way someone might mention the name of a family prep school.

"What does your mother feel, with all of you in prison like that?" the woman asked.

"She like it," he said. "She say, 'You safer in Jackson than in the city.'"

"The city isn't so bad," said Gerald defensively.

Floyd stirred, his professional opinion challenged. "Shit, man, it is, too, bad. That motherfucker be a war. Onliest thing, I ain't never been shot or stabbed." He sounded a bit amazed at his own good fortune.

"You ever stab or, ah, shoot anyone yourself?" asked one of the guests, trying to sound matter-of-fact. Floyd shook his head. "Naw, man," he said. "I leave that shit up to my friends. I got a whole lot of friends down there." He nodded at the street, where the guests knew they would be, on the way to their cars, in an hour or two.

Without further preliminaries, Floyd closed his eyes and fell off to sleep. He snored softly and put his hand on his crotch. An angelic look came over his face. Everyone made small talk and tried to act as if an ex-convict dozing in the living room was a common social occurrence. No one said anything about it because Gerald was there and because Floyd might be listening, even in his sleep, monitoring the conversation with some sort of prison sixth sense.

After half an hour or so, Floyd stirred. He must have been dreaming about sex, because he turned to an attractive black woman in her forties and, in a soft voice, said, "Mama, what you doin' Saturday night?"

The woman, who has a grandchild, couldn't believe her ears. Floyd repeated the question. "You gotta be kidding," she said, sounding more amused than frightened. "Listen, boy, you ain't ready for me on Tuesday night, and I know you ain't gonna be ready on Saturday." Floyd shrugged; Saturday night was a long time off in any case.

Floyd rubbed the sleep out of his eyes, drank another orange juice and gin, and stretched. Gerald, sensing that there had been enough interfacing for one night, told him it was time to be going.

I nervously escorted them to the door, where I made a last-minute (and deeply insincere) offer to be of any help I could to Floyd. He didn't even bother to say thank you.

"When I come up here, I didn't think you was cool," he said. "But you cool, you all right. Maybe I help *you.*"

"What kind of help do I need?" I asked uncomfortably.

"Man, there's a lot of dudes out there. Somebody might be watching you right now, y'know. They could be wanting to do you something. I just say a word around, you know, let people know you mah friend." He stepped out into the hall, leaving behind in the cozy apartment a chill intimation of the street below.

I returned to my guests, shaking my head. "Imagine that," I said. "His mother would rather have him in jail than on the street." I expected agreement, but I had assumed too much.

"Well, I can understand her," said the grandmother who had rejected Floyd's advances. "Sometimes I wish somebody would put my daughter in jail, too. That's where she belongs."

The statement shattered the "we're us and they're them" mood. "You want your daughter in *jail*?" I asked.

"Well, I don't know what to do about her anymore," said the

woman. "She's strung out on crack cocaine, and I just can't get through to her anymore."

The woman, who is the mother of five, began to talk in a subdued voice about her seventeen-year-old child. "The girl steals everything. She took my microwave oven, brass plates, a floor-model TV. One time, when nobody was home, she got her boyfriend to bring over a U-Haul trailer and they cleaned out the house. I was lucky to find out where it was before they sold it. I had to send my son over there with a shotgun to get it back. I can't leave her at home alone—one of my sons stays in the house at all times."

Only a short time before, her daughter had gone out with some friends to buy drugs. She wound up in an argument, and another teenager hit her across the face with a two-by-four. The girl lost an eye.

"Why?" asked the woman. "Why? My other kids are fine—they don't mess with drugs, they don't even drink. I've done everything I can—psychiatrists, threats, beatings, praying—but nothing works. She says, "I'm gonna be all right now, mama, but she doesn't *stay* all right. It's got to where we have to protect her own baby from her."

She was an educated woman, the grandmother in the living room. She had been through the civil rights movement, given her children African names, encouraged them to read James Baldwin, Richard Wright, Toni Morrison. Her daughter would sell her books if she could get her hands on them. She had already sold herself, and she might someday try to sell her only child. The lady shook her head. "You ever hear about the bad seed? I hate to say it but I'm afraid of my own daughter."

Chapter Three

SOSAD

In the fall of 1988, two white Detroiters were tried for burning down a crack house on their street. Although they admitted the act, which was patently illegal, they were acquitted by a mostly black jury. The police department deplored the arson and denounced the two men as vigilantes, but most people applauded. There was a perceptible law-and-order mood in the city and Tom Delisle's question—"Where's the outrage?"—was beginning to resonate.

Many blacks were concerned, not only for their personal safety but also by the fact that violence, especially teenage violence, was frightening away whites. This view was forthrightly expressed in an article, published in the black-owned *Michigan Chronicle*, by col-

pumnist Jim Ingram. Entitled "Wanna Come Over to My House?"
it addressed the city's teenagers:

> To errant Detroit youth: Imagine, if you will, my house. I, no one
> else, have broken out most of my windows, so the blame's on me.
>
> I throw trash in my backyard. I get bored, so I set fire to my attic
> or a bedroom.
>
> When visitors come, I might attack them. I may get mad and stab
> one upstairs or I'll shoot one or two in the kitchen.
>
> It's hard to fix the place up. Why? Well, when I get some money I
> go to houses ten miles away and spend it to repair their windows,
> clean up their litter or paint their porches. And you know what? They
> even take some of my money to hire people to keep me out when I
> try to act like I do at home.
>
> So will you come over to my house? But you can't come in my
> living room. I shot a guy in there and it's all boarded up, you know.
>
> And you have to watch yourself. Some of my friends carry guns
> and they sometimes come over and you might get shot or your
> woman might get raped or something like that. But come on over
> anyway, won't you?
>
> See, I really need you over because I was going to ask you . . . uh
> . . . for some money. See, I need some money to fix it up so more
> people will want to come over. . . .

Since arriving in the city I had met a number of kids, and on the
surface they didn't seem too different from Charles and his friends.
Pontiac had been considered a rough town, and there were sometimes bloody incidents, but actual bloodshed was rare, and basically
rational. I once saw a kid stab another kid at a dance, in a fight over
a girl. A released convict shot and badly wounded a guy who had
been seeing his wife while he was in prison. But these were excep-
tional events. Judging from the stories I heard in Detroit, many of
the city's teenagers seemed to be engaged in mindless mayhem.

This impression was confirmed by an FBI study published on the
front page of the *Free Press* in September.

DETROIT TOPS BIG CITIES IN RATE OF YOUTHS SLAIN

Detroit, whose children have died for gym shoes, drugs or a dirty look, has the highest juvenile homicide rate of the country's ten largest cities, according to a computer study of FBI crime reports from 1979 through 1986.

By 1986, Detroit's children were being killed at more than triple the combined rate for the nation's 10 largest cities. . . .

Shortly after this article appeared, I met with a black journalist about my age who writes with sensitivity and insight into the problems of the city and its people. In the course of our conversation I asked her why Detroit's kids seemed so violent.

The reporter regarded me with disdain "Drugs, unemployment, babies making babies," she said, reciting the causes in a bored tone, like a train conductor calling off stops. I had asked a naive question and she was letting me know it. I also detected a note of resentment in her voice. Who was I to come poking around, snooping judgmentally into the business of black folks and their children?

"But there must be more to it than that," I said. "There were drugs and unwed mothers when we were growing up. And a lot of these kids come from good homes. Why them? Why now?"

She shrugged and stared at me, professional courtesy wearing thin. Throughout my stay in Detroit, the only real hostility I encountered was from members of the black intelligentsia. Some were better at concealing it than others, but very often there was an unspoken question in the air—What the hell do you care? White apathy regarding the fate of blacks in general, and black children in particular, is so pervasive that interest is automatically a cause for suspicion.

This is reflected in the antipathy that many blacks, including black journalists, feel toward Detroit's newspapers and television stations. The major media are all white owned and operated, and most of their editors and reporters live outside the city. Several years ago, black reporters at the *News*, a Gannett newspaper, staged a week-long byline strike to protest discrimination in assignments, and most, at the *News* and elsewhere, continue to believe that press coverage of black affairs swings between the sensational and the apathetic.

Certainly this is true in the case of teenage violence. Particularly gruesome killings, especially when the victims are white, get front-page treatment; but average murders get reported on the inside pages under laconic headings like IN THIS WEEKEND'S SHOOTINGS. Partly this is a simple variation on the old journalistic rule that a dog biting a man is not news; every year, upwards of three hundred kids are shot in the city. But it is also true that black teenagers killing one another is of scant interest to the upscale suburbanites who are the media's target market.

In the city, however, where hardly a family has been untouched by adolescent violence or drug addiction, the question of the kids—how to raise them, protect them, defend yourself against them—was a constant topic. In a strange way it reminded me of Israel, where parents are universally concerned about their children's compulsory military service. Yet the chances of a teenager's being shot on the streets of Detroit are far greater than those of an Israeli soldier's being wounded in combat.

Clementine Barfield learned that in 1986, when her sixteen-year-old son, Derick, and his fifteen-year-old brother, Roger, became two of the 365 children shot in Detroit that year. Roger, critically wounded, survived. Derick died. And their mother, a large, gentle-faced woman with a lilting Mississippi accent, decided to try to put a stop to the violence.

"After Derick was murdered, about a month later, I began looking for a support group," Mrs. Barfield told me as we sat talking in her office on the second floor of an old schoolhouse on Martin Luther King Boulevard. "But there was none. So I went out and started one." The name of the group is Save Our Sons and Daughters—SOSAD.

Half a dozen women, mothers of slain children, were in the SOSAD office that day, performing the menial tasks that go with running an organization. They worked quietly while Mrs. Barfield, a frequently interviewed woman, patiently retold the story of the day in July 1986 that changed her life.

"The day before it happened, there had been an argument in school, and a boy pulled a gun on Roger," she recalled. The next day Derick and Roger went looking for the boy. He saw the Barfield brothers first, sitting in their car in a gas station. Afraid that they had a gun, the boy fired four shots into the car, and fled. The murderer was eighteen years old and he is in jail now. "The family of the killer lost their son, too," said Mrs. Barfield. "It's a thin line between victim and murderer in the black community.

"The kids in this city want to get away as fast as they can," she continued. "Derick planned to go to Georgetown University. He should have graduated this June. Next fall he would have been in college. This should have been his new beginning." Her voice faltered. "All I have now are memories."

Mrs. Barfield handed me a copy of the program for SOSAD's first annual Mother's Day benefit. It was a glossy booklet, a testament to the organization's professionalism—and the pain in which it was founded. It featured page after page of ads from bereaved parents, with pictures of their murdered children.

IN LOVING MEMORY OF A GIFT OF LIFE. ANDRE STREETER:
If I were to take stock of all my worldly treasures, the memories I have of the few years spent with you would be my most cherished possessions. Your mother.

RONALD 'LIL MAN' WEBSTER:
The love you spread, the good you've done, will never be forgotten by anyone. Your loving family.

And, next to a picture of a little boy with a smiling, open face:

IN LOVING MEMORY OF JEFFERY HILSON:
To the son we lost.

"There is a war in Detroit," Mrs. Barfield said, when I finished looking at the booklet, "and young black men are the targets. Our sons are at risk—to suicide, murder, jail and hopelessness. Really it's genocide; the enemy is the society that has forced the situation on them. Right now, the largest employer of young men in Detroit is drugs."

Genocide seemed a strong word; after all, the vast majority of black victims, including Mrs. Barfield's own son, are killed by other black teenagers. "Statistically that's true," she conceded, "but it's misleading. The real enemy is hopelessness. This is the first generation that hasn't done as well as its parents."

One of the women who had been stuffing envelopes when I arrived was listening to our conversation. Suddenly she began to sing, in a soft, mournful contralto. "Reach out and touch somebody's hand, make this a better world, if you can . . ." she sang, and the other ladies in the office put down their papers and joined in. A phone rang but no one answered it. Instead they sang on and on, "Reach out your hand, reach out your hand," mothers of the dead who were lamenting a generation of hopeless, furious, defenseless children.

When I was growing up, Detroit made one promise to its young people—a good job. A place on the line at GM, Ford or Chrysler was part of our birthright, a legacy to the city's children. And then, in the early seventies, that legacy was withdrawn.

After I graduated from Pontiac Central High School in 1965, I followed a route that was being traveled by eighteen-year-olds throughout the Detroit area. The prom, a few days of r&r and then, on Monday morning, the hiring line at Pontiac Motors.

Getting a job was as easy as showing up. We filled out a couple of forms, took a perfunctory physical exam, went to Montgomery Wards to buy work clothes and a lunch bucket and the next day found ourselves turning screws and fastening bolts for $3.65 an hour and all the overtime we could handle.

My first paycheck was close to $180, a fortune in those days. To earn it, I loaded sheets of metal into a giant press, hit a button, and watched the metal turn into panels. I never knew what the panels were for—nobody told me and I wasn't curious enough to ask. My orientation took approximately two minutes, and it was conducted by a scraggle-toothed hillbilly named Lucky who had thin tattooed arms, a greasy ducktail and a mean nasal twang. The foreman brought me over to him, said that we would be working together on the giant machine, and told him to explain my duties.

"See this press, kid?" Lucky snarled. "I'm the boss of this press. The last guy I worked with didn't think so, but he happened to fall in. They just covered this thing up with a black sheet and cleaned him out with a toothbrush."

I didn't say anything, but the look on my face must have convinced him that he had made his point. "Just do what I tell you, and you're gonna get on real fine," said my new mentor.

I have no idea whether Lucky's story was true or not, but I loved it—it was just the sort of initiation into the world of industrial manhood that I had been looking for. Working in the plant was more than just a way to make good money; it was a rite of passage, induction into the brotherhood of workingmen.

I didn't stay in the factory too long because I didn't have to. I blew most of the money I made on a trip to the Bahamas at the end of the summer, and used the rest for college. There were other kids working for tuition or travel money, but many signed on for the duration. Even then, you could easily support a family on an auto worker's salary.

Today you can do a lot better than that; a job with one of the Big Three is a blue-collar dream. Figuring in benefits, workers can easily earn sixty thousand dollars a year, and some make more. The problem is, there aren't any jobs.

The story of the rise and fall of the auto industry in Detroit has been told often. In the early part of the century, Henry Ford lured tens of thousands of semiliterate southern farm boys and European immigrants to Detroit with the offer of a magical five-dollar-a-day wage. Ford was a paternal tyrant who turned his operation into a giant plantation. A service department supervised the personal lives and private morality of his workers, and a private goon squad, led by the infamous Harry Bennett and manned by a collection of gangsters and ex-prizefighters, kept the unions out of the plants.

Throughout the thirties and early forties, the UAW and the auto companies, led by Ford, fought fierce battles. But following World War II, a new policy of cooperation was put in place by Henry Ford's grandson and successor, Henry II. The young Ford realized that fighting the unions was both wasteful and unpopular. In 1946, shortly after assuming control of Ford Motors, in a speech to the Society of Automotive Engineers, he introduced his new approach. "There is no reason that a union contract could not be written and agreed upon with the same efficiency and good temper that marks the negotiation of a commercial contract between two companies," he said.

Over the next quarter century the UAW, led by Walter Reuther, won ever more generous contracts from the Big Three. These concessions were, in turn, passed along to the consumers in the form of price increases. While it lasted, the system kept Detroit prosperous, but, in the mid-seventies, it fell apart. Japanese cars were cheaper, better and more economical. The OPEC-inspired rise in oil prices depressed the market for American gas-guzzlers. Automation made thousands of workers redundant. And the riot of 1967 encouraged management to locate new factories far from the urban battlefield.

The decline of the American auto industry was a national phenomenon, but it has been most painfully felt in the Motor City. In 1978, the UAW had about 1.5 million members; ten years later, it was struggling to stay around 1 million. During that period, the number of auto workers in the Detroit area dropped by fifty thousand.

Union economists know that this is not a temporary phenomenon; the best they can hope for is a slow, managed retreat. Once the UAW was a powerful progressive voice in Detroit, but today its role is largely reactionary. Its primary task is protecting the jobs of its members, which means keeping young people *out* of the plants. "The chance of a high school graduate in Detroit getting a job in an auto factory today are zilch," a union official told me without evident distress. "His best bet is fast foods." Fast-food jobs pay the minimum wage, $3.35 an hour in 1989. And you can't live on that.

Finding a job in an auto factory today is harder than getting into Harvard. In 1987, Mazda opened a new plant in Flat Rock, south of Detroit. The company had two thousand jobs—and one hundred thousand candidates. People who had been hired off the street twenty years before couldn't even get an application form.

Of the Big Three, only Ford has been doing any real hiring in recent years in the Detroit area. It can afford to be picky, and it is, recruiting new workers with the care of a country club screening committee. Candidates who hear about jobs apply through the State Employment Agency, which weeds out the obviously unqualified; high school dropouts or recent graduates aren't even considered. To make the first cut you need a record of successful previous employment.

Applicants who reach the personnel department are required to take a thorough physical examination, which includes a drug test and a battery of psychological tests aimed at judging attitude, motivation, reliability and teamwork. Only an elite few make it through the screening process.

Those who do are then called in for personal interviews. If they pass, they are sent to a special forty-hour orientation course. Some drop out at this stage; some are put on a waiting list; a few are given jobs for a ninety-day probationary period, which can turn into permanent employment.

Under this system, my old boss, Lucky, would never have got a job. Neither would I. The impoverished and poorly educated kids in Detroit don't have a prayer, and they know it. The complexities of international business, oil politics and modern technology have conspired to disinherit them.

Most of the auto jobs that do become available will go to well-educated whites from the suburbs. The simple truth is that a great many of the kids in Detroit do not have the skills—reading, writing and simple arithmetic—to work in a modern factory.

Like other urban problems, bad schools are not unique to Detroit. But the situation there is more stark, the numbers more depressing than in other places. Experts say that as many as 70 percent of the city's teenagers do not finish high school, and the overwhelming majority of those are barely educated. A senior state official told me that, of the twenty thousand or so kids who start the first grade each year, only five hundred will graduate with the skills needed to do college work. And, of the five hundred, four hundred will be girls. In other words, only a tiny fraction of the black males educated in Detroit can expect to attain the earning power associated with higher education.

One obvious reason for the breakdown of Detroit's schools is its diminished tax base: the white exodus left the system impoverished. Detroit spends about half as much as many of its suburban neighbors on education—and it shows.

In 1971, a federal judge named Stephen Roth ruled that de jure segregation existed in Detroit's schools and that there was no way to remedy it within the city itself. The judge decided that the only solution would be to bus students—suburban whites into the city, urban blacks out to the suburbs.

Roth's prescription was based on a revolutionary notion— that Detroit and its satellites were all part of one metropolitan community. This idea aroused fierce opposition from white people who had left town precisely because they didn't want anything to do with blacks. Bumper stickers saying "Roth is a child molester" became common, even after the United States Supreme Court overruled the decision. Three years later, when it was announced that Roth was dying, the hospital was flooded with hate calls wishing him a happy bus trip to hell.

Since then, the situation has become, if anything, worse. "Detroit schools are more segregated today than they ever were," according to Father William Cunningham, a Catholic priest who works with inner-city kids on job programs. "If the enrollment of the Detroit schools was all white, industry and the state government would come down here and put the Board of Education in jail for fraud and failure. Corporations would be screaming. But in America there is a marvelous neglect of what is black. The white administration of this state doesn't give a goddam for black kids."

Faced with the dangers and difficulties of raising kids in Detroit, parents with enough money move out of the city, or send their sons and daughters to private schools in the suburbs. But most people have no such option. Some put their faith in God and hope for the best. Others simply give up. A few, like Louise McCall, dedicate their lives to protecting their offspring.

In the case of her only daughter, Lisa, Louise McCall has a dual mission—to safeguard both the girl and her talent. Lisa is, at nineteen, perhaps the best young dancer in Detroit. A lithe, dark-skinned girl with a giggly voice and long ponytail, she is beautiful enough to have been a contestant in the Miss Black World pageant. Entering the competition was her mother's idea. So was applying for a scholarship, which she won, to the Alvin Ailey dance troupe in New York. With a little luck, Lisa and her mother hope she can dance her way out of danger.

I first met Lisa at a folklore festival, where she was performing with a group of young dancers. We were introduced by the program's director, who hoped to get her a little publicity. I asked a few questions about her career, but Lisa didn't really want to talk about herself. "My mother is the special one in our family," she said, and invited me to visit them the following Sunday afternoon.

Louise McCall was widowed when Lisa was small. She took her husband's insurance money and bought a house in the northwest corner of the city. Today the neighborhood, a well-tended area of middle-class homes and leafy trees, is mostly black, but when the

McCalls moved in, Lisa was one of only two black children in her school.

"On the first day of class, I brought Lisa in," said Mrs. McCall, a large, handsome woman with dark skin and a serious demeanor. "Her teacher was surprised to see me, I guess. She said, 'I didn't know you people cared about your children.' I realized right then that there might be a problem, so I started going to school with Lisa. I went every day for the next five years."

As Lisa grew older, Louise McCall went to work as a secretary. She also enrolled at Wayne State University, where she now lacks only a few credits for a B.A. in journalism and psychology. But even working full-time and studying at Wayne, Louise McCall has kept her daughter on a very short leash.

"I've never really done anything but study and dance." Lisa said. "I always had a fascination with dance, ever since I was a little girl. I'd see things when I watched other people." Louise McCall noticed that her daughter could duplicate the moves she saw on stage, and enrolled her in classes. By the time Lisa was twelve, she was dancing in productions around the city. Lisa's talent and protective upbringing made her an outsider at school and in the increasingly black neighborhood. "We aren't like other people," she said, looking fondly at her mother. "We go to plays, ballet—we never really fit in. I know that behind our backs we've been called E-lites, but were not. We're just different."

The McCalls are different in another way, too: They are Catholics in a Protestant fundamentalist city. Lisa occasionally attends church with friends, out of curiousity, but the gospel tradition, so formative for most black entertainers, is basically foreign to her. "I like Motown," she said, "but we listen to a lot of jazz and classical music. We just don't fit the stereotype. We're them, but we're not *like* them. As far as I'm concerned, I'm not really black or white. I don't care if the place I live is all black or all white. I just want to live in a safe environment."

The McCalls' neighborhood seems safe enough; its streets are wide and well lit, its homes substantial and respectably middle-class. But there are bars on the doors, and Louise McCall, still a young woman herself, seldom goes out after dark. "I'm afraid," she said, speaking for her daughter as well as herself. "People get shot at clubs and parties in Detroit."

As we sat chatting in the living room, we were joined by Lisa's current boyfriend, James. Boy trouble is one of the most common kinds in Detroit, and Mrs. McCall keeps a sharp eye on Lisa's friends. Clearly, she approved of James, a neighborhood kid who was studying architecture at Lawrence Institute of Technology. Like Lisa, he saw himself as an outsider on his own block.

"People think we're too white to be black," James said. "I can't even speak black English. My mother kept us in the house and made us learn how to study." Louise nodded approvingly.

James took a jaundiced view of his hometown. "I mean, when's the last time you heard a game show give away a fabulous trip to Detroit?" he said. Once again, Louise McCall nodded in agreement. Detroit is her home, too, the place where she was born and raised. She is committed to staying in the city; but she has also spent the better part of the past twenty years trying to keep it at arm's length.

People like the McCalls, members of the black middle class, have created an assimilated, American way of life for themselves. They are, in Lisa's words, different. But, despite Lisa's assertion that she feels neither white nor black, it is impossible to escape the reality of race.

On the night of Jesse Jackson's address to the 1988 Democratic National Convention, I returned to the McCall's to watch the speech on television with Louise. Together we heard Jackson tell his audience that he understood—the wounds of discrimination, the pain of poverty, the dreadful struggle of young mothers to raise their children on their own. As he spoke, I imagined that Louise McCall, safe in her comfortable home, proud of her talented daughter, was congratulating herself for having overcome these obstacles. But when I looked at her, tears were running down her dark cheeks. "Tell it, Jesse," she murmured. "Tell it just the way it is."

Carrie Baker* did not watch Jesse Jackson's speech because she doesn't have a television. Besides, she didn't need a presidential candidate to remind her of where she had been—she was still there, on welfare, an unwed mother of three.

I met Carrie at PACT, a program run by Wayne State University that helps parents get back children who have been taken by the court. She is a thin, intense woman with an intelligent, heart-shaped face and a soft-spoken manner. Despite the fact that her three children were taken away from her, and she went to jail briefly for child abuse, she didn't seem embarrassed or ashamed. Instead, she described her life, and her recent ordeal, with the dispassion of a professional social worker.

Carrie Baker was born in 1955, and raised in Highland Park. Her father, who worked on the line at Ford, was a "party person"; her mother, quiet and strict. She dropped out of school in the ninth grade and had her first child, a boy, at seventeen. A year later, she gave birth to a daughter. When we met, her son was sixteen, her daughter fifteen. She also had a five-year-old boy. The children have three different fathers, but she was never married to any of them.

For years, Carrie and her kids struggled along on welfare. Trouble started, according to her, early in 1987, when the father of her daughter, Beverly, got out of jail and demanded to move in.

"He was an alcoholic and a drug addict," she said, "and I didn't want him. So he started to harass me." Even sitting in the safety of the PACT office, I could see the fear in her eyes as she recalled what had happened.

"Bev's father tried to break in a couple of times, and I didn't know what to do. The harassment went on for months. My mother sug-

---

*The names of Carrie Baker and her children are fictitious.

gested that I get a shotgun and shoot him, and I considered it but I couldn't," she said. "I'm not a violent person, and I was too afraid."

Instead, Carrie turned inward. "I got depressed and I couldn't clean the house. There was a dope pad across the street, and people used to fight on our lawn. The situation began to affect Bev. She went on a rampage. She wouldn't go to school, and when she did, she looked like she was nobody's child. I just couldn't control her.

"Right about Easter, Bev stayed out all night. When she came back I told her that I was going shopping, but when I got back I was going to take her to the gynecologist. When I came back home, Bev had taken the baby to the Second Precinct and said I was abusing them. I guess she was mad because I yelled at her, and she wanted revenge. The next day I got a summons. I didn't see my children for two months.

"The police came and arrested me for prostituting my daughter, grand larceny and other trumped-up charges," she continued. "I had no idea what they were talking about. I stayed in jail for three days. I didn't have a lawyer and I was in a panic. But they never pressed any charges, and they just let me go."

Despite the fact that Carrie was innocent, when she got home she found that all three of her children were gone. The baby was put in a foster home, her daughter and son sent to youth centers.

"A lady came out from Social Services and looked around my house. 'Your windows are broken, your house is filthy,' she said. 'You must be on drugs'—although I wasn't. She went down the basement, and it was flooded. I couldn't get the landlord to fix it. 'You won't be getting your kids back,' the lady said, 'because your house is filthy and there's derbies in the water in the basement.' Derbies, you know, shit."

In an effort to get her kids back, Carrie enrolled in the PACT program. It was one way to demonstrate to the court that she was a conscientious parent.

"At first I thought it was, you know, just some more changes they were putting me through—but it worked," she said. "The counseling sessions taught me to look at myself. I realized that I was always trying to please other people. I thought if other people were happy, if I did things for them, it would make them care about me. I had to learn to be my own person, not what everybody else wanted me to be."

She also had to find a new home—her old place had been part of the reason that her kids were taken away. But she was broke. "Welfare took care of the rent, but I had no furniture, no money to heat the house and no transportation," she said. "For six months I looked for a new place to live and a job that would bring in more than the welfare—that's what I did while my kids were gone."

Where were her relatives while all this was going on, I wondered; didn't she have anyone to turn to for help? Carrie shook her head. "For a while I moved in with my mother, but I left because she wanted to use me as her tidy maid," she said. Her sister, who lived nearby, wouldn't take her in at all. So she went back to her unheated house and wrapped herself in blankets, waiting out the cold weather.

Finally, she found a new place on the west side, furnishing it with secondhand furniture and appliances. Her mother gave her a hot plate. Finding the house was a major step in getting her kids back. Six months after they had been taken away, her two sons were returned to her. Bev was still required to live in the youth home, but was allowed to visit her mother on weekends.

"When my baby came home, he didn't laugh or play or talk very much," Carrie said. "At night he would wake up screaming. My oldest boy hated Bev for what she did, although he's getting over it now. The two boys are very close. And I'm learning how to get along with Bev on a one-to-one basis. When she comes home, she'll have to learn that she can't just run wild. She'll have to work for what she gets."

By this time we had been sitting in the PACT office for half an hour, and Carrie had to go. Before she left, she invited me to visit her the following Saturday afternoon.

The house that Carrie searched months to find is a small, wooden bungalow on a quiet street in northwest Detroit. When I arrived, neighbors were watering their lawns and engaging in laughing porch-to-porch conversations, while their children rode bicycles on the sidewalk and ran from house to house. As I walked up to Carrie's door I noticed them noticing me; probably they thought I was another welfare inspector.

I found Carrie, wearing a red sweater and jeans, sitting in her living room, on a Salvation Army couch. Bev, home for the weekend, sat on the other end. Carrie's eldest son, Arnold, was at work, but Clarence raced around with a manic, six-year-old's energy. The place was clean but spare, the only wall decoration a hole punched through the plasterboard in the living room.

Bev was in a bubbly mood that afternoon, still excited about her high school homecoming game the night before. Although she lives in a girls' home, she attends a regular school on the west side. Like ninth grade girls everywhere she was worried about her appearance. "I'm only five-two and I weigh one hundred and twenty-four pounds," she said ruefully, dipping into a bag of potato chips on the coffee table. "And I'm the darkest one in the whole family."

Despite her ingenuous manner and baby face, Bev has had experiences that most American teenagers couldn't even imagine. In the two years she had been away she had run away from the girls' home half a dozen times. During one of her escapes, she and two girlfriends wound up in a crack house, where they spent two traumatic weeks. Bev saw people beaten bloody, stabbed, and one customer shot to death. After the shooting, the man who ran the house tried to keep her there by force; he was afraid she would tell the police. One day, while he was out, she fled. A few weeks later, her girlfriend, also fifteen, was murdered by the pusher, who accused her of stealing money and drugs.

She told this grisly story without prompting, in a high, girlish tone, while her mother sat on the other end of the couch and shook her head in dismay. "I know some people won't like this," Carrie said, "but whenever you got a whole lot of black people, you're gonna have problems. Blacks are ignorant and rude. Like that Suicide boyfriend of yours."

"Oh, Mama, he was just a friend," Bev said.

"She had a boyfriend named Suicide," said Carrie in a grim voice. "*Suicide*. He called up here and I answered, and he said, 'Yo, mama, Bev be home?' That's what I mean. Just an ignorant, crude nigger."

Bev was only a year older than my own daughter, Michal. I tried to imagine how I would feel if she came home with a boyfriend named Suicide. But of course she wouldn't, I thought. Where would she meet someone like that? And even if she did, I'd put a stop to it. Or could I? I tried to imagine myself duking it out with a young hoodlum. Then I tried to imagine Carrie doing it. It wasn't an easy picture to conjure up in either case.

Suicide was now out of the picture, but Carrie also disapproved of Bev's current boyfriend, a twenty-four-year-old musician. "I don't *do* anything with him," Bev protested, sounding like a teenager on a sitcom. "And I don't like it when he calls me his woman. I'm too young to be someone's woman. I just want a friend to talk to." Her mother, who first got pregnant when she was just about Bev's age, listened skeptically.

"You better think about what you're doing, Bev," she said. "This boy is a man. I tell this girl—wait for marriage to have sex. But if you can't wait, I'll take you to the doctor to have some pills. I'm telling you, every guy who tells you 'I love you,' what he means is 'I love *it*.' Just look at me and try to learn from my mistakes."

"Mama, I know that," Bev said. "I want to have a career, I want to be a policewoman. But, Mama, babies are so cute. You can dress them up and play with them."

"If you don't have any money, you can't afford to dress anybody up." Carrie sighed. Suddenly Bev sounded much younger than fifteen, and her mother seemed a lot older than thirty-three.

It was lunchtime, and we went to a neighborhood pizza parlor. Although Carrie and her kids have spent most of their lives on welfare, they seemed perfectly comfortable in the restaurant, expertly picking through the salad bar and the Italian menu. Clarence asked for a stack of quarters and amused himself at the Pac-man machine.

At the table, Bev took out a small mirror and a comb. "I have a white brother and a Jewish cousin, and they both have such good hair," she said. "Not like me."

"There's nothing wrong with your hair," said Carrie. She explained that Bev's white 'brother' is actually a trick baby, the child of her father's wife—a prostitute—and one of her customers. The Jewish cousin is the daughter of Carrie's sister and a man named Herb. Carrie explained these things without evident embarrassment. One of the things she learned at PACT is that it is permissible to talk openly with her children about sex.

"In my house, you didn't talk about sex," she recalled. "Once I asked my mother about the pill. When I got up off the floor, she said never to mention it again. I couldn't communicate with my mother at all. She was too busy working and entertaining guests. My parents were very straightlaced. I'm glad my father wasn't alive to see my children taken away—it would have destroyed him."

The food arrived and Clarence left his Pac-man game to join us. He seemed happy and content, until his mother rose from the table. Suddenly a look of panic crossed his face. "Mama, where you goin'?" he demanded.

"Just next door for some cigarettes, baby. I'll be right back," she said. Reassured, he rubbed a small hand across his eyes and returned to his pizza.

Bev ate with foster-home etiquette, primly and efficiently. Once she reminded her mother not to sit with her elbows on the table. Carrie smiled, proud of her daughter's manners. When Clarence spilled some of his Coke, Bev wiped it up with a napkin, saying nothing. He waited for a moment, surprised.

"Hey, ain't nobody mad at me?" he piped.

"Why should we be?" asked Bev in a matronly tone. "It was an accident."

"Seems like if you waste food, somebody gonna be mad," said

Clarence, sounding disappointed. Carrie leaned across the table and stroked his cheek.

Watching the interplay between Carrie and her kids, I had to remind myself that they were prime examples of the "urban underclass"—an unwed welfare mother, a rebellious teenage daughter who had lived in crack houses, and a small boy who had already spent almost half his life in foster homes. The conventional wisdom is that such people are irresponsible at best, and possibly evil. But the truth, it seemed to me, was more banal. Bev was a sweet, confused adolescent girl; her mother, a bright, harassed woman with no money and no resources to fall back on. I wondered if, in similar circumstances, I could have done better—and I wasn't sure.

Clearly, despite the differences in our backgrounds, Carrie wants the same things for her kids that I want for mine—to finish school, go to college, stay away from drugs and violence, and wait for babies until marriage.

These are the values she preaches to her children, but her authority is limited; unlike Louise McCall, she is not strong enough, financially or personally, to provide security or impose discipline. She can only tell them what she thinks and hope they listen.

On the way home from the restaurant, Bev mentioned a fourteen-year-old cousin who just had her first child. "That girl has ruined her life," said Carrie sternly. "She'll never get an education now, or a decent job."

"I know, Mama," said Bev in her bubbly teenage voice. "But, Mama, that baby is so cute. . . ."

Carrie sighed and said nothing. She saw what might be coming, but was powerless to stop it. Only thirty-three herself, the woman who was still fighting to get back her daughter knew that she soon might have a grandchild to raise.

Northwestern High School shares Detroit's Grand Boulevard with two citadels of the city's faded dreams: General Motors World Headquarters, and Hitsville USA, the former Motown studio.

Northwestern is also near the place where Clementine Barfield's son Derrick was murdered. The day before he was killed, Derrick Barfield, knowing his life was in danger, had gone looking for Kim Weston for protection. He never found her, and by the time she heard about it, it was too late. "I don't know what he thought I could do," she said. "But I sure would have tried to do *something*."

Thousands of young people have sought the protection and support of Kim Weston. The director of Festival, the city's performing arts program, she is a quiet, dignified woman, nearing fifty, with dark skin and a face that belongs on an African coin. When she enters a room, the toughest street kids in Detroit stand up and take off their hats. When she holds up her hand, an auditorium full of noisy teenagers falls into immediate silence. And when she sings, usually gospel, the most talented young artists in the city listen with openmouthed awe.

People in the music community of Detroit say that Weston is one of the finest female singers the city has ever seen—a considerable compliment in a town that has produced Diana Ross, Anita Baker, Martha Reeves and Aretha Franklin. Weston herself makes no such claim. In the early sixties she had a string of hits as a Motown artist, but she was never a superstar.

In 1966, Weston left Motown and moved to Los Angeles, but she didn't feel at home. Her husband, former Motown A&R director Mickey Stevenson, wanted to live in Hollywood near the show business community, but Weston hated its glitz and pressure. She missed being among black people, and used to drive miles across town, to Watts, to work with Jesse Jackson's Operation Breadbasket. She missed Detroit and the people she had grown up with on the city's east side. And so, in 1972, Kim Weston came back home. Five years later, she founded Festival.

For her faculty, Weston chose Motown alumni—Beans Bowles, the musical director of the Motown Revue; Hank Cosby, who played horn on many of the old Motown hits; former personnel director Dorothy Carey; Teddy Harris, Jr., who worked with Diana

Ross and the Supremes; costume designer Margaret Brown, who created the stage outfits for the Temptations and other Motown acts, and a number of others. She recruited them both for their professional skills and as role models for aspiring teenage performers. They serve as reminders that kids from the streets of the city can do something special.

"Did you ever see any of the old Motown artists?" Weston asked me as we walked down the hall of Northwestern High. It was a sweltering August afternoon, and I had come to see Festival in action.

"I saw you at the Fox Theater in the Motown Revue," I said. "It was back in about 1962. You wore a tight red dress and you sang a show tune. How's that?"

"Shut up!" Weston said, laughing and embarrassed. "You must have been a fan."

"A fanatic," I said. And I was. Our parents didn't understand Motown, but we did. At one time I was even in a group—King Mellow and the High Earls of Jive—that dreamed of becoming Hitsville's first integrated act. I was debating whether to demonstrate a few bars of our unforgettable rendition of "Two Lovers" when Weston was stopped by a pretty sixteen-year-old named Piper Carter. She was scheduled to perform in one of the minishows that Festival puts on at old folks' homes and community centers around the city, and wanted to talk to Kim about her act.

"Is that what you want to do, be a professional rapper?" I asked.

"No, actually I want to be an attorney," she said. "I'm planning to go to Harvard. What I really like to do is write poetry. But rapping might be a good way to make some money while I'm in college. It's expensive, you know."

Weston beamed and led me into the vocal music workshop. As soon as she entered, the room came to a respectful silence.

"We have a visitor with us today," she said, pointing to me. "I want you to let him know, are you as good as the singers from Motown?"

"Yes!" the class erupted.

"Are you better than we were?"

"Yes!" they chorused.

"Okay," she said, pleased. "Let me hear you prove it."

A small, dark young man left his seat and stood at the head of the class. A pianist hit the opening chord and he began to sing "Amazing Grace" in a pure, clear baritone. When he hit the high notes with a flourish, the room erupted into cheers of "Sing, George, sing." He closed his eyes and improvised, daring his own range, and the kids clapped wildly. Weston stood in the corner, listening intently, arms folded across her chest.

When the song ended, George walked across the room. Weston unfolded her arms and hugged him. There were tears running down her cheeks. Happy and embarrassed, George turned to the class. "Hey, give me two," he said, and they responded with two sharp claps of applause. "Give me one," he commanded, and they clapped once more. "Now, give me a half," he yelled, and they moved their hands together, stopping just short of contact. The silence was a surprise, and Weston doubled over, laughing.

The kids sang on and on. A frail, pretty girl with reddish hair performed "Somewhere over the Rainbow." The entire group sang "Now We Sing Joyfully unto God," sounding like the Mormon Tabernacle Choir. Then choir instructor Rudy Hawkins sat down at the piano and played one of their favorites, a rousing gospel number called "Spirit of the Living God." Weston sang along, quietly, careful not to upstage her young protégés.

The gospel spirit is part of Kim Weston, and of Festival. When you ask her how she is, she answers, "I'm blessed." On especially good days she says, "I'm better than blessed"; on bad ones, "I'm blessed anyway." And in private moments, when she is asked what she wants to accomplish with Festival, she says, "I want to be a blessing in the lives of these young people." Coming from any other show business personality, such sentiments would sound corny, but for

Weston they are natural expressions of a personality molded by a life of deep, fervent faith in God.

Kim Weston was raised, literally, in church. Her mother was an officer in the Apostolic Overcoming Holiness Church, a sanctified denomination with a stern moral code that forbade secular music, dancing, and even riding the bus for fun. She and Kim lived in a small apartment over the sanctuary. In the early morning, before she went to school, Kim would accompany her mother downstairs, where, together, they dusted the pews, swept the floor and lighted the stove in winter.

Kim's mother spent her days cleaning white people's houses, her nights looking after church business and her weekends singing in the choir and cooking barbecue to raise money for the congregation. At the age of three, Kim sang her first solo at a Sunday evening service, and by the time she was a teenager, she was a featured performer in the Wright Specials, a local gospel group.

One of the reasons for Weston's amazing rapport with her "young people" is her authenticity. Although she rarely discusses her background, they can sense that she has been where they are now— black, poor, the child of a single mother with nothing more to fall back on than belief in God and her own talent. And there is something more; Weston was there, at Hitsville, a part of the Motown legend that motivates and haunts the city's talented teenagers.

Kim Weston came to Motown in the early sixties, after songwriter Eddie Holland heard about her singing and invited her to record some songs. At first she refused because she felt uncomfortable singing secular music. But Holland was persistent, she needed the money, and eventually she made the trip across town to Hitsville, USA.

In those days, Hitsville was more than a company headquarters. It was a fraternity house, an exclusive club where black teenagers came together to make music and money under the tutelage of homeboy Berry Gordy. They sang together, partied together, toured together and often married one another. Like the cast of *Saturday*

Night Live a decade later, the Motown stars were the envy of young America, permanent guests at the hottest party in the country.

Like a lot of parties, this one ended with a hangover. In the early seventies, Berry Gordy moved his operation to the West Coast, taking a few of his most popular acts with him and leaving the rest to fend for themselves. Gordy's defection meant little to the white establishment. A scan of the Motown file at the *Free Press* reveals the extent of this apathy; the paper published only two articles—one a denial, one a confirmation—about Motown's departure. There was virtually no editorial discussion or op-end comment. Thus did Berry Gordy move Motown, a multimillion-dollar industry with inestimable public relations value—out of the city.

White adults never saw Motown as more than a bunch of black kids in capes and ball gowns. But for blacks, losing the company was a demoralizing blow. The auto companies promised young Detroiters a job, but Motown offered more—a chance for greatness. Every kid who sang in church dreamed of following Smokey and Diana, Martha and Little Stevie—and Kim Weston—into Berry Gordy's star-making machine on West Grand Boulevard.

Today, now that it is too late, people understand what they lost. The state of Michigan uses Motown songs in its promotions and the governor was on hand to dedicate the Motown Museum, located in the old Hitsville studio, which is all that is left of the Detroit show business dream.

The museum attracts more than a thousand visitors a month, most of them from out of town. People come to pay homage to the Motown sound and to gaze at the tiny Studio Number One, a primitive facility where most of the early hits were recorded. A Lebanese Christian told a tour guide that he used to listen to "My Girl" while his village was being bombed by Druze artillery. A Japanese tourist fainted from excitement in the control room. A lady from England stood on the spot where the Supremes had recorded "Stop in the Name of Love" and cried.

"This is the first place I came when I arrived in Detroit," said

Gerald Clark, the man who had brought Floyd to my cocktail party. Clark, who often speaks in fragments of old rock and roll lyrics, arrived in Detroit from Springfield, Massachusetts. "I wanted to be a songwriter, and this was Mecca. I drove from Springfield, and I listened to Motown songs the entire way." He looked lovingly around the studio he never managed to penetrate, and remembered an old Smokey Robinson tune. "You really had a hold on me," he said to the empty room.

Clark's friend Bob Kerse came a little closer. In the late sixties he worked at Motown briefly as an assistant technician, and he had dreams of becoming a producer. "I didn't take it seriously back then, though," he said. "I was a young guy and I goofed off. I thought there would be plenty of time. Nobody ever dreamed that Motown would leave Detroit. Motown *was* Detroit."

In the summer of 1988, Clark and Kerse were trying to revive the dream. They were promoting amateur shows, attempting to locate and sign new singers, just as their idol, Berry Gordy, had done a generation before. But, they admitted, things were going slowly. The talent was still there, an unending stream of church-schooled crooners and shouters, but the magic was missing, and so were the audiences. "Some nights we don't get more than fifty, sixty people," said Kerse. "I don't know what the problem is, but it's pretty discouraging."

The shows were staged at the Palms, a downtown movie house just a few blocks from the Fox Theater, where the Motown Revue once performed, and this proximity gave a haunting, melancholy flavor to the effort. Many of the contestants were kids from the Festival program. Kim Weston encouraged them and helped them prepare. She takes a proprietary interest in their careers, and her greatest frustration is that she has been unable to help most of them find outlets for their talent.

When they do perform, Weston is often in the audience to cheer them on. That is what brought her one evening to the Latin Quarter, a downtown showroom where Martha Reeves and the Vandellas were staging a bon voyage show on the eve of a British tour. Weston, who dislikes nightclubs, was there because Martha is an old friend from Miller High and Motown, but mostly because some Festival graduates were performing that night in the New Breed Be-bop Society Orchestra.

When she arrived at the club, there was a sense of excitement and reunion in the air. The tables on the mezzanine had little white place cards reserving them for "Miracles," "Contours," "Spinners," "Tops" and other members of the Motown royalty. The entirely black audience sat at long tables on the sprawling main floor and looked up at the empty places with anticipation. The parking attendants under the club's marquee inspected the new arrivals closely, searching for stars.

Backstage, Martha Reeves sat in a red-sequined gown and fussed with her long, straight wig. When she saw Kim Weston, she jumped up and gave her a warm kiss. The two women, about the same age, made an interesting contrast. Reeves looked like an aging teenager; Weston, who had just come from a reception honoring civil rights pioneer Rosa Parks, wore glasses and had her hair pulled back primly in a knot.

One of the Vandellas spotted Weston and came over to give her a hug. "You got back together a year ago, right?" Kim asked, and the Vandella nodded. "Well, y'all started a year before me last time, so maybe I'll start up again pretty soon myself," Weston said. The two women giggled, remembering their first years at Motown, more than a quarter century before.

A tall, open-faced man with thick glasses came up behind Weston and the Vandella and embraced them both. Kim spun around and her eyes went wide with pleasure. "Bobby Rogers of the Miracles," she exclaimed, giving him his full title. "I didn't know you were in Detroit." Many of the Motown people who stayed at home have a feeling of being left behind. Some are bitter, some philosophical; either way, they take an obvious comfort in each others' presence in the city.

Rogers, who started out with Smokey Robinson when they were teenagers, surveyed the room.

"Just like old times, isn't it, Bobby?" the Vandella said.

"Yeah, things are coming back the way they used to be," he replied. He didn't sound as if he meant it, but he didn't sound too unhappy, either. The Motown teenagers have all grown up since the sixties.

Rogers is a friendly man who used to make a point of signing autographs for ugly girls. Unlike many former Motown artists, he still receives substantial royalties, which supplement his income as an interior decorator.

"Smokey made sure we got our money because he was close to Berry," he said. "I got to say that Smokey was very fair with us, very fair. He invited me to write with him, and you know Smokey Robinson doesn't need any help from me to write songs. The only hit I ever wrote was 'First I Look at the Purse.'"

Cocktail waitresses circulated with drinks and people began to take their seats. Many of the celebrity tables remained vacant. The Tops were on the road, somebody said. A lone Spinner represented his group. "Where's the Contours?" someone asked, and a loud laugh went up from the others. "Man, them Contours were something else," Rogers said fondly.

The old Motown people gossiped about Smokey and Stevie, Marvin and Diane (never Diana)—legendary names to most people, old pals to them, nothing more. The gossip was good-natured, affectionate. "We were just a bunch of kids together," said Kim Weston. "And we honestly liked each other."

"And still do," said Rogers, raising his brandy glass in a toast to old times.

The house lights dimmed and the show began with a number of amateur acts. Most of them were second-rate, but Bobby Rogers and his friends laughed hard at their jokes and clapped enthusiastically along with their music.

Weston asked Rogers if he was still singing. "Only in church," he said, and squeezed his wife's hand. He was once married to Wanda Rogers, lead singer of the Marvelettes. His second wife, Joan, has worked for United Airlines for twenty years. "Bobby had to learn all the songs," she said.

"Never did spend too much time in church as a kid," said Rogers, a bit sheepishly. But after all, who needs a church when you are a Miracle?

Unlike Rogers, most of the Motown stars started out singing gospel. In Detroit, where there is a Baptist or Sanctified church on nearly every block, there was an enormous pool of talent, but the same could be said for other cities. Chicago, New York, Philadelphia, and New Orleans all produced their share of black teenage r&b artists. Nowhere else, however, were these singers picked, packaged and provided with material like at Motown; and nowhere else did they work for a black man and a black company.

This was a part of the magic of Motown for black Detroiters. Berry Gordy created more than a sound and a fortune; he proved that a black man was smart enough and tough enough to control a black product. Yet, that night Gordy was in California, and other members of his family, the brothers and sisters who have stayed in Detroit, were conspicuously absent. Martha Reeves had wanted the chance that Gordy gave to Diana Ross, and she slammed the door after her when she quit Motown. The Gordys have a long memory.

The New Breed Be-bop Society Orchestra struck up "Jimmy Mack," and Reeves came charging out. She looked lithe and youthful, although her voice, still strong, sometimes fumbled around for notes like a drunk searching through his pocket for a coin. The Motown fraternity didn't seem to mind, though; they watched her with smiles on their faces. "Good for Martha," Kim Weston said, and the others nodded.

Throughout the show, people approached the Motown tables to pay their respects. Some asked for autographs, others hauled one or another of the artists to their feet for a photograph. They mentioned shows they had attended, called out the names of old hits.

Weston was less concerned with the past than the future. "The band up there is all Festival graduates," she told Rogers. "Believe me, some of the kids I have are better than we ever were."

Rogers considered. Behind his thick glasses you could see his eyes grow hazy as he recalled the glory days with Smokey and the group. "Better than we were?" he finally said, in a gentle tone. "Yeah, I suppose they are better than us. But there's only one thing, Kim. They aren't us."

"They're better," Weston insisted softly. "All they need is a chance."

After my first visit to Festival, I came back several times, partly because the sight of so many happy, talented kids cheered me up. One day I mentioned to Weston that it must be fun working with the city's teenage elite.

Weston shook her head. "We get a cross section," she said. "The kids you see here come from every high school in the city. They're no different from everybody else. They have their problems."

I was skeptical and said so. The kids at Festival seemed too well-behaved and gentle to be representative of the fierce generation of the homicide statistics. But Weston was adamant. "I'll let you talk to some of the young people and you can judge for yourself," she offered.

Late that afternoon, I was introduced to three Festival participants. "This gentleman wants to interview you," Weston told them, and left the room. The kids stared at me across a great gap of age and race, waiting to see what I wanted.

We began with a little what-I-want-to-be-when-I-grow-up. Perrin, a light-skinned sixteen-year-old with a B average at Southwestern High School, said she intended to be a foreign ambassador. George, the baritone from the choral workshop, was out of school and trying to break into show business. Joycelyn, who had sung "Somewhere over the Rainbow" in a Judy Holliday voice, was older than the others, and hoped to get a job at the Mazda factory while she looked for work as an entertainer.

"We're chosen to be part of a dream," said George. Shifting into a mock-sermonic voice, he turned to the others. "Can I get a witness, children?" he demanded, and they said "Amen." He was obviously the class clown, and the preacher parody is one of his stock bits.

"I came to Festival as a gospel singer," said Joycelyn. "And you know what? I found out I can do opera. Imagine that."

"The girl can do opera," said George. "Great God Almighty, we got us an opera-singing young lady here with us today! Let us say 'Amen.'" Joycelyn and Perrin giggled.

"What it shows is that people can accomplish something, not just go out in the street and act the fool," said Perrin, sounding adult and serious. "Smokey Robinson lived on my grandmother's street. We know him real well. He sends me little tips sometimes. And my family is good friends with the Four Tops, too."

"People say Detroit is dead without Motown, but if they'd only give us half a chance, I do believe we could make the Motown of old come back to this fair city," said George.

"That's right," said Joycelyn. "We've got everything they had. We have a Berry Gordy in Kim Weston."

"None of this would be here without Sister Weston," said George.

"None of *us* would be here without Kim," said Joycelyn. "If I have a hero, it's her." The others nodded in agreement. "Praise God for Sister Kim," George half-sang.

"My mother is my hero," said Perrin. She hesitated. "See, my mother is black, and my father is white, although he's semiprejudiced against whites. At school the kids know about it and, being mixed, I get it from both ends. When I came here, I had to decide what I was, whether I was black or white. On the form I wrote 'Amgriques.' That's what you call what I am," she said, pronouncing the strange-sounding word. "I'm amgriques."

"How do you get treated when you leave the city?" George asked.

"Like a black," she said. "I went out to the suburbs to spend the night with a friend one time, and the cops knocked on the door to find out who I was."

The others nodded knowingly. "Those suburbs are taboo," said George. "I don't even bother going out there anymore. Once I was just driving around, out in Bloomfield Hills, and a cop stopped me and hit me. I just called on Jesus." He lapsed into his preacher's voice. "I said, 'Lord, let me get out of this mess and I'll never come back out here again.' And I never have."

"One time I got a job out in Bloomfield, taking care of some people's child," Joycelyn added. "They left me in a big old house with a sauna and Jacuzzi and their little baby. He used to just fall out and have fits like something got a hold on him. And you know what they did? They left a fifty-dollar bill in a kitchen drawer. I said, 'What's fifty dollars doin' in there with the spoons and the forks?' They were testing me, trying to find out if I was thief. So I quit and came back to the city. I'm no thief, just because I'm black."

"Sometimes white people act crazy," George said, and the others nodded assent. They have grown up in a black city, and they can't remember a time when Detroit wasn't divided by the invisible barrier at Eight Mile Road. On their side of the line they are at home, but they know all about the kind of trouble that faces blacks who try to break out into the larger world.

Talking about the suburbs had turned the conversation gloomy. To break the mood, I asked George whether his comic talents were inherited. I expected a wisecrack, but his eyes registered alarm.

"Inherited? I don't know if I should talk about what I inherited or not," he said, and paused a long moment, weighing the matter. Finally he said, "Okay, you asked for it," and took a deep breath. "A couple of years ago my father got up on the wrong side of the bed, you might say. He, ah, well, he killed my stepmother and baby brother. Then he burned down the house. Then he killed himself. Kind of a tough day, know what I mean? That's my inheritance." He tried to smile. The others, who clearly hadn't heard the story, looked at him in shock.

"After that, I went through the drug thing," he said in a steady voice. "At the time, it was severely critical. I took the insurance money and put it up my nose—fifty thousand dollars. And I lost two years of my life after Daddy took his scenic cruise."

There was a long silence. Finally Perrin said, "There's drugs in every house around me, but I've never even seen them. Because of my mother."

"My mother is said to have ESP," said Joycelyn. Then she stopped, looked at George, and her lip began to quiver. "I had a tragic incident too," she said, averting her eyes. "I got involved with cocaine and—well, there is time I can't account for. I don't remember where I was or what I did. I can't account for a year and a half of my life." She began to cry silently, and it was George's turn to look on helplessly.

At the beginning of the conversation, I had suspected a setup; three model students to represent the program. But Kim Weston had a different point to make. The media have turned "teenage drug addicts," "high school dropouts" and "unwed mothers" into clichés of the black metropolis, stock phrases meant to convey an image of menace or immorality. But just as there is a thin line between victim and murderer in the black community, there is a blurred distinction between "good" kids and "bad" ones.

After a few moments, Joycelyn wiped away her tears. "Three years ago I went to Solomon's Church," she said. "I spoke in tongues and caught the Holy Ghost, and I was saved."

"Amen to that," said George, serious this time. "Amen," the others whispered. "If it hadn't of been for God, and Festival, I'd be lost," Joycelyn said. "Instead, I'm saved."

Several months after my first visit to Festival, Kim Weston invited me to a dinner-dance sponsored by the National Law Enforcement Practitioners, who were holding their annual convention in Detroit. By day, the practitioners discussed the ways and means of fighting crime; by night they partied. And in Detroit, partying still means Motown.

The dinner was an elaborate spread. The Detroit Police Department laid on a full buffet, open bar and entertainment by Weston, Ivy Hunter (who wrote "Just Ask the Lonely" for the Four Tops) and the Earl Van Dyke Band, once the house band at Hitsville.

Like the Martha Reeves show, this was something of a reunion. George Gordy was there, representing the Gordy family. A tiny man with a shining bald head, gold-framed granny glasses and a giant gold medallion dangling from his neck, he looked like a diplomat from some Afro-American foreign planet.

Maxine Powell sat at our table. She wore a fedora and green suit, and looked as proper and forbidding as she had in the days when she ran a charm school—chaperone operation for the company's young stars. She munched fried chicken wings, holding them daintily with her pinky finger sticking out, chewing with her mouth tightly shut. When she wanted to pick her teeth, she put her head almost under the table and covered it with a white linen napkin. The legend is that she turned Diana Ross and the others into little ladies, and the aging musicians at our table behaved like children forced to dine with a strict schoolmarm.

The band sat together, old men who still make young men's music. That night Earl Van Dyke played mostly left-handed because his right was arthritic. The others, pushing sixty, wore thick glasses and sported potbellies that hung over their cummerbunds.

Pistol Allen, the old Motown drummer, came escorted by his twenty-eight-year-old daughter. He produced pictures of all nine of his children and passed them around. "Every one of them is a professional," he said, beaming, and the others, mindful of the pitfalls of child rearing in Detroit, nodded appreciatively.

The emcee that night was a middle-aged police officer who told the crowd that he had originally come to Detroit from Ohio to join Motown. Before starting the show, he introduced Katherine Shaffner of the Marvelettes.

Once the Marvelettes communicated in three-minute bursts of rhythm, little poems with cautionary messages: "Watch out, here comes that playboy"; "Don't mess with Bill"; "Danger, heartbreak dead ahead." Tonight Shaffner had a different warning, and it was delivered in dry, measured prose.

"Some of you may know," she said, "that last year my nineteen-year-old son, Tony, was shot to death here in Detroit." She said it with such dignity and reserve that it took a moment for the words to sink in. The musicians exchanged looks—most of them hadn't known. There was an uncomfortable rustling in the audience. The officers, mostly white, had come to party, not to listen to another hard-luck story. But if Shaffner sensed their mood, she ignored it. She took her time, telling them about the son she had lost.

These stories are all depressingly similar. There wasn't a Detroiter there who hadn't heard them, and many had experienced them personally. Jacqueline Wilson; Jackie Wilson, Jr.; Tony Shaffner—the sons and daughters of the famous rate an item on the evening news, a visit from *Entertainment Tonight*, a brief mention at the flatfoots' ball. The others get six lines in the newspaper and a gospel song.

"I'm telling you this," she concluded with composure, "because you are on the front lines of the battle, and you need to know what a mother feels. You need to see this from the family's point of view. We are all the victims of what's going on. There's a war going on out in the streets."

There was an awkward moment when she took her seat. Then the musicians filed up to the bandstand to start the show. They struck up a Motown medley, and the assembled officers and their wives lumbered out of their seats. The white cops danced with thick-ankled determination, and their black colleagues showed solidarity by moving sedately to the beat. Gradually, as Van Dyke played and Ivy Hunter sang, the gloomy mood lifted, and a sense of tentative festivity took its place.

Closing the show, Kim Weston took the microphone and belted out one of her old hits, "Take Me in Your Arms." People danced, clapped at the tables or bellied up to the open bar for a nightcap. The evening was coming to a successful conclusion.

During Shaffner's speech, Weston had been in the ladies' room, preparing to go on. She had missed the story, and knew nothing of Tony Shaffner's death. Now, as the band swung into "Dancing in the Streets," she called on the former Marvelette ("My Motown sister Katherine") to join her onstage. Schaffner hesitated for just a moment, and then rose from her seat. The two women stood side by side and sang: "Summer's here and the time is right, for dancing in the streets; don't forget the Motor City, dancing, dancing in the streets. . . ."

The officers and their wives danced and sang along, transported by the tune and the memories it evoked. Memories of a time when Detroit was Motown, not the Murder Capital; a time when children walked to school in safety and there was dancing, not warfare, in the streets of America's sixth largest city.

Chapter Four

A CHRISTIAN WOMAN NAMED VIOLENCE

When I told Bea Buck about some of the kids I had met—the fearsome Floyd; George, with a year missing from his life; Matthew, stabbed and bleeding on the lawn near the Seawinds—she looked up from the colored people's spaghetti she was preparing and said, "Somebody ought to cut them little fuckers' heads off with a sword." She pronounced the *w*, giving the sentiment a biblical flavor, and then went back to stirring her pot in the narrow kitchen of her downtown apartment.

Ms. Buck is not a cook. She is police communications specialist by profession, an amateur playwright by avocation, and something of a social commentator. Close to sixty, she is a handsome, ample-breasted woman with a high-pitched laugh and sparkling almond eyes. Her round, caramel face contrasts nicely with a sharp tongue, and she dispenses mordant observations on the human condition in the barbed aphoristic style of a Motown Ambrose Bierce.

I had offered to bring some wine for dinner, but Ms. Buck told me she doesn't drink wine. When I remarked that most Americans don't, she was quick to correct me.

"I am not an American," she said, stiffly.

"Then what are you?" I asked.

"A colored person," she replied, a note of challenge in her voice.

"Let me ask you something. Did you ever think what it would be like to be white?"

"No, I never thought about it and I never want to," she said. "The idea horrifies me, if you want to know. White people will steal the taste right out of your mouth."

Ms. Buck went into her bedroom and emerged with a photograph of her maternal grandfather, who was white. "I never liked that man," she said. "He scared me when I was a little girl."

"But you've got his picture. That must mean something."

"That's right, I do. Well, the truth is that nobody else in the family would take it, so I did."

She was so obviously enjoying the chance to shock a visitor that I persisted. "You can't tell me that you never wondered what it would be like to be white. You're a writer—aren't you at least curious about what white people's lives are like, what they think about, talk about . . ."

"I know what they talk about," she said. "They talk about niggers." She laughed and asked for my plate. "I fixed you some colored people's spaghetti," she said.

"Okay, what's colored people's spaghetti?"

"That is spaghetti that ain't cooked right," she said with a loud laugh, dishing a mound of it onto my plate.

Bea Buck was born and raised in Detroit. As a young girl she worked as a switchboard operator at the Gotham Hotel, the city's fanciest black establishment, where she became friendly with the entertainers, politicians and other celebrities who patronized the clubs and cabarets of nearby Paradise Valley. Despite poverty and segregation, Ms. Buck regards the late forties and early fifties as a golden era, a time when black Detroit had safe streets, glamorous nightlife and obedient children.

"Don't get me wrong," she said. "We had plenty of problems back then, too. But we certainly didn't have the opportunities that these children have today. The only thing they've been deprived of is a functioning brain. They've been raised without any values. There's only one answer: Somebody needs to cut the little fuckers' heads off with a sword."

Fred Williams, spokesman for the Detroit Police Department, was both appalled and diverted by Bea Buck's sanguine solution to the city's crime problem. She and Williams are old friends, and he is well acquainted with her hyperbolic style. When I asked him if the department was laying in a stock of swords, he shook his head and said fondly, "Bea Buck is crazy."

"She cooked me colored people's spaghetti," I told him. "You know, spaghetti that ain't cooked right."

The conceit did not amuse Inspector Williams. "You come by my place and I'll cook you a real dinner," he said. "And bring Ms. Bea Buck with you. I'll show you what colored people's cooking is all about."

"Freddie Williams is crazy," said Bea Buck fondly, as we rose to the twenty-first floor of the Jeffersonian, a luxury high rise on the Detroit River, on the way to dinner. "But I'll admit one something—that man does know how to cook."

In Williams's apartment, which might be more accurately described as a bachelor pad, hundreds of videotapes lined the walls and elaborate stereo equipment was stacked neatly next to an electric organ in the tasteful living room. Art books lay primly on the coffee table, in marked contrast to the sybaritic king-size bed in the bedroom. As Williams led me to the balcony to gaze at the lights of the city and his fishing boat bobbing below in the marina, the aroma of New Orleans gumbo wafted out of his small, immaculate kitchen.

The gumbo was as good as it smelled. Williams is a perfectionist, and as we ate he discoursed on the intricacies of Cajun cooking, one of his many hobbies. He produced literature—cookbooks and guides to New Orleans restaurants—and explained every aspect of preparing the complicated dish.

An ex-amateur boxer and high school football star, Fred Williams became a cop in the fifties. "In those days, the only time you saw a picture of a black man in a white newspaper, it had 'wanted' printed over it," he said. "Black policemen were locked into three precincts. We couldn't even patrol Woodward Avenue. That was in preliberation times. Hell, they used to have a black holdup squad with all white officers. People talk about the good old days? Well, what was so good about them?"

During those years, before the Young administration, Fred Williams was known as a militant. He led protests against discrimination in the department, and was considered a troublemaker by many of the white officers. He went into his bedroom and emerged with several photos of a younger officer Williams, with a formidable Afro, dressed in a dashiki.

Along with the photos, Williams brought out a police scanner. It crackled with reports from the street below. A man was cut in a knife fight on Chicago Boulevard. "We've got to rid ourselves of drugs and guns," he said. "We've been waiting for a knight on a white horse ever since Martin Luther King died. These kids today, now that the civil rights bills are in, they think they have a free ticket. Young parents don't realize that the fight isn't over. Hell, we haven't even begun. We're going backwards. Blacks can't sit around and wait for whites to do for us. The trouble with us is us."

"Freddie, did you ever think about what it would be like to be white?" Bea asked, a mischievous twinkle in her eye. Williams snorted. "I wouldn't be white for nothin'," he said. "I would have missed a lot of living. The heritage we have is so rich and so proud, we've done so much with so many handicaps."

"What I can't stand is these *siditty* folks who move out of town, them little bourgeois-ass niggers," said Bea Buck. "They go out there and just tear up. They don't know anything about lawns, anyway. The only thing a black person wants to do with something green is put it in a pot and boil it with some ham hocks." She laughed happily.

"I go out to the suburbs for a drive, and police cars follow me," said Williams. "Now, what in hell is suspicious about me? When I get into an elevator with a white woman, she looks at me like I'm going to mug her. Because that's what she's been conditioned to think about black men.

"Basically this is a problem of image. We got a problem with the media. And it's not just the way they make us look to other people; the media make you feel bad about Detroit, bad about yourself. They call it a hellhole. Is Detroit worse than other cities? Hell no. Are the Dallas Cowboys 'America's Team'? Same thing, it just PR."

The radio crackled again—a fatal shooting on the east side.

Williams cast his gaze toward the glistening lights of the city below. "Things are building up out there," he said in a low voice. "Could we have another riot like 1967? Shit, yeah. The police were the catalyst last time, but it would have happened anyway. The lack of jobs, the despair, the bullshit by the politicians—read the Kerner Report, you could adjust it to today. It's building up, and if something isn't done, it could happen again."

"I'll tell you something," he continued. "Detroit was the first city to get a lot of these problems, and it's going to be the first city to find solutions to them. We're going to solve these urban problems and blacks are going to do it. The real answer is moral—the family and especially the church. We need moral rearmament; this is basically a very moral city."

Ms. Buck, serious for once, nodded in agreement. "The church is a sleeping giant," she said. "And it's about time it woke its tired self up."

Williams rose from the table, dimmed the lights and sat down at his small electric organ. He is a self-taught musician who, with typical thoroughness, learned to read music as well as play by ear. He ran his fingers over the keyboard with a professional flourish and began to play "Tenderly." Bea Buck closed her eyes and sang along quietly. Twenty-one floors below the lights twinkled merrily while the police radio crackled, bringing news from another planet.

Wherever I went that fall, people talked about the need for what Fred Williams called "moral rearmament," a return to a perhaps mythical time of traditional values and accepted authority. And, not surprisingly, they tended to look for leadership to the city's most powerful institution—the church.

"In this city, people *stay* on their knees," a woman told me, and it was true. In Detroit, Christianity—specifically black Protestant fundamentalism—approaches the status of state doctrine. It touches every aspect of public life—politics, government, art, culture, education—in a way unknown in other American cities. Public school choirs sing gospel songs and classrooms are decorated with pictures of prominent religious personalities. Political meetings begin with prayers and hymns. Clergymen write columns in the newspapers and serve as precinct captains for the Coleman Young machine. In 1988, four of the nine members of the Common Council were ordained ministers.

One day I came across a copy of a form letter sent by a city department to thousands of citizens. It was signed "Yours in Christ."

"How can you send something like this?" I asked the official. "Haven't you heard that there is separation of church and state in America?"

"Maybe in America," the official said with a grin. "But not here."

Nobody knows for sure just how many churches there are in Detroit (the usual estimate is upwards of 2,500, one for every 400 people); with the commercial exodus from the city, banks, grocery stores and theaters have been transformed into houses of worship, and there are some blocks with a church on every corner. In most of them, the majority of worshipers are women, often accompanied by small children or grandchildren, and elderly men. A generation ago, several ministers told me, there was a more even balance between the sexes. "Used to be, the women came to pray with their menfolk," a deacon told me. "Today, they come to pray for them."

I attended a different church almost every Sunday for months, and I was usually the only white in attendance. My reception was always warm and welcoming. Ushers smiled and nodded when I arrived; members of the congregation supplied me with prayer books and stenciled church bulletins, and made it a point to shake my hand at the end of worship. Often I was acknowledged from the pulpit and asked to stand and introduce myself. Invariably, when I did so, I received a round of encouraging applause.

Predictably, these congregations came in all sizes, shapes and shades of black. They ranged from the flinty respectability of the elite black churches, such as Hartford Memorial, to frenzied storefronts and cultist shrines. Taken together, they are an institution that might someday spearhead the moral rearmament that Fred Williams talked about.

Despite their denominational diversity, the ministers in the city can be divided into two primary groups—those who emphasize works, and those who preach faith. Jim Holley, a short, powerfully built, light-skinned preacher from North Carolina, is a works man.

Holley is the pastor of Little Rock Baptist Church, one of the largest and most prominent in Detroit. Its chapel seats around one thousand, and it is usually full on Sunday mornings, when Reverend Holley preaches. Thousands more listen to his sermons on the radio, see his billboards advertising Little Rock Baptist's philosophy ("Don't Worry, Be Happy") as they drive along the freeways, or read about his various political campaigns and social programs in the newspapers. Since he came to town fifteen years ago, Jim Holley's activism and outspoken eloquence have made him one of Detroit's most visible clergymen.

His credentials are impressive—a B.A. from Tennessee State University, M.A.s from Tennessee State and the University of Chicago, and a Ph.D. in education from Wayne State. Despite his degrees, however, Holley affects a down-home style and calls himself "a country preacher," a title he appropriated from his friend and political mentor, the Reverend Jesse Jackson. Most of Little Rock's 3,500 members are working class people, and a good many come from the South. Holley wants them to feel at home.

Little Rock is an impressive mock gothic building on Woodward Avenue, next to Northern High School. On an August Sunday morning, sunshine filtered through the stained-glass windows of its high-ceilinged chapel, and the polished wood pews were crowded with worshipers dressed in accordance with the church's informal summer dress code—jeans, sport shirts, jogging outfits and even work clothes.

After some gospel music by an excellent choir, Reverend Holley, dressed in a sparkling white robe, rose from his seat on the pulpit, prayed briefly, and then began the service by reading his personal want ads from a stack of three-by-five note cards. "Channel Two is looking for a television technician and a secretary," he said, and shuffled the cards. "A lady's clothing store downtown is looking for a stock boy." Shuffle. "The federal government is hiring air controllers. Say amen!" The congregation dutifully responded. "Now, you can get that job, church," he said. "There are jobs out there, but it's a job finding a job. So while you're looking, touch up your skills. Out of eighty-five thousand pilots in this country, only two hundred are black. You can be a pilot. But you gotta get trained. Say amen. Now say amen again. If any of y'all are interested in applying for these jobs, you come and see me. I'm not letting anybody go out on any job interviews without getting past me first." A laugh rose from the pews. When I asked him later what he had meant, he smiled and said, "Oh, it's just a charisma line."

Satisfied, Holley moved on. "This winter we'll be giving out ten thousand pair of shoes," he said. The announcement was greeted with silence. "Now, that's ten thousand *pairs* of shoes, church," he reminded them. "Y'all ought to clap or faint or somethin'." The congregation laughed and applauded.

Riding the applause, Holley expounded his self-help vision for the black community. "We got to teach our children to read. Open up the school of Little Angels, teach our kids foreign languages, computers. We don't want them dancing da butt all day long. There's more to life than da butt. There's more to life than drinking, selling drugs and getting buried. We've got to teach them to appreciate the Detroit Symphony Orchestra [applause], the ballet [louder applause], the ah, ah, *opera*." The congregation cheered at the prospect of their children's trading da butt for Debussy.

In an effortless transition, Holley went from the secular to the sacred, preaching on the story of Hosea, which he transformed into a dialogue between the prophet and God, with himself playing both parts. When the Lord (Holley) tells Hosea (Holley) to marry a faithless woman, Hosea protests: "God, you're tellin' me to marry a prosti-tute!" ("And I know a lot of y'all can relate to that,") he added, to loud laughter.

The congregation grew silent again as Holley led to his dramatic conclusion. "God," he screamed in anguish. "This woman has broken my heart. But she hasn't broken my love."

"And that's the way it is with us, here in Detroit," he said quietly. "God says, 'I took black people off the plantation and gave them houses and cities, mayors and leaders. And now they're killing each other, hating each other. They broke my heart, but they haven't broken my love."

There was a chorus of amens, and suddenly everyone joined hands. A young black man standing next to me took mine, fixed me with a sincere stare and said, 'Brother, God loves you and so do I." Surprised, I managed to murmur "Me too," feeling foolish. He released my hand, the choir began to sing "The Old Ship of Zion" and the angels of Little Rock Baptist filed out into the street, where the sinners were just starting to wake up from another Motown Saturday night.

Jim Holley is one of Detroit's best preachers (the *Free Press* once ranked them, like college football teams), but his real interest is politics and community organization. He regards Martin Luther King as his "spiritual father," and four years ago he headed the Jackson campaign in Michigan. He has obvious political ambitions himself, not an unreasonable thing in a city with so many divines in public life, and he uses his church as a base.

Like many fledgling politicos, Jim Holley is not averse to publicity, which is why he invited me to accompany him on his rounds one day. "We're glad to have you with us this morning, Reverend," he said when we met at his church. Although I was flattered by the honorific title, I didn't want to mislead my host. "I'm not really a reverend," I told him modestly. "In fact, I'm not even a Christian. I'm Jewish."

Holley took the news with good humor. "I'm a rabbi myself," he said. "A black rabbi. A Jewish rabbi serves only Jews, right? Well, my calling is only to serve blacks. We need to help ourselves."

And yet, our first destination that morning was Temple Baptist Church, a wealthy white suburban congregation. Holley planned to ask its pastor for assistance in setting up several outreach programs. "They send missionaries to Africa, Reverend," he said to me. "I want to get them to send a few to Detroit."

Despite his prominence and his Ph.D., Holley seemed ill at ease when we arrived. We parked near the church, walked past its gleaming white pillars and entered the building. No sooner were we inside than we were startled by the loud ringing of a school bell. "That's the alarm for when niggers are in the church," he told his driver, only half joking.

The church secretary, a crisp, smiling woman, greeted us with polite confusion. According to her calendar, the meeting was scheduled for the following day. She ushered us into an audiovisual room while she went to call the pastor, who was taking the morning off. As we waited, Holley spread out his papers on the desk. "I'm sure that meeting was for today," he said, "but maybe I misunderstood.

I been in the battle for sixteen years and I still don't understand white people. No offense, Reverend."

The lady returned, full of apologies for the mix-up, and promised to reschedule the meeting. Holley gathered up his carefully drawn proposal and put it back in his briefcase. He seemed more relieved than annoyed.

On the way out, we conducted a quick, nervous inspection tour of the building. Holley looked wistfully at the modern classrooms and the auditoriumlike chapel with its color-coordinated seats. As we reached the entrance, another school bell rang, and children spilled into the halls. They regarded us with total apathy. Holley's driver spotted two small black kids among the throng. "Hey, Rev, they got some of us out here," he said in wonder.

Once this would have been a cause for rejoicing, especially for a man who regards himself as a spiritual son of Martin Luther King. But Holley is no integrationist. "It's just an admission that we don't have the ability to care for ourselves," he said. "When we bus our kids to white schools, it just says we're not able to educate our own children. Education doesn't come by osmosis, it's hard work. Being around white people doesn't do it."

On the way back to the city, Holley looked out the window at the green parks and neat homes and reflected on the lure of the suburbs. "Upper-middle-class blacks have the responsibility to reach back and help other blacks," he mused. "They're gonna let the middle-class Negroes have Southfield, keep the poor Negroes in Detroit. I can move my body to Southfield but not my soul. Isiah Thomas, all these other sports stars—here I am, having to ask white people for help. Why can't I ask Isiah? He's making enough. Most of these Negroes don't even belong to the NAACP. They have moved body, soul and mind from the streets where they learned to play ball in the first place. This pisses me off to the highest pissitivity. They don't do anything, man, anything."

"Why do you call them Negroes?" I asked.

"Negro is just another word for nigger, Reverend," he said. "Now that I have a wider audience, I have to be more polite."

I asked Holley what he would do with the money he wants to raise, and he spoke about establishing church-based institutions—health-care clinics, recreational centers and especially schools.

"Negroes know how to sing—that's nothing," he said. "We got to teach our children how to play the harp, the violin. I want them to be cultured, to speak properly, to be able to compete. We in the church have a responsibility to them, but so far we're just not making a difference. We've got to give them the right skills, and the right values.

"If someone in a family tells a teenage girl that pregnancy is all right, then that person must be made responsible for the baby," he continued. "I had a seventeen-year-old girl come to see me, with six children—two sets of twins. Teenage mothers have no right to their children. White folks can't say that, but it's true. They ought to be given to an extended family member or to the state. Those kids are nothing more than walking zombies.

"Two years ago, I took seventeen young men down to Alabama State University and I registered them personally," he said. "Three are left. One got thrown out for rape. Two more got thrown out for jumping on the pizza boy. Some people we just can't change. We have to stop spending so much time on the generation we've already lost and put emphasis on those kids who are infants, the ones that can still be saved."

As we talked, the car sped from the suburbs back into the city. We hadn't passed any checkpoints or border signs, but when we looked out the windows we saw another country of burned and blasted houses and knots of aimless-looking young men on street corners. Holley shook his head with sorrow.

"This is a strong city, although it appears weak," he said. "The strength is in the spirit of the people. In the last few years, there has been a hairline fracture of the spirit, but not a break. The problem is, we lack community. No white man in America is smart enough to do to us what we're doing to ourselves—killing, selling drugs, raping, not teaching our children, not helping one another economically—every process, social, political and economic. But it doesn't have to be this way. We can change things; the church can change things." He was silent for a long moment, as he gazed at the cityscape, and then turned back to me. "Reverend," he said, "if Dr. King could see this, he would weep, weep, weep."

To many whites, all black churches seem pretty much alike, congregations full of ferver and rhythm. Within the black community, however, the differences—social, theological and ritual—are substantial. Jim Holley, with his burning social commitment, represents the activist wing; but at the Universal Liberty and Christ Temple, a small congregation on Detroit's east side, a more personal gospel of salvation is dispensed. Its proponent, the Reverend Ralph J. Boyd, doesn't mind rendering unto Caesar what is his, providing the rest is rendered unto the man known to his followers as "the Living Christ."

Boyd is an elegant man in his late sixties who, despite recent heart surgery and the implanting of a pacemaker, fully expects to live forever. He came to Detroit from Alabama in the 1940s with his mentor, the estimable Prophet Jones, and he continues to preach Jones's doctrine of eternal life on earth and prosperity for the faithful of the Kingdom, as his congregation calls itself.

Prophet Jones confounded his own beliefs by dying in 1973. But at his height, during the 1950s, he held his services at a converted downtown theater and claimed several hundred thousand adherents across the country. The Prophet boasted that he could heal the sick, predict the future and talk directly to God. It was he who established the essential theology of the spiritual church in Detroit, which includes not only the doctrine of eternal life and prosperity but the dictum that "God don't like women." Jones claimed that sexual intercourse with a female was a life-threatening sin; his detractors said that he simply wanted to keep the young men of his congregation for himself.

Eventually Boyd split with Jones and established his own church. Soon after, Jones ran afoul of the city's morality laws and ended up in exile in Chicago. But his flamboyant style lives on in places such as the Universal Liberty and Christ Temple, and in other storefront sanctuaries throughout the city.

Boyd's church is more elaborate than most, but it is still a modest edifice for a man who claims to be in direct, personal touch with God: blond wood pews, a small altar and walls decorated with neon signs—DIVINE GOD and 7 (God's perfect number)—that look like beer advertisements. Adjacent to it is the House of Holiness, a combination sacristy, meditation facility and boutique where Boyd meets with congregants.

When I went to see him on a Saturday afternoon, there was a long line of people ahead of me. As I waited I browsed through the merchandise in his store, which runs to the exotic. Holy hyssop bath oil ($5.00), hyssop floor wash, Voodoo dolls ($3.25), Jinx Remover, Triple Strength Cast-Off Evil Incense, Holy Vision Bath Oil ($5.25), High John the Conquerer Soap ("It conquers all evil forces"), and cards inscribed with the Reverend Boyd's revelations (sample: "I am, I am in perfect harmony with the law of prosperity") for $2.50.

The label on the hyssop bath oil advises, "Read Psalm 51." The psalm says, "Purge me with hyssop, and I shall be clean; wash me, and I shall be whiter than snow." It was, I assumed, a figurative wish; Boyd's followers are all black.

Off the boutique there were prayer rooms equipped with meditation couches and brass stands, where people leave written requests. I opened one and read: "Help me get a high-paying job. Give me health. And help me control my son."

An attractive woman who used to be a high-fashion model in Europe and now serves as the Prophet's secretary, informed me that he was ready to meet with me. She ushered me into a spare room where Boyd sat behind a desk, wearing an expensive-looking camel

hair sport jacket and a blinding amount of jewelry. When I compli-
mented him on his diamonds, he beamed. "The earth is the Lord's
and the fullness thereof," he intoned. "And we are each the Lord in
our own world. The things that God put on earth, he put here for
our use."

Judging from the note I found in the meditation room Boyd's followers—who include prosperous professionals as well as domestic
workers and welfare women—want pretty much the same things as
the Reverend Holley's. But unlike the city's more mainline pastors,
Boyd doesn't believe they can be obtained through works. At one
point he considered opening his own school, but funds were not
forthcoming. "I just brought my mind in instead," he said. Communication with the holy spirits, prayer and the proper use of roots
and herbs are his prescription for the social ills of Detroit.

Reverend Boyd, like his mentor, Prophet Jones, claims to be
psychic. According to him, he can see, feel and sometimes hear the
voice of God. "In Detroit people know of prophecies I have made,"
he told me. "Sometimes it's frightening. I fell out during a trance
one time. My spirit went to Russia, to a very beautiful place where
men were in conference discussing the world. A man at the head of
the table said, 'We'll release an object that will give us up-to-date
data.' I came back into my body, and that night I prophesied that
the Russians were going to put an object in space. The church was
packed with people that night, dear. And the next week it was up
there—Sputnik."

The prophet didn't have much time for me that Saturday, but
before I left he offered to tell my future. He closed his eyes for a
moment and concentrated. "You are a wonderful and beautiful person, dear," he said. "You're going to have great success. Amen."

This sort of perceptive genius has won Boyd a large following in
Detroit. Two hundred or so of the faithful, mostly well-dressed
women and a smattering of men, were in church on a Sunday night
in October. When I arrived, about eight o'clock, they were singing

gospel songs and dancing in the aisles as they waited for the arrival of their leader.

After about half an hour Boyd entered from a rear door, wearing a vicuña topcoat over a splendid white silk robe. The singing and clapping rose to a crescendo as he was assisted out of his wrap by Angel Bishop Dorothy, a teacher in his College of Higher Wisdom, and assumed his seat, a thronelike chair that seemed entirely appropriate to his regal manner.

A few minutes later, the singing was interrupted for a reminder that the Kingdom's Christmas would be celebrated on November 14, Reverend Boyd's birthday (participation fee, one hundred dollars). Boyd smiled at the assembly with benign modesty. Then the church band, which included electric guitars, tambourines, drums and an electric organ, struck up "I'm a Royal Child, Adopted into a Royal Family," and the dancing and singing re-commenced.

Finally, Reverend Boyd took the rostrum to announce a collection—the first of four during the service. Many of the people there made offerings all four times, and some had done the same that morning. Eternal life does not come cheap on the east side of Detroit.

After the collection, Reverend Boyd introduced Prophet Dawson, his 'spiritual son,' who was to deliver the evening's main message. Dawson acknowledged the honor gratefully, telling the worshipers that "spiritual bread is baked by God, but delivered by the King," and then launched into his sermon. A small, dynamic man with the stage presence and intensity of Wilson Pickett, he half sang, half preached his gospel of salvation through Reverend Boyd. There were no want ads, no admonitions about community solidarity, no calls for a new board of education from the pulpit—just straight, old-time religion, interrupted by an occasional commercial.

Dawson's text centered on immortality: "The King teaches that it was not the plan of God for man to die. The Bible says, 'The wages of sin is death, but the gift of me is eternal life.' If you think you can live and you qualify, then there ain't nothin' you can do but live." People cheered, shouted amen and beat on tambourines.

The primary qualification for immortality is the ability to call on spirits. Sometimes this is done by Boyd himself, sometimes on a do-it-yourself basis by the congregation. That night Prophet Dawson hollered and danced, cajoled and thundered in an effort to summon them, and as the service progressed, more and more people joined in.

After a time, Dawson paused to ask for a second offering to buy Reverend Boyd a new Mercedes Benz. "He's a king," he said, "and a king needs a chariot." White-robed ushers passed buckets through the crowd, and women with callused hands snapped open their change purses to contribute to the royal transportation fund.

Following the second offering, Dawson stepped up the intensity another notch, and people began to fall out. A fat woman in a white pleated skirt and middy blouse danced up the aisles in total ecstasy, eyes closed and feet thudding on the threadbare carpet. She was quickly surrounded by other women who held their arms out to keep her from crashing into a pew. A young girl no more than seventeen, dressed demurely in a suit and small pearl earrings, stood rigidly at her seat and howled. Nearby a tall man in a black pin-striped suit began to chant "Thank you, Jesus; thank you, Jesus," a mint Lifesaver bobbing on his tongue throughout the incantation. Ralph J. Boyd surveyed the scene with great equanimity, but a woman in a white hospital uniform and nurse's cap peered closely at the congregation. From time to time she descended from the pulpit to lead one of the more emotional worshipers to a seat.

In the midst of all this frenzy, I was forgotten, although earlier I had been the subject of considerable curiosity. White visitors to the Kingdom are rare, and when I first came in, the congregants—perhaps mindful of Prophet Jones's problems with the law—regarded me with a circumspect interest. Blacks are expert at looking at whites without seeming to, and I had felt, rather than seen, their scrutiny.

Now, however, transported by the music and the dancing, they were no longer concerned about outsiders, or about the outside world. They were applying medicine to wounded spirits, stoking their emotional fires for another long, hard week. One song led into another, the tambourines and drums providing a steady beat. People sat passively and then were suddenly ignited, like the houses I had seen go up in flame on Devil's Night.

Prophet Dawson allowed the frenzy to continue for almost half an hour before he calmed things down again. He produced a white garment and a pair of scissors, and told the congregation that he had decided to cut up his robe ("blessed by Reverend Boyd") and sell the pieces for five dollars each. Once again purses clicked open, and a number of people came forward to buy a patch of the garment.

No one seemed uncomfortable with this blatant fund-raising. At one point a visiting soloist told the congregation that Reverend Boyd was the first man she had ever seen wearing a full-length mink coat. The congregation shouted 'Amen' and Boyd himself smiled, taking the remark, correctly, as a tribute. "You have inspired me both spiritually and materially," the singer told him.

It was nearing midnight, and although Dawson had issued mock warnings ("The spirit is in here and we just might stay all night") things began to wind down. People were spent, and they sat quietly while Reverend Boyd addressed them in a surprisingly low-key manner. He talked about the need for prayer all through the week, not just on Sunday; reminded them again about Christmas, and prayed for the ill and shut-in.

When the prayer was concluded, the band struck up a tune that sounded very much like "Mamma's Little Baby Loves Shortnin' Bread" and the congregation began to sing—"Money, money, money, money, money, money, money, a whole lot of money is coming my way." They sang it over and over, while about thirty people lined up at the side of the church, each with twenty dollars in hand. One by one they approached the altar, handed the bills to the white-robed church ladies, and paused in front of Reverend Boyd, who cupped his hands over their right ears and whispered a brief, personal message to each one. It was a simple, practical benediction from the Living Christ on Earth—the lottery number for the week.

Later I discussed what I had seen at Reverend Boyd's church with a friend. She is a woman of great sophistication, intellect and social consciousness, and I expected her to be outraged by the blatant materialism and egocentricity of the Living Christ and his doctrines. But she herself was raised in a holiness tradition, and she was surprisingly sympathetic.

"There are all kind of people in the black community, just like in the white community," she said. "Not everyone can relate to a Martin Luther King, or the intellectual approach of some of the ministers here in Detroit. They need something, too, and they get it from the Reverend Boyds. When they give him money, they're really just supporting their church. It's basically no different then paying dues or a tithe to any other church; they feel that they're getting something for their money. And besides," she added with a mischievous smile, "you never know. Somebody's liable to hit that number."

Over the years, the essential religiosity of the black community has made Detroit a fertile ground for sects and doctrines of all kinds. Some, like the spiritual church of Prophet Jones and Ralph Boyd, have been introverted and self-centered. Others take a broader, harsher social view. The Nation of Islam was founded in Detroit by W. D. Fard in the summer of 1930; Temple Number One, ministered by the brother of the late Elijah Muhammad, is still located there. And, in the late sixties, the Reverend Albert Cleage established a nationalist denomination, the Pan African Orthodox Christian Church, as a militant alternative to traditional, white-oriented Christianity.

Cleage was deeply influenced by Malcolm X, and his church reflects the black nationalism and racial separatism of the Muslims. Its chief theological tenet is that Jesus was a black political figure; its main social doctrine, that integration is a pipe dream and that blacks must gain economic and political power to liberate and defend themselves from white oppression. Following the riot of 1967, Cleage terrified whites with talk about burning down the rest of the city; but, in recent years, he has toned down his rhetoric, if not his basic message, and his adherents have become a part of Detroit's establishment.

Cleage, who Africanized his name to Jaramogi Abebe Agyeman, has a significant national following. The sect does not divulge membership figures, but it has major churches in Atlanta and Houston as well as Detroit, where the membership of the Shrine of the Black Madonna is estimated in the thousands.

Most suburbanites (and some Detroiters) have never heard of it, but the Shrine is a powerful force in the city's political life, a place where church and statecraft intersect. Its Black Slate endorses candidates, and sometimes runs its own. In the summer of 1988, in the Thirteenth Congressional District's primary, the Black Slate put its muscle behind one of Jaramogi's most faithful followers, Barbara Rose Collins.

At first glance, Collins seems like an improbable militant. She is an ample, almond-eyed woman with a round, pleasant face and a cheerful manner. But, despite her jovial appearance, she is, in her own words, the political creature of Jaramogi and his church. Professionally she uses her American name, but at the Shrine she is known as Makunda Najuma Fela. "That means daughter of a king, lovely to behold, and violent," she explained. "I chose that last name— violent—because the time may come when we have to defend ourselves. The people who call me Makunda are the older ones, the ones who came through the struggle with me."

In 1973, the Shrine and the Black Slate played a key role in the election of Coleman Young. Now, they were hoping to accomplish the same thing for Collins against one of the mayor's closest allies, George Crockett. Young, who is politically indebted to the church, was officially neutral; but even with the mayor on the sidelines, few of the city's political pros thought that Collins had a chance. Crockett was the incumbent and incumbents are rarely beaten in general elections, let alone primaries. It would take all of the Shrine's energy and commitment to defeat him.

The Thirteenth District is a mixed bag. It is about 75 percent black and includes the WASP suburb of Grosse Pointe; neat, working-class neighborhoods, once known as "the black suburbs," in the southwest part of Detroit; and the city's east side, perhaps the poorest urban area in the country. On the Saturday before the election, I accompanied Collins to a settlement house meeting there, not far from the neighborhood where she was born and raised.

"Most of this city is like a national disaster," she observed on the way to the meeting. "Drugs, crack, assembly lines shutting down—it all comes here first, the good and the bad. Whatever happens in America happens here first—Detroit is like a laboratory for the rest of the country."

Collins was especially upset by the absence of black-owned stores along the crumbling business streets. "This is a phenomenon of the black community in Detroit," she said. "It's really a question of racism. Businessmen have learned that the blacks will go where they are—to the suburbs."

Black economic self-sufficiency is one of the basic teachings of Jaramogi. The Shrine runs cooperative ventures based loosely on the Israeli kibbutz model, and it encourages its members to go into business. "We thought we could get it through political power, but we've learned that we need economic power, too," Collins said. "Anytime you don't have a major department store in a city this size, you know you're oppressed." It was a strikingly American criterion for oppression—the absence of a downtown Macy's—but not a frivolous one; a great deal of the money earned by Detroiters is, in fact, spent in the suburbs.

There is a strong strain of Calvinism in the Shrine's doctrine. "Jaramogi says that blacks have a different mind-set from whites because of slavery," she explained. "When you work for massa, you work slowly, and that's not good if you're trying to hold a job. White people declared blacks to be inferior—and when we act it out, we turn that myth into a fact. If you are willing to work hard, you can accomplish anything you want. And if you have a black city administration, it's our fault if the city deteriorates."

Collins's campaign was largely based on her ability to deal with this deterioration. She contrasted her local expertise with her opponent, casting Crockett as an apathetic absentee representative who spent most of his time dealing with foreign affairs. "People over here are interested in issues that are close to home," she said. "I care about Third World issues, too; Jaramogi teaches us that nothing is as sacred as the liberation of black people. But first things first."

Foreign affairs were not on the minds of the hundred or so blacks who came to hear Collins that afternoon at the settlement house. They were the substantial burghers of a disaster zone, and the candidate focused on their concerns.

"You sit on valuable land," Collins told them. "You don't like the way it looks, do ya?"

"No!" they hollered in unison.

"This was a beautiful area. What went wrong in Detroit? We lost our jobs and our young boys went to sellin' drugs. And a new type of slavery took over—welfare. We're supposed to be urban, but we've become rural—that's how much vacant land we have here. Politics is power and there ain't nothin' wrong with it. Either you have it or you give it to someone else. We need to go up yonder where the money is, to Washington, D.C. And I need to get you excited."

There were shouts of "Amen" and "Tell it, Sister Barbara" from the crowd. One by one they rose to testify to the difficulties of daily life. They complained about the lack of police protection, the city's failure to demolish dilapidated houses, and the shortage of jobs. Collins listened with sympathy and, from time to time, jotted down a note.

An elderly woman in a white hat and pigtails rose and began talking about the new city airport that had opened nearby. "They say it's supposed to provide jobs," she said, "but if it provides jobs to the colored people like the highway does—forget it. You don't even see a colored man digging a hole for a tree out there." The audience murmured its agreement.

"It's a disgrace, it's the county's fault and I'll look into it," the candidate promised. Once again, there was applause and scattered amens, but this time there were a few boos as well.

A man in a white painter's hat rose from his seat and pointed his finger at Ms. Collins. "It's very hard to see you when you're not running for office," he said. "You only come around at election time. What do y'all do on that council?"

"We can't get a loan from a bank to put a roof on our house," yelled a woman.

"Why don't you folks on the council do somethin' 'bout these drug houses?" called an old man. And, all of a sudden, everyone was shouting at once.

The chairlady, an officious woman with a large gavel, began banging for order. "You people just be quiet," she said in a shrill, school-marmish tone. "Nobody has the right to talk unless I tell them to."

At this, a stout woman in a floral dress stood up and shook an admonishing finger at the chairlady. "You don't know how to talk to people. We're not children, we're citizens," she said, and the crowd applauded. The stout woman turned to them. "I don't know what y'all are so excited about," she told them. "I been sitting here for a hour's time and still didn't nobody say 'Thank God for bringing us here today.' How many get up on Sunday morning and say, 'I'm a child of God'?" This seeming irrelevancy struck a responsive chord; people began to nod and say "That's right" and "Tell it." In Detroit, religion is never irrelevant; amens syncopate the beat of the gavel at every public meeting.

Collins sensed the new mood of the crowd and smiled benignly. She is a church lady, and this was familiar turf. She began gathering up her notes and shoveling them into her oversized purse—it was early afternoon, and she still had a number of campaign stops.

"Good luck, everybody," she called to the luckless inhabitants of the east side. "God bless you and don't forget to vote."

In marked contrast to Collins's frenzied effort, George Crockett was not even campaigning for reelection. Three days before the balloting, the waiting room of his office on Woodward Avenue seemed more like that of a small law firm than an election headquarters. Two secretaries typed quietly at their desks. One or two constituents sat leafing through old copies of *Ebony*.

Crockett had come back from Washington the day before. At the airport, he asked a cabbie about his chances and was told "Everything's cool." That was the extent of his polling. He planned to confine his campaign to a rare Sunday morning visit to his church. Like his old friend the mayor, George Crockett belongs to a generation of secular revolutionaries for whom religion is a matter of only passing concern.

The congressman's self-confidence was based on more than the calculation that incumbents seldom lose. He is a legendary figure in Detroit, one of the founding fathers of what is viewed as black liberation. Born in Jacksonville, Florida, in 1909, he studied at Moorehouse College in Atlanta, and then took a law degree at the University of Michigan. In 1944, he came to Detroit as director of the UAW's Fair Employment Practices Commission. Two years later he went into private practice, specializing in civil rights cases, and he became a partner in the first major integrated law firm in the United States.

As a lawyer, Crockett developed a reputation as a radical. He represented Carl Winter of Michigan and other American communists in a celebrated case in New York in 1949, and went to jail himself for contempt of court when he vocally maintained that the judge was hostile to his clients' civil rights. He defended suspected subversives, including Coleman Young, before the HUAC, and worked as a defense lawyer in Mississippi in the sixties. Whites in the Detroit area say that he is a communist, although he calls himself "basically a socialist."

In 1966, George Crockett was elected to a seat on the city's Recorders Court. Three years later, he became involved in an incident that secured his place as a hero of the liberation movement.

The incident took place in March 1969, less than two years after the riot. A white policeman was killed by gunshots from the New Bethel Baptist Church, where a group of black militants were meeting. The police counterattacked, fired into the church and then broke through the doors. They arrested more than 140 people, some of them women and children, and held them in a police garage overnight.

In the charged atmosphere of Detroit, this kind of mass roundup could well have set off another riot. At this point, however, Judge Crockett intervened. He set up court at police headquarters, released 130 of the detainees against whom there was no evidence and, more controversially, nine who, nitrate tests showed, had recently fired a weapon. Crockett based his decision on the fact that the tests had been administered while the suspects were being held without counsel, a violation of their constitutional rights.

The judge's ruling enraged the police department and the prosecutor's office, which was fine with him. "Can anyone imagine the police invading an all-white church, rounding up everybody in sight and busing them to a wholesale lockup in a police garage?" Crockett demanded. The tough rhetoric, no less than the quick justice, won him the admiration of the black community.

Eleven years after the New Bethel incident, following the resignation of Congressman Charles Diggs, Jr., Crockett was elected to Congress. He was already seventy, and he proved to be a less than energetic legislator. Now, in the summer heat of primary week, he was noticeably tired.

In person, Crockett is an impressive, somewhat distant figure who had a hard time getting used to white people calling him by his first name when he went to Washington. Despite his socialist leanings, he has a decidedly bourgeois life-style (he and his wife, a physician, are leaders of Detroit society), which has removed him from the grinding realities of the east side.

I asked Crockett about the charge that he had neglected the gut issues of poverty in his district, which has one of the lowest per capita incomes in the country, and had spent too much time on foreign affairs. He looked at me through thick glasses, like a wise old owl, and shook his head. "I don't think of Detroit as very poor," he said.

A few days earlier, in a special report on the thirteenth District, the local NBC affiliate had called him "George Crockett, Third World congressman"—a reference to both his ideology and the devastation of his district. Crockett chose to take the reference as a compliment.

"Third World?" he mused. "Well, there's something to that. Detroit is the black capital of the United States. When I first ran for City Council, back in 1965, I predicted that within ten years Detroit would be a majority black city with a black leadership, and I was right. One problem of postcolonial societies is a lack of prepared leadership cadres, especially in places like Angola and Mozambique, which were under Portuguese rule. We're not quite that bad, but there's room for comparison.

"We had a white outflow that I'm not aware has been duplicated in any other metropolitan area in the United States," he continued. "There is urban-suburban animosity because whites lost money in running, and because they still want access to the library, the symphony, the ballpark, and getting to them is inconvenient. So, in that way, too, there is room for comparison to a postcolonial situation."

Crockett's district includes the decidedly first-world suburb of Grosse Pointe, but he is not exactly a familiar figure there. "I've been there twice I think, since 1982," he said. "Those people don't really need a Congressman." He smiled with a grim satisfaction. "And never in their worst dreams did they think they'd get me."

There were a couple of white candidates from Grosse Pointe on the primary ballot, but Crockett didn't take them seriously; nor was he particularly concerned about Barbara Rose Collins. "In past years,

I got about ninety percent of the vote," he said. "This year I'm up against a Barbara Rose Collins, a real tough candidate . . . so I think maybe I'll get, oh, eighty-five percent." The hero of New Bethel leaned back in his seat and smiled the confident smile of a politician with a safe seat.

But Crockett was smiling too soon. On the Sunday before election day, Collins pulled a last-minute surprise. Hundreds of reinforcements, dispatched by Jaramogi, arrived by bus from Houston and immediately hit the streets to "leafletize" the Thirteenth District for the Shrine's favorite daughter.

"You should have been in church when the people came," she said at her headquarters on election night. "It was a holy explosion. It scared Crockett to death. That's when his workers started spreading the word that I have a lot of Jews supporting me so they could get diamonds out of South Africa. They said I was for apartheid." She shook her head at this absurdity, her "Barbara Rose for Congress" straw hat almost spinning off her flowing black hair.

The entrance to the Collins headquarters was guarded that night by bearded men in white shirts with identifying arm patches who form the Shrine's security detail. The room was packed with modestly dressed women and neatly groomed men. They milled around the television sets and greeted one another with African salutations. An out-of-town friend of Collins regarded the scene with interest. "This fascinates me," said the lady. "We don't have anything like this in New Jersey."

As the early results came in, it became apparent that the race would be very close. Fried chicken wings—the national cuisine of Detroit—were passed around, and Collins chewed on one reflectively as she went over the figures with several aides. Suddenly she set down the wing and began singing: "Nobody told me that the road would be easy, nobody told me that the road would be easy." The others took up the song, and the room filled with gospel fervor.

Only the candidate's mother seemed unmoved by the reverent mood. A spry, energetic woman dressed in modish good taste, she listened with wry dispassion as she sucked away on a black olive. When the hymn was completed, she punctured the silence. "Olives make you sexy," she said loudly. "I told people that at my New Year's party. Normally, now, black people don't eat olives. But they ate up every one that night." She laughed and took a big sip of Old Granddad from a paper cup.

The candidate's mother gazed at the political groupies in the room. "People are just like cattle," she remarked. "Barbara, this is the slowest campaign. Where are the results, girl?" Collins shrugged, and her mother turned to a press photographer for a discussion of horse racing.

Around eleven, the numbers began to roll in. Crockett had won—but by only a couple of thousand votes. The voters he considers "not very poor" had come out for Collins. If it had not been for the two white spoiler candidates, who siphoned off a small but significant number of potential Collins voters, the hero of New Bethel might well have lost his seat in Congress.

The guards stood at stoic attention while the Shrine's campaign workers wrapped up their chicken wings and ballot sheets. There was disappointment on their faces, but it mingled with an unmistakable look of optimism. Like Fred Williams, they knew that things were building up on the streets of the Black Capital of America. For the moment, the secular revolutionaries were still in control, but there would be a next time. Two years from now, Crockett would be older, the city's problems more acute, and Detroit might be ready to send to Washington a smiling Christian woman whose name means violence.

Chapter Five

THE HOSTILE SUBURBS

There is a lovely park across the street from Dudley Randall's house, on the west side of Detroit, but at three in the afternoon it was deserted. At the curb, almost directly opposite the house, two very tough-looking young men sat in a late-model Pontiac. They passed a bottle between them and gazed out the windows, as if they were waiting for someone.

I rang the bell and Dudley Randall had to open several locks to let me in. At seventy-four he was a stooped, tired-looking man with bifocals, dressed in a flannel shirt and khaki trousers. His living room was lined with books, the walls were covered with African art and there were *National Geographic* magazines and anthologies of poetry stacked on the coffee table. Above a bookcase I saw a plaque, signed by the mayor, proclaiming Randall the Poet Laureate of Detroit.

Randall looked out his front window and gestured at the car in front. "I moved across from the park because I thought it would be nice," he said. "But those two sit there every day and drink whiskey. And then they urinate in the bushes." He made a sad face, offered me a seat and took one himself.

Randall has lived his life with books. For years he was a librarian and poet-in-residence at Wayne State University. During that time he founded the Broadside Press, a forum for black poets. But now, retired, he doesn't write anymore, nor does he bother much with literature. "I no longer find truth in the great poets or the great books," he said. There was a pause. "I still read Tolstoy," he added, and fell silent again.

"What's it like being the Poet Laureate of Detroit?" I asked. Randall considered for a moment. "Poetry isn't such a big thing in Detroit," he said finally, in a flat tone.

"What do you think of the city?" I asked, trying hard to make conversation. Friends had told me that Dudley Randall was one of the smartest, most perceptive people in Detroit, but he seemed too discouraged to talk. He looked out the window at the car. "I want to move away," he said. "I'd like to go someplace where it's warm."

A few weeks earlier, on a visit to the mayor's office, I had noticed a poem of Randall's, entitled "Detroit Renaissance," which is dedicated to Coleman Young, hanging on a wall in the reception room. Now I asked Randall about it, and he rose slowly, returning with a slim volume of his work, which includes the poem. He sat in silence as I read it to myself.

> Cities have died, have burned,
> Yet phoenix-like returned
> To soar up livelier, lovelier than before.
> Detroit has felt the fire
> Yet each time left the pyre
> As if the flames had power to restore.

First, burn away the myths
Of what it was, and is—
A lovely, tree-laned town of peace and trade.
Hatred has festered here,
And bigotry and fear
Filled streets with strife and raised the barricade.

Wealth of a city lies,
Not in its factories,
Its marts and towers crowding to the sky,
But in its people who
Possess grace to imbue
Their lives with beauty, wisdom, charity.

You have those too long hid,
Who built the pyramids,
Who searched the skies and mapped the planets' range,
Who sang the songs of grief
That made the whole world weep,
Whose Douglass, Malcolm, Martin rung in change.

The Indian, with his soul
Attuned to nature's role;
The sons and daughters of Cervantes' smile;
Pan Tadeysz's children too
Entrust their fate to you;
Souls forged by Homer's, Dante's
Shakespeare's, Goethe's, Yeats's style.

Together we will build
A city that will yield
To all their hopes and dreams so long deferred.
New faces will appear
Too long neglected here;
New minds, new means will build a brave new world.

"Do you still believe it?" I asked. "Will you ever be able to rebuild this city together?"

Randall looked at me and shrugged, a slow movement of tired shoulders. "I guess not," said the Poet Laureate of Detroit. "All the white people have moved away."

And that is the simple truth. The week I met with Randall, the Detroit papers published a University of Chicago study that found, to no one's surprise, that the suburbs of the Motor City are the most segregated in the United States.

Many blacks look beyond the Eight Mile Road border and see America—an undifferentiated, uncaring world of suburban affluence where they are neither liked nor wanted. Actually, the almost four million people of the Metropolitan Detroit area—Wayne, Oakland and Macomb counties—are subdivided by ethnicity. Macomb, to the northeast, is blue-collar territory; a large percentage of its people are second- and third-generation Polish and Italian refugees from Detroit. Oakland, to the northwest, is the second wealthiest American county among those with a population of over one million, and it is dominated by WASPs and, to a lesser extent, Jews. Detroit itself is located in Wayne County, whose population, outside the city, includes a good number of working-class southern whites, Hispanics, Arabs and ethnics.

In most ways the towns of the tri-county area have little in common; what they share is an estrangement from Detroit. Unlike the suburbs of other major cities, they are not bedroom communities. The average suburbanite almost never visits the city for any reason. As Arthur Johnson, head of the local NAACP, observed, Detroiters know they aren't loved by their neighbors. During the early years of the great white exodus this antipathy was impersonal. It got a face in 1973, with the election of Mayor Coleman Young.

The problem started with Young's inaugural address, in which he warned hoodlums ("whether they're wearing blue uniforms or Superfly suits") to "hit Eight Mile and keep on going." The idea of Detroit policemen crossing the boundary didn't seem to bother suburbanites, but they were mightily exercised by the prospect of a legion of Superfly badasses invading their turf.

A more politic mayor would have tried to mend fences, but Young is not a fence-mender. He dubbed his neighbors "the hostile suburbs" and mounted a campaign of verbal and political harassment that still goes on today. They responded with a hatred usually reserved for enemy heads of state—which, in a way, he is. The mention of the mayor's name is enough to set off tirades from the ritzy salons of Grosse Pointe to the redneck suburbs—places such as Melvindale, "The Little Town with the Big Heart."

Melvindale is a hamlet of modest, neatly tended tract houses, located not far from the Ford factories that employ many of its twelve thousand citizens. Like other working-class suburbs heavily dependent on the auto industry, it has experienced hard times since the seventies, although not so hard as the city of Detroit, where most of its people were born and raised.

The nerve center of Melvindale is Tom Coogan's barbershop, a two-chair emporium with a homey, Mayberry feeling—bear rugs and stuffed moose heads on the wall, brown-and-white-checked linoleum on the floor, and a sign in the window: BURGLARS BEWARE. And, in back of a barber chair, over a Pinaud Clubman Talc advertisment, there is another sign: TOM COOGAN, MAYOR.

When I arrived at his shop, Mayor Coogan had a constituent in the chair and three more waiting for haircuts. Coogan is a genial, cautious man in a pale blue barber's smock whose thick glasses give him a scholarly appearance. He was in the middle of trimming a sideburn when a woman with a Tennessee accent came in to complain about overgrown weeds in a lot near her house. A believer in direct action, Coogan put down his scissors and called the police chief on the walkie-talkie he keeps next to his barber tools. He spoke briefly, then picked up his shears once again. "The violation is in the mail," he told the lady.

"Can you imagine Coleman Young doing something like that?" I asked, hoping to get a rise. I got one. A waiting customer snorted. "You have to change your color, you want any help from him," he said.

"No, Coleman is responsive," said Coogan with collegial solidarity.

"Shit, that son of a bitch don't even take care of black people, let alone white," said another man. "Back in the fifties, Detroit was a beautiful city. You could get drunk in Detroit."

Coogan snipped reflectively. "The city started deteriorating when they took off STRESS [a tough police unit, established after the 1967 riot, which deployed white cops as decoys in mostly black areas]. It kept people honest, being subject to search. Now everybody packs a piece downtown."

The old man in the chair, who was getting a marine crew cut, cleared his throat. "Back in the old days when I was in Detroit there were colored but they knew their place. They knew right from wrong. They wanted to work then, not like today." The others said "Damn right" and "Goddamn Young," but Coogan snipped away in silence.

Except when Tom Coogan is conducting municipal business, his barbershop is a male preserve, a sort of club where fellas drop in every so often to get their ears raised whether they need it or not. They are talkers, and they weren't at all averse to chewing the fat with a visiting writer, especially when the subject was the city they once lived in and now view as an alien colony.

"Detroit is real squalor," drawled one of the regulars. "All Young cares about is the great big monuments he's building himself."

"Shit, they enjoy the environment they're in. That's the way they are," said another man.

The blue phone that Coogan uses for official business rang. He picked it up and said, "Mayor Coogan." As he spoke, the old fellow in the barber chair said, "This here is the only place in Michigan where you can insult the mayor. Ol' Tom's the best mayor we ever had. Even the best ain't too damn good, but he's the best anyway." It got a laugh, and Coogan, hand over the receiver, nodded in agreement.

The mayor completed his conversation, finished the flattop and another man climbed into the chair for a six-dollar haircut. "Every community has crime and drug problems," Coogan said, "and we've got our share. But we try to keep Detroit from spilling over into

Melvindale. We run police cars up and down Schaffer Road at night—that's our border with Detroit—and we feel it's a deterrent. We've been able to keep the crime under control out here."

"Control, hell," said one of the men. "My insurance guy called the other day and said, 'Bill, we've got to raise your premiums because of Detroit.'"

"Hell, the insurance companies will use any excuse," said the fellow in the chair.

"Yeah, well ninety-five percent of prisoners are black," said Bill. "Now, what does that tell ya?"

"Where is the mom and dad, that's what I wonder," said a young man who had come into the shop and assumed one of the Naugahyde seats along the wall.

"Hell, they can't even count their kids. I used to walk three miles ever' day to Southwestern High School, for cripes sakes," said Bill.

The mayor snipped away and said nothing.

"Last time I was in Detroit, some big black come up and asked me for some money," said the young man. "I told him, 'If you ain't out of here in two seconds I'll kill ya.' But I'll tell ya something, I wouldn't drive my car down Woodward Avenue today. Them big black dudes standing down there—shit."

A heavyset middle-aged man named Carl, wearing a soiled T-shirt and work pants, came in to the shop and was enthusiastically greeted. He is considered the town wit, and he immediately went into his routine—a series of jokes about Catholic priests and Jewish rabbis, dagos and A-rabs, and Greeks who, according to him, have a universal passion for anal sex. Then, surprisingly, he offered a minority opinion on Coleman Young.

"I think Coleman's good," he said. "He's fast, forward and he tells it like it is."

"Shit," said the young man, whose name was Angelo. "You're the first white guy I ever heard say something good about him."

"Yeah, well where was my car stolen, Detroit or Melvindale?" Carl demanded. "People are afraid to go into Detroit just because of the fear instilled by the news media. Blacks are human, you know. Just don't go looking for problems and you'll be all right."

"This guy is crazy," said Angelo. "He'll go anywhere. I ride with him and I start to shake. Shit, Detroit, man. My old house is gone. Wiped out."

"Yeah, well you fuckin' I-talians abused the houses. Blacks didn't want them no more. You left them a ghetto," said Carl.

Angelo was furious. "Tell them about that incident on Belle Isle— you never tell that to anybody," he almost shouted.

"Shit, all that happened is some blacks hassled my car over on Belle Isle. They didn't hurt nobody," said Carl.

Mayor Coogan continued snipping, and said nothing.

"1967?" said Bill. "I was over at the Stroh's Brewery when the riot broke out. Blacks and whites were shooting each other all over the place. They say that only forty-three were killed but that's a damned lie—I counted more'n a hundred in the hallway at Receiving Hospital."

"Fuckin' blacks, man," someone said, and the others shook their heads. "Fuckin' Coleman Young."

Carl, the liberal, sensed he was losing his audience. "You're from Israel, right?" he said to me. "Did you hear the one about the Jewish Santa Claus? He asks the kids for presents." The men laughed, happy to be back on familiar ground.

"I'll tell you one thing about Detroit," said Mayor Coogan, snipping away at his customer's neck. "I don't know about this other stuff, but it's the best damn sports town in the world. I think we can all agree on that."

Not every politician in suburban Detroit is as circumspect as the barber-mayor of Melvindale. Few, on the other hand, are as outspoken as Brooks Patterson, who served as prosecutor of Oakland County for sixteen years before stepping down in 1988, and made a career out of Detroit-bashing.

Patterson's headquarters was the Oakland County courthouse, a modernistic building set down in the vacant land in the northern tip of Pontiac. On the day I visited him, the halls were quiet. A dorky-looking young couple wearing his-and-hers matching dental braces walked hand in hand, holding a marriage certificate. Outside a courtroom, a white lawyer and a black defendant were in conference, the lawyer saying, "I can't promise, I can't promise, I can't promise . . ." while his client peered off into the distance. But there was no tension in the air, none of the hurly-burly normally associated with places where people's fates are determined. Clearly, in Brooks Patterson's domain, things were under control.

Patterson himself appeared relaxed and jocular. He was only a few months away from voluntary retirement and there was an end-of-the-semester informality about him. Nearing fifty, he was wearing a sport shirt, a boating jacket and moccasins without socks. A boyish-looking man with a round face and a dry "heh, heh, heh" kind of laugh, he had the air of shrewd efficiency normally associated with the security chief of a medium-sized corporation.

Patterson, like his nemesis, Coleman Young, is known to local journalists as "good copy." One reporter who came to interview him found a miniature electric chair, complete with a battery-charged shock, on display. To another, who asked him if he would be defending felons in private practice, he replied that he wouldn't "unless they're members of the family." But, despite his sense of humor, Brooks Patterson is a highly unpopular man in the city of Detroit, where he is regarded as the symbol of suburban racism.

Patterson considers the charge unfair. "I'm color-blind," he said. "But out here we don't plea-bargain on breaking and entering cases, assault and other violent crimes, and black defendants don't like it. Oakland County is less than ten percent black but eighty five percent of the jail population is black."

I wrote down the statistic, but the prosecutor suddenly seemed unsure. He picked up a phone and asked an assistant for the racial breakdown of the county's prisoners. "Actually, that number is about fifty percent," he corrected himself in a same-difference tone of voice.

It is rare for a suburban politician to talk so specifically about blacks. In the established code, they are "Detroiters," and whites are "suburbanites." A few years ago, when Patterson became embroiled in one of his epic battles with Coleman Young, these terms came into wide public use.

That was back in 1984, when the Detroit Tigers won the World Series. Following the final game, gangs of drunken revelers celebrated by attacking passersby and burning a car. The incident, which drew national attention, was a major embarrassment to the city, and Young blamed it on his neighbors.

"When Coleman Young talked about marauding gangs coming in from the suburbs, I checked the figures," said Patterson. "It turned out that on that same day, thirty of the last thirty arrests in Southfield [an Oakland County city that abuts Detroit] were of Detroiters. Now, is that racial? Bullshit. The fact is, Detroiters present a serious law enforcement problem to Oakland County."

Although he denies being a racist, Patterson began his public career as the attorney for NAG (the National Action Group), a Pontiac-based organization dedicated to fighting school busing. His high profile in that struggle won him election as prosecutor in 1972. Twice he led unsuccessful state-wide petition drives to institute capital punishment, and he established a policy of refusing to plea-bargain in cases involving serious crimes.

He also developed an appetite for political advancement. A hard-line Republican in a basically Democratic state, three times he ran for higher office—governor, senator and attorney general—and three times he lost. In each race, his base of support was conservative suburbanites, many of them former liberals, who applauded his law-and-order attacks on Detroit.

"In this county, robbery is a crime," said Patterson. "In Detroit, it's an occupation. It's warfare in the city, it absolutely is. A baby born in Detroit has a bigger statistical chance of being killed than a soldier in World War Two. If I was the mayor, I'd call in the National Guard."

I mentioned that, in their defense, Detroiters often say that there is crime in the suburbs, too, but Patterson wasn't having any. "We've got a crime problem? Bullshit! We have crime, sure; there's more than a million people here. But by percentage, we're light-years ahead of Detroit when it comes to protecting the public."

Hundreds of speeches to Kiwanis Clubs and Rotaries have given Patterson a ready command of the statistics. "In Wayne County in 1987, out of a population of two-point-two million, there were close to one thousand homicides," he said. "Here, in Oakland County, with one-point-one million, there were between forty-five and fifty."

The great suburban nightmare is that the violence of Detroit will spill out beyond Eight Mile Road. In the mid-eighties, Grosse Pointe, which abuts the city, tried to build a "flood-control wall" along the border, and the town of Dearborn passed an ordinance forbidding the use of its parks to nonresidents.

"The walls will be up for a long time," he said. "Is there hatred between us and them? Okay, I don't deny it. We see ourselves as a target. In this situation you see the evidence of one man's hatred for the honkies. He's the racist. Things will quiet down when Coleman leaves."

This is the predominant suburban feeling—that whites are the victims, not the perpetrators, of racism. People like Brooks Patterson, who was born and raised in Detroit, view themselves as innocent refugees and regard their native city with a mixture of contempt and anger. They do not accept the notion that Detroit is still the big city; to them, it is an irrelevancy.

"Coleman calls the suburbs 'cornfields,'" Patterson said angrily. "But in fact, in no sense are we dependent on Detroit. They are dependent on us. The truth is, Detroit has had its day. I don't give a damn about Detroit. It has no direct bearing on the quality of my life. If I never crossed Eight Mile again I wouldn't be bereft of anything."

"What about the quality of life for Detroiters?" I wondered. Patterson looked at me as if I were simpleminded. "It's like the Indians on the reservation," he said. "Those who can will leave Detroit. Those who can't will get blankets and food from the government men in the city."

Brooks Patterson sees the post-Coleman era as a time of potential rapprochement between the cornfield and the battlefield. "But they've got to see that crime is the bottom line," said the prosecutor of Oakland County. "They have to kick ass and take names. Without getting crime under control you have no solution. All the city's problems have their origin in a lack of safety."

"And until they do?"

Patterson smiled bleakly and rubbed his hands together. "Until they do, you move to the suburbs and defend yourself," he said.

Moving to the suburbs isn't so simple though, even for blacks who want to. Open housing statutes make it legally impossible to select your neighbors and make sure they stay selected, but there are ways. Detroit's suburbs did not get to be the most segregated in the country by accident.

A generation ago, residential separation was simpler. When I was growing up in Detroit, Grosse Pointe had a "point system" to keep out undesirables. Prospective buyers were rated by skin color, accent, religion and other criteria, including a "typically American way of life." Under the system, blacks, Mexicans and Orientals were automatically given a failing grade, as were virtually all Jews and southern Europeans.

In Dearborn, the seat of the Ford empire, racism was less scientific, but equally virulent. Mayor Orville Hubbard, a vocal segregationist, was kept in office for more than thirty years by an admiring populace composed of ethnic Italians, Poles and southern whites, who subscribed to his antiblack attitude. "I just don't believe in integration," he said in 1967. "When that happens, along comes socializing with the whites, intermarriage and then mongrelization."

This sort of blatant race-baiting has all but disappeared from the public discourse of metropolitan Detroit. The fact is, civil rights legislation and black political activism have chipped away at many of the institutionalized forms of overt racism. In the summer of 1988, for example, Dearborn was forced to accept its first black police recruit. A smattering of blacks now live there and in Detroit's other working-class suburbs. Even Grosse Pointe has a handful of wealthy black residents.

The main obstacles to integration are economic and social. Realtors say that there is no place in the Detroit area today where a black can't buy a home, but the cost is often prohibitive. The most modest white neighborhoods in the suburbs are more than twice as expensive as comparable areas in the city—precisely because they are white. And those blacks who can afford to move often feel unwelcome.

Nowhere is this truer than in Warren, a small city just to the north of Detroit, inhabited largely by Poles and Italians. Twenty years ago, a mixed couple tried to move in, and police had to be called to protect them from outraged mobs. A few years later, the city fathers turned down badly needed HUD money because it meant building integrated housing. The only important black institution there is the Detroit Memorial Park Cemetery, the Metro area's largest black burial grounds, and most Warrenites want to keep it that way.

"The attitude isn't as much racist as one of fear," said Richard Sabaugh, a county commissioner and public relations executive who as a Warren city councilman helped lead the HUD fight. "People don't see every black as bad. But the image of Detroit is of a decaying, crime-ridden city headed by a mayor who makes racist remarks. We view the values of people in Detroit as completely foreign. To us it's like a foreign country and culture. The language is different and the way people think there is different. We just want to live in peace. And we feel that anybody coming from Detroit is going to cause problems."

Sabaugh, who ran unopposed in his last contest, faithfully mirrors the views of many of his constituents. "It's all one complex—blacks,

Coleman Young, crime, drugs, Detroit. People feel they've been driven out once, and it could occur again."

Considering the conditions in the city, I wondered if anyone felt compassion for its residents. Sabaugh seemed amazed at the notion.

"Any sentiment to help Detroiters? Not at all. I've never heard that. If you ever asked to raise taxes to help Detroit, it would go down fifteen to one. Guilt to help people who won't help themselves? That's a thought that's not even tolerated. If they saw a young kid in a destitute situation, there might be some compassion. But otherwise, no. There is no feeling of pity for Detroit in the suburbs. Maybe the bottom line is they've given up on Detroit. You want to hear what people think, the best place is the senior citizen picnic. Most of those people used to live in the city. Ask them how they feel about Detroit," Sabaugh suggested.

The Warren perspective was on display at the annual outing, held in a wood pavilion in one of the city's verdant parks. The seniors were bland, mild-eyed veterans of the auto factories and their equally bland wives. The men wore polyester sportsclothes, the ladies sported Lurleen Wallace bouffants. They played cards at long wooden tables, or lined up for free eye examinations and blood pressure checks at booths along the sides. Mayor Ronald Bonkowski moved among the old people shaking hands and exchanging family gossip. Among the thousand or so picnickers, there wasn't a single black.

At a table in the center of the room, two old men, who turned out to be brothers, sat in stoic silence while their wives chatted happily. They were glad to divert themselves by talking about their old hometown.

"It's a war zone across Eight Mile rode," said one, a grizzled former toolmaker named Steve. "They should put up a big wall, like in Berlin. I'm afraid to go back there—it's like going into some Russian-held city. You don't know if you're coming back alive." The women, who had fallen silent, nodded in agreement, but Joseph, Steve's brother, shook his head.

"I'm an old union man," he said, "and one thing I learned is that you have to get along with blacks. It's worse to be a bigot than a black. It's against the law to be a bigot, and it's not against the law to be black. I think we're better off in this country because we got blacks, Chinese, Japanese . . ."

Steve cut him off impatiently. "What's wrong with the colored? I'll tell you what's wrong. No one ever taught them how to live. They destroy their own houses. They should live in a tent, like a Boy Scout, until they learn to live in a house. They can't get it into their head that a house should last more than five years."

"Well, I built a house on Waldo, and it's still there, paying taxes," said Joseph.

"Yeah, well maybe you should go back there and live with them," said Steve, and the women giggled at the absurdity of the suggestion.

"I don't mind living next to them," said Joseph. "In time, people will recognize that the black fella is just like them."

"Maybe they're just like you, but they sure as hell ain't just like me," said Steve. "And I don't want any out here in Warren. You want to live with 'em, go right ahead. You know what you are?" He hesitated before continuing; this was his brother, after all. But anger overcame family sentiment. "I hate to say it, Joseph, but you're nothing but a damn liberal."

Twenty-five years ago, Detroit prided itself on being in the vanguard of American liberalism; today, the term has become an epithet. One of the few places where it is still respectable, if not exactly fashionable, is Southfield, often considered to be the "Jewish" suburb just north of Detroit.

When I left for Israel in the summer of 1967, the majority of Detroit's eighty thousand Jews were clustered in the northwest corner of the city. Dozens of synagogues, religious schools, community centers and delis dotted the areas's main commercial avenues, and families lived in spacious brick homes built along quiet, tree-lined streets. But the riot touched off a mass exodus; six months later, when I came home for a visit, I literally didn't recognize the place. Not a single one of my friends' families was still there.

Most of them had moved to Southfield or even farther north, to the WASP suburbs of Birmingham and West Bloomfield. Only a few years before Jews felt unwelcome in such places, but in the racially charged atmosphere they now had the primary qualification for acceptance: if blacks considered Jews "almost white," WASPs seemed to feel that they were "white enough." Seemingly overnight, synagogues and day schools sprouted in the cornfields of suburbia, while, in northwest Detroit, abandoned temples became AME churches and pastrami parlors were transformed into barbecue joints.

In the eighties, Southfield became the new downtown of white Detroit. Glittering gold-painted business towers and massive shopping centers tipped the commercial balance away from the city. In the fall of 1988, there were 23 million square feet of office space in Southfield and another 1.5 million were under construction—more than in the entire city of Detroit, whose population is ten times larger.

For three generations, blacks have followed Jews northward, and the pattern is now being repeated in Southfield. In 1970, there were less than one hundred blacks in the town. By 1980, the number had grown to about eight thousand. Today, the city administration estimates that there are twenty thousand—about 20 percent of the population—making Southfield the most integrated city in the area.

Ironically, it is also the least popular with Detroiters. They see it as their primary competition for the black middle class and many regard the black yuppies who live there as defectors. Moreover, the huge Northland shopping center, whose stores are white-owned and patronized largely by blacks, has become a symbol of suburban commercial exploitation. It is a mark of social consciousness not to shop there. Arthur Johnson told me proudly that he hasn't bought more than a pair of shoes north of Eight Mile Road in years. Federal circuit judge Damon Keith, who lives in Detroit and whose court is in

Cincinnati, prefers to shop in Ohio rather than drive a mile or two
to Northland.

This antipathy has little to do with the Jews; Detroit has been
remarkably free of the acrimony that has often characterized black-
Jewish relations in Chicago and New York. Partly this is because
Arab store owners in the city have become the main focus of black
resentment; partly because the Jewish community, especially its
leader, multimillionaire Max Fisher, has been active in supporting
Detroit projects. And a good deal of credit goes to Coleman Young,
who is something of a philo-Semite.

During the 1940s and 50s, when Young was involved in radical
union politics, many of his associates were Jews who supported him
in battles with the UAW establishment. In office, he has reciprocated
by appointing several to key city positions. From them Young
learned to appreciate Jewish cooking and Jewish humor. Throughout his incumbency, he has gone out of his way to encourage Jews—
even those who now live in the suburbs—to remain involved in the
life of the city.

There is, in fact, more intimacy and complexity in the Jewish-
black relationship than in any other. "We were always closer to Jews
than to the others," said Arthur Johnson, "and we miss them more."
Indeed, for generations, Jews were the only community willing to
sell homes to blacks, and to contemplate living next to them. But
each time, as poor blacks arrived in the wake of the middle class,
contemplation gave way to flight.

The cost of these repeated exoduses—in new homes, synagogues
and institutions—has been crippling. This time, the Jewish community is trying to make a stand. Its Federation offers grants to young
Jewish couples who buy homes in Southfield and neighboring Oak
Park. "It's not so much that Jews still believe in integration," a Federation activist said. "We just don't want to run again."

Southfield officials are extremely concerned that the efforts to
maintain a stable white population will fail. "The media say that we
will be a throw-away city in ten to twenty years," said Southfield

mayor Donald Fracassi. "I'm frightened, I admit it. But I'm not about to let the city fall without a fight. We understand the cost of a city becoming all black, and we're ready to take on the threat of resegregation. If we lose, at least they'll have to say we tried."

The Southfield strategy is based on another irony—the only important city in the Metro area that has declared integration to be a policy goal wants to maintain it by recruiting whites and steering blacks away. "Our approach to racial problems is unorthodox," admitted city manager Robert Block. "Since we're naturally attractive to blacks because of our quality of life and the fact that they feel welcome here, our target market is the white community."

The man in charge of implementing this strategy is Nimrod Rosenthal, a transplanted Israeli who chain-smokes Winstons and mixes business jargon with liberal platitudes in fast, Hebrew-accented English. He was hired to use the expertise he acquired as a marketing whiz for the Hudson's Department Store chain to help sell the city to white people.

Part of Rosenthal's plan is based on the Shaker Heights model. The Cleveland suburb has fought resegregation by actively directing urban blacks to other suburbs, and Nimrod Rosenthal admitted that Southfield is considering doing the same. The idea is to set up a non-profit office in Detroit that would help those who want to leave find housing elsewhere in Oakland County. In late 1988, the notion was still under discussion, and Southfield made little effort to publicize it; it is not the kind of program likely to be popular among its less liberal neighbors. Its officials were unmoved, however, by possible negative reactions. "They can't hurt us," said one. "Fair housing is the law of the land."

Southfield's leaders were counting on blacks to go along. "The minorities here understand that if we can't maintain a racial balance, they will be the losers," said the mayor. "Their kids will go to poor schools and live in filthy neighborhoods. So the minorities will have to get out of the comfort zone, and move to other suburbs."

If the Shaker Heights plan represents push, Southfield has also mounted an impressive advertising campaign to pull in young whites. Its centerpiece is a series of thirty-second television spots that Nimrod Rosenthal screened for me on his office VCR.

The ads depict aspects of life in Southfield—young couples dining in fine restaurants, relaxed businessmen able to drive to their offices within minutes, happy children frolicking in a safe schoolyard, youthful families walking hand in hand across well-tended lawns with brick ranch houses in the background. After watching half a dozen of the commercials it became clear that they had a common denominator—the only blacks visible were little girls and light-skinned women.

When I pointed this out, Rosenthal seemed a bit defensive. He continued to run the ads, and after a few minutes he shouted, "Hey, there's a black guy," in an excited tone. He rewound the tape and played it over, so I could see a fleeting frame of young black executive sitting in a plush office.

On and on went the commericals. Handsome yuppies playing tennis, shopping, clinking glasses of shining crystal, all against a background of glossy neo-rock. No one who saw the ads could possibly have guessed that nearly half the students in the Southfield schools are black, or that elderly people make up a large part of the city's population, or that there are more than twenty thousand blacks (not to mention ten thousand Chaldeans and Arabs) already living in the suburb.

"I have to overcome the perception of what whites think of as an integrated city," Rosenthal explained. "People are interested in quality of life." This, of course, means a quantity of whites. Southfield's marketing director has a product to sell—and who can blame him if he doesn't want to hurt sales by giving prospective buyers the idea that there are blacks living in Detroit's most integrated suburb.

Nobody will ever do a commercial like that about Hamtramck, although there are probably more blond-haired, blue-eyed people there than Nimrod Rosenthal ever dreamed of. The little city is, like

Highland Park, an island, surrounded on all sides by Detroit, which expanded around it. Its diverse population includes blacks, Albanians, Ukrainians and other Slavs—but Hamtramck is, first and foremost, a Polish town.

Unlike Chicago and other large northern cities that have experienced suburban flight, Detroit has not retained strong ethnic enclaves. The city is, as Chief Hart observed, one big ghetto all the way to its borders. Aside from a small barrio on the southwest side and a few areas on the riverfront and the outer extremities, all its neighborhoods are heavily black. Only Hamtramck, in the city but not a part of it, remains to remind people what Detroit was like thirty years age.

In those day, the city was dotted with corner shot-and-a-beer joints—ethnic taverns like Lillie's. A summer storm was raging outside when I walked in, and the patrons at the bar were in the midst of giving the weather a Hamtramck spin. When thunder rolled overhead, the young bartender said, "When I was little, my ma used to tell me that thunder is Jesus bowling."

"Yeah," said a man in a blue work shirt, seated at the bar. "I heard that. And the lightning is the scoreboard lighting up."

"God, you guys," a young woman in narrow, dark-rimmed glasses and a beehive hairdo said in mock disgust. "Jeez, bowling!"

"Hey," the bartender said, "I'm a Polack. Whaddaya want?"

"Yeah, well waddaya think I am, Japanese?" quipped the woman, and the guys at the bar, dressed in factory clothes and baseball hats, laughed and raised their glasses in a toast to ethnic solidarity.

Dave Uchalik walked in during the banter, sat down at the bar and chugged a Budweiser. He is a pale man in his early thirties and he was dressed according to local custom, in a work shirt and Tigers baseball cap. But unlike his father, who worked at the nearby (and now defunct) Dodge Main for forty-one years, or Lillie's other patrons, who are still on the line at the GM plant that took its place, Uchalik is no auto worker. He is the leader of a rock band called the

Polish Muslims, the founder of what he calls, facetiously, the Ham-tramck sound.

"Hamtramck is the Liverpool of Detroit," Uchalik said, draining his Bud. "This is heavy-duty industrial territory. When I was a kid, my father and I both wanted me to escape the factories. He said, 'Get an education.' But I figured I'd just play the guitar instead."

Uchalik is a pretty good guitar player, and the Polish Muslims do their share of straightforward rock, but his real forte is as a lyricist and commentator on his native city and its folkways. "We do a kind of Polish rock 'n' roll," he said, wiping his granny glasses on his blue work shirt. "For example, we've got a song called 'Love Polka Number 9' which we sing to the tune of 'Love Potion Number 9.' That's one of our big numbers."

Dave Uchalik's version sounds nothing like the Clovers':

> I went out Friday night with you know who,
> That *bobcia* with the size 12 bowling shoe.
> She feeds me kielbasa and she makes me drink that wine
> And then she likes to dance that Love Polka Number 9.

Uchalik's lyric vision of his hometown comes from his days at St. Florian's school and his nights in the bars along Joseph Campau Avenue, the city's main strip, where Polka bands and Polish dancing are as natural as country music in Nashville. Growing up in the Motown era, he gravitated to r&b as well, and the result is a unique fusion, possible only in the Warsaw of Wayne County.

"I use the things that go with this place," he said. "Polish foods, bowling, overweight people, the polka, *bobcias*—that's Polish for 'old women.'" Although his parents speak Polish fluently, Uchalik admits that he knows only a smattering of the language—just enough to get by in a town of less than twenty-five thousand that still has a Polish language newspaper.

"As far as the name—the Polish Muslims—is concerned, we were just sitting around a bar a few years ago having some cocktails when we came up with it. There was nothing racial about it. A few older people were offended and once a guy jumped on the stage and tried to take the microphone away from me, but most people think the name and the songs are funny. After all, if you can laugh at yourself, you can laugh at anybody."

Uchalik's sense of humor is nothing if not irreverent. When Pope John Paul came to town a few years ago, he composed a tune for the Pontiff, "Traveling Pope," to the tune of Ricky Nelson's "Traveling Man." "I like to think of the pope listening to that one in the Vatican," Uchalik said, popping the top on another Bud. (Uchalik was not the only one inspired by the pope's visit. A local car dealer, Woodrow W. Woody, caught a video shot of His Holiness waving to the crowds in front of his Pontiac dealership. In the picture, the pope's arms are extended in what appears to be a benediction of the auto showroom, and it has become a fixture of Woody's advertising.)

The Muslims, who also feature some female backup singers called the Muslimettes, play mostly around Hamtramck, with occasional gigs in Detroit and the suburbs. A local bandleader, Big Daddy Marshall Lachkowski, has been helping them, and the band has a loyal following. Several of the guys at the bar smiled in recognition as Uchalik recited another of his favorite compositions, "Bowling USA," which is sung to the tune of the Beachboys' "Surfin USA."

> I'm getting my new ball drilled, I'm gettin' it back real soon.
> They're waxing down the alleys, they can't wait for June.
> I'm watching *Beat the Champ* now, you can't tear me away.
> Tell yo mamma you're bowling, bowling USA.

"That's Hamtramck all right," said the bartender as he came over with a refill. "Polacks and bowling balls."

The people at Lillie's are not the only ones proud of their ethnic heritage. Hamtramck's official slogan is "A touch of Europe in America." Surrounded by the Third World city of Detroit, it is an island of Second World sensibility. The street in front of the city hall is named Lech Walesa Avenue, and there is a letter from the Solidarity leader on display on mayor Bob Kozaren's office wall.

Kozaren is a St. Ladislaus boy who has been in office since 1980, and his walls are festooned with Hamtramckania. There is a picture of its Little League championship team making an appearance on the Lawrence Welk show ("This is a great sports town, home of Rudy Tomjanovich and Jean Hoxie"), a bronzed record of "There's a City Called Hamtramck" by local favorite Ted Gomulka ("Mitch Ryder was a Hamtramck boy, too"), and lots of framed photographs of American presidents on state visits to the Polish capital of Michigan.

"There is a saying, 'If you want to be president, you have to come to Hamtramck,'" said Kozaren. "FDR, Truman, they've all been here. JFK was invited for the first time because of his Polish brother-in-law, Prince Radziwill. And when Dukakis came this year, we spelled out his name in Polish sausage. He took a part of it back to his hotel room with him. We got into the *Guinness Book of World Records* with the world's largest kielbasa."

Kozaren is a strong Democrat in the old UAW mold and, unlike other leaders of the towns around Detroit, he had nothing but praise for Coleman Young. Hamtramck was badly hurt by the contraction of the auto industry in the seventies and the closing of Dodge Main. Kozaren and Young collaborated on a plan to open a GM plant on the site of the old factory, on a plot of land partly in Hamtramck and partly in Detroit. This entailed demolishing the Poletown neighborhood, a project that aroused emotional opposition from its mostly elderly residents; but Kozaren believes that it helped save his city. "On the whole, it was the best thing that could have happened," he said.

Coleman Young played a big part in the Poletown drama, and Kozaren is grateful. "Coleman is a dedicated mayor," he said. "Some of the suburbs condemn him because he keeps Detroit in mind. But people didn't leave him with much. He came along after the riots, and everyone wanted to strip Detroit clean. They even took the ball teams. People around here want to separate the suburbs from the city, but it just won't work."

One reason that the Poletown demolition generated so much emotion was the fear that it would lead to a loss of ethnic identity. But that doesn't seem to have happened. The small city looks as if it has been caught in a time warp—its modest frame houses are immaculately tended, its downtown is a long strip of mom-and-pop restaurants, five-and-dimes and friendly taverns. Six churches—four Roman Catholic, one Ukrainian Catholic and one Polish National Catholic—anchor its neighborhoods.

In contrast to the demolished business streets of Detroit, commerce bustles in Hamtramck, and the booster spirit is alive and well. Once a week, its middle-aged merchants gather at the Polish Century Club to eat middle-American cuisine (sample menu: hot canned chop suey with boiled rice, white bread, red Jell-O and milk), sing "Vive Le Rotary" out of a stenciled songster, and listen to motivational lectures. There are outings ("Tuesdee at the yat club, for a swim in da lake"), softball leagues with teams sponsored by sausage companies, church bazaars and, every September, a monster ethnic festival that attracts tens of thousands of former Hamtramck people who now live in Warren and other Polish-American enclaves east of Detroit.

"Growing up in Hamtramck is like growing up in a fraternity," said Kozaren. "People may leave, but they retain their ties. It's a city where we have sidestepped time."

Not every member of the fraternity is happy with the quaint old-world flavor. One dissenter is Bob Zwolak, whose combination bicycle shop and weekly newspaper, *The Hamtramck Times*, shares a block on Joseph Campau with the Ukrainain Reliance Credit Union and the General Sikorski PLAV Post #10.

A strong critic of the local establishment, Zwolak uses his paper to attack perceived malfeasance—even his own. In the summer of 1988, the *Times* carried a front-page exposé of a candidate for Wayne County Clerk who sent registration notices to deceased voters. According to the paper the culprit was—Bob Zwolak. "Of course, there's nothing illegal about it," he explained. "The list comes off the registrar's computer. So a candidate wouldn't necessarily know who had died."

"In other words, you had no way of knowing."

"Well," he said, looking sheepish, "I *was* the city clerk. But what the hell, I believe in freedom of the press."

Zwolak struck me as an honest man, and I asked him how his city had managed to hang on to its identity in the midst of so much suburban flight. People at City Hall had portrayed Hamtramck as an open, friendly city, a picture that caused him to laugh out loud.

"There are about six hundred thousand Poles in Michigan," he said. "That's forty percent of all the people who actually vote in this state. We are the biggest ethnic group in Michigan except for the blacks. And Hamtramck is the symbolic center, the capital. Our officials judge people by their ethnic background. You're Polish, no problem. But other people want something, forget it. No way. This should be America, not an extension of a foreign country. If the church wants ethnicity, that's fine—but not the entire municipal government. What other ethnic group is still left except the blacks? Only the Poles.

"Hey, when I was a kid I lived for a few years in California," said the crusading publisher. "And you know what? While I was out there, I realized something about Hamtramck. It isn't reality—it's Disneyland."

The Polish Disneyland was in full swing on Labor Day, when Hamtramck threw its annual ethnic festival. Pierogi and kielbasa stands lined the streets, and women in *babushkas* carried white cardboard boxes from the Oaza bakery in both hands. On an improvised bandstand near the corner of Joseph Campau and Cannif, Dave Uchalik and the Polish Muslims were entertaining the members of the fraternity.

"*Yak shmash*, Hamtramck," he called, and the crowd cheered. He turned to his drummer. "Ready, Yash?"

"Ready, Stash," said the drummer, and the band struck up "Love Polka Number 9." People began to dance, heavy work shoes clomping on the pavement in time to some internal metronome unheard by the average ear. Uchalik pranced around the stage, the Muslimettes banged tambourines and Polish flags flapped in the damp breeze.

A thin black man in a white robe and turbanlike hat stood on the corner, next to Tondryk's Electric, surveying the scene. Although blacks account for perhaps 15 percent of Hamtramck's population, there were few at the festival, and his outfit aroused my curiosity.

"Excuse me, but are you a Muslim by any chance?" I asked.

He waited a while before answering. "Yeah man, from Kansas City," he finally said, tugging on his scraggly beard.

"These guys are called the Polish Muslims," I told him, and he digested the information slowly.

"Ain't never heard nothin' 'bout no Polish Muslims," he said, after a moment. "Don't look like they servin' Allah up there, not to me it don't."

On the bandstand, Uchalik got ready for his next number, "John Paul One, John Paul Two" (to the tune of the Beatles "Obla Dee, Obla Da"), dedicated to Hamtramck's favorite pontiff. "For all you do, this song's for you," he said, and the crowd cheered, although some boos were mixed in. "Hey," Uchalik said, "I know His Holiness can take a joke. One, two, three, four; ready, Yash?" "Ready, Stash . . ."

Helen Livingstone Bogle was perplexed. "Where *are* all the Polish people?" she asked.

Mrs. Bogle was sitting in her living room in Grosse Pointe, leafing through albums of family photographs and memorabilia. Her life story was there in the yellowing pictures—the family home on the lake, next to the Dodge mansion, where she had been born in 1921 ("I'm not the least bit self-conscious about my age"); photos from Grosse Pointe Country Day School and the Ethel Walker School in

Simsbury, Connecticut, where she had been polished and prepared for society; tintypes of maternal great-grandfather Travgoot Schmidt, who reputedly owned more real estate than any other man in Michigan, and of paternal grandfather William Livingstone ("Just the most elegant teddy bear of a man"), who founded Detroit's Dime Savings Bank and once served as the president of the American Banking Association. There were also more contemporary mementos, including twenty-nine snapshots from "the nifty trip we took last year to Kenya." Mrs. Bogle is a born archivist, and her chosen subject is the history of her family, which is, in its way, the social and commercial history of Detroit.

Reminders of the family's prominence are not confined to Helen Bogle's albums. Her grandfather, William "Sailor Bill" Livingstone, raised the money to dredge the channel of the Detroit River that now bears his name. The marble lighthouse on Belle Isle—the only one of its kind in America—is named for him as well.

Sailor Bill was a close friend of Henry Ford. "He loaned Henry two hundred and fifty thousand dollars to buy out his partners," Helen Bogle said proudly, and showed me a book with a warm personal inscription from the auto magnate to the banking mogul. Next to it was a history of the Republican Party, authored by her protean ancestor.

On the wall in her living room there was a handsome oil portrait of a distinguished-looking man, her father, Seabourn Rome Livingstone, the former president of the Detroit stock exchange, as well as an oil painting of her parents' yacht. The mantelpiece was crowded with pictures of various Livingstones and Schmidts.

Mrs. Bogle's mother was a local golf champion, and her aunt was on the U.S. Curtis Cup team; it is from them that she inherited her athletic bearing and square-jawed, handsome looks. She paced about the house with an energetic stride, rushing downstairs for her childhood silver loving cup, upstairs for a photo of a family summer home (since sold to the state as a gubernatorial mansion), back downstairs to show an ornate dollhouse of her youth that she had found and reclaimed from her grandmother's ballroom. The tour was accompanied by a stream-of-consciousness discourse on glorious times, now gone forever.

"Detroit was a small town in those days," she said. "Everyone knew everyone else. I still can't believe that Henry Ford [II] is gone. He was our link to the outside world, like a head of state. He bought my cousin's house. As a girl I was driven to school in a chauffeured car. I was born with a platinum spoon in my mouth, and I was terribly closely held. But I was curious."

Helen Bogle's curiosity led to her take up a brief, highly unorthodox career as a photographer, and later to go to work as a fund-raiser for the Detroit Institute of Art. There, for the first time, she became the victim of discrimination. "My superior gave me a hard time because I had had a coming-out party," she recalled. Harassment included being assigned a desk without a telephone. The young fund-raiser overcame that particular hurdle by calling the head of Michigan Bell, a family friend, and directing him to have a telephone installed forthwith.

During her years at the DIA, Detroit was still controlled by people Helen Livingstone Bogle knew as uncles—members of the auto aristocracy and their allies, the captains of business and industry. Now that the city has fallen into more callused hands, she rarely ventures into it.

"Very few Grosse Pointe people bother to go downtown nowadays unless it's to the symphony or the museums," she said. "The papers make it seem unsafe [Mrs. Bogle subscribes to one Detroit paper, as well as the *New York Times* and the *Martha's Vineyard Gazette*]. Well, I suppose it is unsafe but there's no need to publicize it on the front pages. Why not have a new society page for criminals? If you want to see who shot whom, just turn to Section D. The colored people—what do you call them nowadays, blacks?—well, I have known marvelous ones. But you *cannot* overlook the crime that is creeping out," she said firmly.

When Helen Livingstone Bogle was growing up, there were no

colored people in Grosse Pointe. "There used to be the point system here, of which I did not approve. We do have some black families now, though." She pondered the change. "I should think they'll be terribly lonely," she said, not unkindly.

Notwithstanding the arrival of several black families, and a handful of Jews and Italians, Grosse Pointe seems to the outside observer to be pretty much what it has always been—a WASP bastion of privilege and wealth. Once restricted by explicit agreement, it remains off-limits to all but the richest and most socially confident, by virtue of custom and the astronomical cost of its stately homes. But Mrs. Bogle is anything but an outside observer, and to her experienced eye, deterioration is everywhere.

"Grosse Pointe is land poor," she said. "My cousin is subdividing the family estate—ten acres. Things have changed so. I don't have one family house that I can show you, except my grandmother's. It's this damn ADC [Aid to Dependent Children]—people don't want to work anymore. You simply cannot get help. Where *are* all the Polish people?"

To demonstrate the fallen condition of Grosse Pointe, Mrs. Bogle donned a mink jacket and led me on a nostalgic tour of the area. Her first stop was her girlhood home, now part of a church, which is situated next to the Horace Dodge mansion. "Mrs. Dodge built the most beautiful house, which was a duplicate of the Petite Trianon. It had a seventeen-car garage with cinnamon-colored doors," she recalled. "And her boat, the *Dolphin*, had a crew of seventy-five."

Near the Dodge mansion she stopped at a nondescript building. "This is the Grosse Pointe Club," she said. "It's known as the Little Club."

"Known to whom as the Little Club?" I asked.

Mrs. Bogle seemed nonplussed. "To whom? Why, to everyone," she said, climbing out of her car for a closer inspection.

Inside, on the Wednesday morning before Thanksgiving, the deserted clubhouse seemed fairly unimposing—thick green carpet on highly polished wood floors, flowered easy chairs, a closed veranda with a view of Lake St. Claire. But its charm lies not in its decor, but its membership.

"Who can belong to the Little Club?" I asked.

"Anyone who's lucky enough," she said. "We have around three hundred members—it's the most exclusive club in Grosse Pointe."

The Little Club's initiation fee is $10,000, and monthly dues are $175. "That doesn't seem exorbitant—unless you belong to a lot of clubs," she observed. Most of the members are old-time Grosse Pointe people, although the club was, on that very day, in the process of accepting its first Jewish member, the director of the Detroit Institute of Art.

A quick cup of Protestant coffee and Mrs. Bogle was back behind the wheel, pointing out local landmarks. The Alger home ("General Russell Alger's daughter was the first woman to go up in the Wright brothers' flying machine"); the house of a childhood friend, actress Julie Harris; and the Merkle house, which once belonged to one of the town's most prominent families but is now owned by two decorators. "Which is the way of it all," Mrs. Bogle observed with weary sadness.

As she headed west toward Detroit, she occasionally pointed out one of the remaining mansions of her girlhood, which were scattered among newer, very substantial, ten- and twelve-room brick homes. "Some of these are originals," she remarked. "And then you get the mix of these funny little . . . poops."

Past Fox Creek, she turned down Alter Road, generally considered the border that divides the Pointe from Detroit. It was midday, but she immediately locked her doors. "Might as well take some precautions," she said warily, although no one was in sight.

On the Grosse Point side of the street there were medium-sized brick homes; on the Detroit side, dilapidated frame houses, some of them boarded up. They were divided by a canal that runs the length of the street and by a chain link fence on its bank. Grosse Pointe wasn't able to build its flood-control wall, but it has achieved a measure of physical separation from the black giant to the west.

Detroit's proximity is a matter of grave concern to many Grosse Pointers. There had been a recent public controversy over the closing of a movie theater, just outside the city limits, that had attracted black patrons. "When your neighbors get funny, do you stay or move?" Mrs. Bogle asked rhetorically.

"What do you mean by 'funny'?"

"Different from you," she said in a silly-question tone of voice.

From Alter Road, Mrs. Bogle turned back to the east, heading away from the city, toward Provencal Road, "the last really nice street in Grosse Pointe," across from the Detroit Country Club. She seemed to know every house on the short street. "That's Kathy Ford's place," she said. "Henry bought it from my cousin. There's the Williams home—you know, Soapy, the former governor. This one belongs to another cousin. And that is Bob Zeff's house. He's the only Jewish gentleman on the street. He was Kathy Ford's divorce lawyer . . ."

Each of the homes on Provencal had a story. This one was the site of an adolescent party, that one the scene of an elegant affair, still another the residence of a local celebrity. "It is really a nifty street," Helen Bogle pronounced.

"What makes a nifty street?" I asked.

"One that is established and doesn't have too many surprises," she said. By that standard, Grosse Pointe is a nifty city indeed.

On the way home, Mrs. Bogle shifted her perspective for a moment to the national scene. The presidential election had just ended with George Bush's victory, of which she thoroughly approved.

"We had a party for George Bush at grandmother's house a few years ago," she recalled. "I like him very, very much."

"That's not surprising," I said. "He's the first president from your class since Kennedy."

Helen Livingstone Bogle was not happy with the observation. "The Kennedys?" she said. "They tried to worm their way into everything. They were pushy. And I don't know anybody of *any* race who is pushy and gets away with it."

In the fall of 1986, the pushiest black man in Detroit, Coleman Young, gave an interview to the Canadian Broadcasting Corporation. The occasion was Detroit's No Crime Day, and the interview, which has become legendary, went like this:

CBC: . . . it's so incomprehensible to us. I mean, you've had what, nine hundred and twenty-five people shot this summer?

Young: You know the figures better than I do. . . .

CBC: What would happen if you went door-to-door and started collecting all the guns?

Young: Well, then people wouldn't have guns to shoot at each other. I have no problem with collecting all the guns if it is done like you do it in Canada. But I'll be damned if I'll let them collect guns in the city of Detroit while we're surrounded by hostile suburbs and the whole rest of the state who have guns, where you have vigilantes, practicing Ku Klux Klan in the wilderness with automatic weapons. I am in favor of everyone disarming; I'm opposed to a unilateral disarming of the people of Detroit."

When the mayor's remarks were reported by the Detroit media, an angry cry went up from Grosse Pointe to Melvindale. Here was another example of Coleman's paranoia and suburb-baiting. Statistics on the number of suburbanites (i.e., whites) shot by Detroiters (i.e., blacks) were brought forth; furious denunciations of the mayor appeared in the letters-to-the-editor columns of the Detroit papers; and even some of Young's supporters admitted privately that this time he had exaggerated.

It was, indeed, hyperbole—the residents of Detroit are in no immediate danger from the dowagers of Grosse Pointe or the crew-cut patrons of Tom Coogan's barbershop. But less than an hour up Highway I-96, in Livingston County, there are some good ol' boys who wouldn't mind teaching the mayor of Dee-troit what the business end of an M16 looks like.

Livingston County is within commuting distance of the city, but few of its seventy thousand residents work there, or even visit. To them, the glitzy northwest suburbs and the ethnic enclaves to the east are almost as foreign as the black metropolis itself. Cross the line from Oakland County to Livingston County and you cross into a rural America right out of Faulkner.

One Saturday night, a street-smart reporter and I drove the forty miles north to check on a report that some of Detroit's white police officers were attending the Ku Klux Klan cross burnings that are a regular weekend attraction in Gregory, a little town in the poorest part of the county. The reporter, who is white, covers the mean streets of Detroit with a fearless professionalism; but the eerie rural darkness was something else, threatening and oppressive. When we passed a sign, just outside Pinckney, advertising a survivalist camp, he instinctively clicked the locks on his car doors, just like Helen Bogle had on Alter Road.

Survivalist camps were in vogue in 1988. That summer some entrepreneurs opened a paint-ball facility in an abandoned factory complex in Detroit where suburbanites could don army fatigues and take part in simulated urban violence by shooting one another with paint guns. The gallery was originally called Little Beirut, which sparked an outraged protest from Detroit's large Arab population. The name was changed, but the idea caught on, and hundreds of people came into the city each weekend to play Dirty Harry.

The owners of Little Beirut argued that their mock battlefield offered nothing more than good, dirty fun; and, in any event, it was in Detroit, where Coleman Young's police force could keep an eye on it. But a survivalist camp in Pinckney was a different proposition. "They've got army trucks out there and a tank," said a local law enforcement officer who met us in Gregory. "They say they shoot paint at each other, but you'd swear it was automatic weapons from the way it sounds."

The officer sat at a table in the back corner of the Gregory Inn and ate the turkey-and-mashed-potato special. It was raining that

night, and the place was full of hunters in dripping parkas. Tacked
to the walls were posters advertising farm auctions and an ad for
Carol's Plucking Parlour and Slaughter House.

"I don't know how the rain is going to affect the cross burnings,"
said the lawman. "I don't know if you can burn a cross in the rain
or not." He spoke with a neutral curiosity, as if he were discussing
a possible rainout of a softball game.

"Do you know where they take place?" the reporter asked.

"Right down the road," he said, gesturing with his head. "Cross
burnings aren't illegal up here. You don't even need a permit. This
is Klan country."

The Klan and other white supremacist groups have been a prominent feature of Detroit's political culture for decades. The city's
modern founding father, Henry Ford, was also America's most outspoken Jew hater, a man whose picture hung on Adolf Hitler's wall.
And in the 1930s, Detroit's best-known Catholic clergyman, Father
Coughlin, was an open defender of Nazi racist doctrines.

Ironically, Coughlin began his public career when the KKK
burned a cross on the lawn of his church, the Shrine of the Little
Flower. In those days, there were said to be two hundred thousand
Klan members in Michigan. A Klan offspring, the Black Legion, was
a power in city politics, and the *New Republic* estimated that the
group carried out some fifty murders between 1933 and 1936. The
Reverend Gerald L. K. Smith, another nationally known bigot, was
headquartered in Detroit. Ford, Coughlin, Smith and the Black
Legion found fertile soil in the religious and racial xenophobia that
Eastern European Catholics and southern whites brought with them
to Detroit; they, in turn, created the climate for the race riot of
1943, the bloodiest of its time, in which thirty-four people died.

The modern repository for this legacy of racial violence is Livingston County, where there are hundreds of active Klan members
and thousands of sympathetic fellow travelers. Robert Miles, who
lives in Cochatca, near Howell, is the closest thing to a celebrity that
the county can boast. Miles once served as a national grand dragon

of the Klan, and he is a beloved figure in white supremacist circles. He advocates the establishment of an Aryan nation in a part of North America, which would presumably be created in the image of Livingston County.

The Klan is not the only hot organization up there. Not far from the Gregory Inn was a devil worship church, and townpeople claim to have sighted their breeders—young women who produce babies for the cult—shopping on Main Street. "I don't go near them or their church," said the lawman. "I hear they have animal sacrifices, and that's against the law I suppose, but devil worship isn't illegal around here, either." Livingston County is nothing if not tolerant.

Local law enforcement personnel spend most of their time combing dirt roads for poachers, breaking up bar brawls and performing other mundane police tasks. There were only three homicides in the county in 1988—less than on a fast Saturday night in Detroit.

"The people out here, they moved here most of 'em because the KKK keeps the corruption out," our host said. "Most of them are farmers, and they like the peace and quiet."

The last time the Detroit reporter had been in Livingston County, he had attended a holiday party at the home of some acquaintances. "They had a big sign," he recalled. "It said 'Don't shoot Jesse Jackson; we don't need another national holiday.' And these were liberals."

"We don't need another national holiday," said the lawman, savoring the punchline. "Don't shoot Jesse Jackson. Ha, ha."

Jesse Jackson is not likely to venture into the Gregory Inn anytime soon. There are only three black families in the entire county, a statistic that is closely monitored. "Why would *any* blacks want to live up here?" the reporter asked, and the lawman shook his head. "Got me by the balls," he said.

It was still raining heavily but our guide had promised a cross burning, so we headed down D-19 toward a small farmhouse with a traffic light attached to its roof. When we arrived, the light was red. "Hate to disappoint you but it looks like the burning got rained out after all," said the lawman. "They use that light as a signal. When something's going on, it's green. And usually, when there's a burning, there are hundreds of cars out here. Looks like you picked the wrong weekend." There was genuine regret in the officer's voice, like a Floridian apologizing for unseasonably cold weather in January. He was not a member of the Klan himself, but outsiders had shown an interest in his territory, and he was sorry not to be able to oblige.

Instead he took us for a ride to Hell. Howell is the county seat, but Hell, Michigan, is the spiritual capital of Livingston County. Presumably its founders intended the name as a joke, or as a tourist gimmick. A general store stocks postcards with captions such as "I've been to Hell" and "Why don't you go to Hell?" But with hundreds of gun-toting Klansmen on the loose, and a Satanic cult just up the road, the jocular name seemed spookily appropriate.

"Doesn't anyone object to this kind of stuff?" asked the reporter. "I mean, how about the people who live next door to the devil worship church?" In the city, people have been known to picket unwelcome neighborhood incinerators, but the ethic in Livingston County is live and let live. "People around here stay out of each other's business," said the lawman broadmindedly.

The rain began to let up and we cruised out of Hell, searching the back roads for an alternate-site cross burning. We passed through a quiet little town whose residents all come from Kentucky, drove by the devil worship church to look for signs of activity, and went by the survivalist camp, but we didn't see a single burning cross that night.

Half an hour and many miles later, we were about to turn in when we met another patrol car coming down a dirt road in the opposite direction. The two stopped side by side, and the lone officer in the other car rolled down his window. He was glad to goof off for a few minutes and to engage in some friendly banter.

Hoping to salvage the evening, our host did a little fishing. "I hear rumors that your chief is in the Klan," he said. "Know anything about that?"

"Yep, I heard that one too," said the cop. "But I don't know. I don't like niggers much myself, but I ain't in the Klan."

As cops always do, the two men got to swapping combat stories. "Tell them about the time you busted that beer party," the other man said, and our host laughed modestly.

"Hell, it was just a bunch of teenagers having a party," he said, in the tone of the man who captured Dillinger. "Some dickhead and a bunch of his friends, including a guy in a wheelchair, were making a commotion. And their dawg was barking his head off."

"He wanted to shoot that dawg," said the other cop.

"Yeah, I sure did. Anyway, these kids started mouthing off, giving me a hard time, so I grabbed the guy that was giving the party and dragged him out in his front yard. In the rain. And I put that dickhead down on his knees and made him recite the Lord's Prayer. Right there in the yard." He laughed and his friend laughed. Police work, done right, has its satisfactions.

"Made him say the damn Lord's Prayer," said the lawman, shaking his head. "Right in the damn yard."

"Yeah, but you still should have shot that damn dawg," said the other. "That's what you shoulda done." The two cops raced their engines and thought about the lost opportunity. Then they put it in gear and headed down the dirt road in opposite directions, looking for poachers.

My friend the reporter and I drove back to Detroit. It was late, but the city was only forty minutes away, and we couldn't wait to get back home.

Chapter Six

"THANK GOD FOR MAYOR COLEMAN YOUNG"

In the fall of 1988, shortly after the Collins-Crockett campaign, a Detroit television station ran a profile on Mayor Coleman Young. Young's relations with the local media have been stormy, but the documentary was highly complimentary, and the mayor seemed to be enjoying himself. The high point of the show came when he discussed his warm personal relations with former president Jimmy Carter.

In 1976, Coleman Young had, typically, done the unorthodox and endorsed the unknown Georgia governor early in his campaign. Once in office, Carter reciprocated with generous federal assistance. Young talked about the strange friendship between a white southerner and the militant mayor of Motown. "He is a very moral, very religious person," said Young, and his eyes crinkled and shoulders shook in the mirthful gesture that usually precedes his one-liners. "Now, I'm not *immoral,* but I've never been accused of being *too* moral, either."

It is one of the few accusations he has escaped during a public career that spans almost fifty years. Young has been called a communist, a radical and a crook, denounced as a heartless big-city boss and a ruthless dictator. In the suburbs he is considered a black racist; in the city, following his refusal to support Jesse Jackson's presidential bid, some people labeled him an Uncle Tom. There is only one thing that everyone agrees on: Coleman Young, who was first elected mayor of Detroit in 1973, is a formidable and fascinating man.

Many Detroiters can never remember another mayor. Kids at the Whitney Young elementary school believe it is named after Whitney Houston and the mayor—a not-unlikely supposition in a city where Young's name adorns everything. There is a Coleman A. Young community center on the east side and a seventy-five-acre Coleman A. Young civic center downtown on the Detroit River. Accomplished schoolchildren receive financial aid from the Coleman A. Young Scholarship Fund. The mayor's picture hangs in virtually every city office, like the visage of some postliberation African leader—photographs of the young Coleman, handsome enough to have earned the nickname "the Black Clark Gable" in Detroit's Black Bottom neighborhood; or of the older, Big Daddy Coleman, light-skinned and gray-haired, with a Redd Foxx twinkle in his eye. Young's name is inscribed on the stationery of city officials, and on their personal calling cards. And a few years ago he had it plastered in huge letters on the tower of the Detroit Zoo, which is located in suburban Royal Oak. This was vintage Coleman Young, an in-your-face gesture to the white suburbanites he loves to taunt and harass.

Political observers in Detroit sometimes call Young "the last of the great Irish political bosses." There is, in fact, something Skeffington-ian in his audacious, often charming, sometimes ruthless domination of Detroit. But Young is more than a tribal politician; to many, he is a hero and a savior. Fittingly, there is a hagiographic flavor to the mayor's biography, which is usually depicted as a series of challenges heroically overcome, stations of the cross successfully executed.

The story begins with Coleman the Gifted Student, denied a scholarship because of his race. Then there is Coleman the Officer in the Tuskegee Airmen, who went to a military stockade for opposing wartime Jim Crow regulations; Coleman the Labor Leader, tossed out of the UAW for radicalism; Coleman the Defiant, dragged before the House Committee on Un-American Activities, lecturing his white inquisitors on the proper way to pronounce *Negro*; Coleman in Exile, unable to find work for almost a decade, scratching out a living "driving a little taxi, handling a little beef"; Coleman Redux, elected to the Michigan State Senate in the mid-sixties; and Coleman the Underdog, defeating the white establishment and the Negro E-lites to become the city's first black mayor. And, finally, Coleman the Liberator, the man who dismantled the colonialist occupying forces and brought self-determination to the people of Detroit.

An anonymous poem, published as an ad in the playbill of a city program, put it this way:

> Coleman Young, Coleman Young
> There's Only One Coleman Young
> Coleman Young, Coleman Young
> Thank God For Mayor Coleman Young
> A Man With Integrity
> A Man With Personality
> He's So Brave, He's So Smart
> Yet He's A Man With A Great, Big Heart
> Coleman Young, Coleman Young
> Thank God For Mayor Coleman Young.

When I saw the poem, I wondered what Brooks Patterson would think of it, or the boys in Tom Coogan's barbershop. The mayor's enemies concede that he is smart; some admit that he is brave; and few would disagree that he has personality, at least the kind that appeals to his own people. But *integrity* is not a common adjective for Coleman Young in suburbia; nor do many see him as a man "With A Great, Big Heart." Unlike other black mayors, such as L.A.'s Tom Bradley or Atlanta's Andrew Young, he has never sought the approval of white people, never attempted to portray himself as a comfortable bridge between the races. Young is not the credit-to-his-race type of middle-class black whom whites find reassuring. You deal with Coleman Young on his terms, or no terms at all.

Young has been divorced twice and lives alone in the Manoogian mansion on the Detroit River. He travels the city in a midnight-blue limousine ("You want a Cadillac mayor, you buy him a Cadillac") with two bodyguards and a police escort, earns $125,000 a year (the second-highest mayoral salary in the country), and dresses in quietly elegant, double-breasted silk suits. The trappings of wealth and power convey a message, but they don't conceal, and are not meant to conceal, the fact that he is still a street man, a signifying mayor who uses the style and language of Black Bottom to delight his supporters and shock his opponents.

It took me about three days in Detroit to realize just what a powerful man he is. For one thing, whites—in and out of the city—couldn't stop complaining about him. For another, none of the municipal officials I contacted for appointments would return my calls. "In this city, nobody will say anything without Coleman's okay," a reporter explained. "You better see him and let him know what you're up to."

I tried, but it wasn't easy; the mayor's press policy could not be described as open-door. You need a sponsor to get an appointment. Finally I found somebody who knew somebody who talked with Young's spokesman, Bob Berg. After a few weeks of negotiation, I was eventually granted an audience.

I admired the technique. Young was letting me know that he

wasn't the mayor of some second-rate town; a meeting with him was a rare gift, something to be valued. This approach worked (it always does); I went to our first interview feeling like the Cowardly Lion on the way to Oz.

I arrived at the mayoral mansion at three o'clock on a sweltering August afternoon. An aide ushered me into the living room and told me to wait. I used the time to browse through a stack of books on the coffee table—*The Holy Koran, Billyball, The Book of the Dead* and *Rare Breeds—A Guide to Horses*—that testified to the eclectic tastes of a man who educated himself in the public library. The room was filled with memorabilia from his various trips—a Samuri sword and Japanese suit of armor, African sculpture—and a larger-than-life bust of His Honor. It is a bachelor's living room, seldom used except for official occasions.

After half an hour or so, Bob Berg appeared and walked me upstairs to the mayor's study, a cluttered and mercifully air-conditioned room. There, at half past three in the afternoon, I found the mayor of Detroit, dressed in blue pin-striped pajamas and a checkered bathrobe.

The television set in the room was tuned to CNN, and a deck of playing cards sat on the desk. Interviewers often mention the fact that the mayor conducts conversations while watching the tube and playing solitaire. The implication is that he is easily distracted, or perhaps a bit eccentric. But, as I came to discover, there is a white interpretation of Young's actions, and a black one. Toward the end of our conversation that day, I asked him why he kept the television on.

"I don't really watch this thing," the mayor said, gesturing toward the set. "But I like to have it on in the background. See, I don't want people listening in on my conversations." This is not paranoia; several years ago, during an investigation into a municipal scandal, the FBI bugged the mayor's private townhouse.

And what about the solitaire? I asked.

"I only play when I get bored," said the mayor dryly, and his shoulders shook with silent laughter.

Humor is Coleman Young's great solvent. He uses it to shock and deflate, charm and conciliate, or just to amuse himself. Young has the timing of a professional comedian, and the keen ear of an impersonator. Bilingual, he is able to switch back and forth effortlessly between perfectly crafted English and street talk. The latter is used primarily to disconcert what he calls "the black boogie wazzie" and other "phoney-ass people." Since unknown white visitors are all suspect, he usually prefers to begin with profanity and jive, enabling him to size them up on his linguistic turf.

That afternoon, when I entered his office, the mayor was engrossed in some official papers. After a time he looked up and shook his head. "They want me to pass out free condoms, because of this AIDs thing," he said, dropping the documents on the desk with an exasperated gesture. "Hell, why do I have to get involved in this? I neither condemn, nor do I condone, ah . . . fuckin'." He paused and peered out of narrowed eyes for my reaction.

"Mr. Mayor," said Berg, "this interview is on the record."

"Oh," said Young, in mock alarm. "Well, in that case, you better say that I, ah, condone fuckin'. I don't want people to get the wrong idea about me."

I laughed. I had no idea if this was the appropriate response, but the remark struck me as funny. What the hell, I thought, at least I got one good quote.

Switching subjects but not tactics, the mayor mentioned a construction project that had run into some opposition because it would require uprooting part of a cemetery. "They got this Greek priest who's leading the protests," he said. "I found out that the motherfucker is from Warren. He doesn't even have a got-damned church." Again he turned his eyes on high beam and peered across the desk. I don't know what he saw, but he was apparently satisfied; he con-

ducted the rest of the interview in more or less conventional
language.

Later, Berg, a white former newsman, explained that Young has
an infallible way of gauging white attitudes toward blacks. The cursing is a part of the test, and people who flunk have very short audiences with His Honor.

Young's conversational style is rambling and circuitous, but he
always returns to the point, which is usually connected in some way
with white racism and its crippling effect on blacks. Some of this is
posturing; the mayor is far too sophisticated to believe that his city's
problems—especially its crime problem—can be attributed wholly to
discrimination, past or present. His enemies say, with justice, that
he uses suburb-bashing as a tool for deflecting criticism, much as
southern segregationists a generation ago hollered "nigger" to make
poor whites forget their own misery. Young's attacks on the "hostile
suburbs" are calculated to rally support, create an us-against-the-
world atmosphere that he, as supreme commander of "us," can use
for political gain.

But there is no doubt that militance is more than a tactic; Young
genuinely sees the world in racial terms. And when it comes to
assessing guilt, he refuses to play the liberal game of dividing the
blame and splitting the difference. "I view racism not as a two-way
street," he once told a conference on race relations. "I think racism
is a system of oppression. I don't think black folks are oppressive to
anybody, so I don't consider that blacks are capable of racism."

Young also rejects the popular notion that the problems of black
people—and of black Detroit—are a seamless web. "I'm not going
to buy that vicious-cycle theory," Young told the *Detroit Free Press*
in 1987. "It starts with economic pressure, and the first economic
pressure was slavery. . . . It reminds me of something Martin Luther
King said. 'How do you expect us to pull ourselves up by our bootstraps when we don't even have boots?'" Improving on Dr. King, the
mayor added a coda: "The motherfuckers *stole* our boots."

The sense that Detroit has been fleeced and abandoned runs through Young's conversation. So does resentment of whites who have left but continue to meddle in the city's affairs. "I don't know of any other city in the nation where there's such a preoccupation in the suburbs for control," he said. "The same people who left the city for racial reasons still want to control what they've left."

Paradoxically, some blacks feel that Young himself has opened the door for white interference. Since taking office he has concentrated on rebuilding the downtown, and most of his grandiose projects have been financed and built by whites such as Henry Ford II and Max Fisher. The mayor is unapologetic about the strategy—which he views as necessary for creating jobs—or the tactic of marshaling suburban help. He is realistic in assessing the problem: "Ain't no black people wielding any of the major power—economic power—in this city," he said.

The inability to translate political control into economic self-sufficiency is perhaps Young's greatest frustration. He goes through life keeping score: how many for us, how many for them. The dominant theme of his administration has been to get more black numbers on the scoreboard, but judged by that standard, he has been a disappointment. Only fourteen black-owned companies in Detroit earned more than $10 million in 1987, and six of them were auto dealerships. Even more revealing, of the twenty-five largest black-owned companies, just two were building firms whose combined income was $6.6 million. "The head of the Minority Contractors Association runs a soul food restaurant on Seven Mile Road," a columnist for one of the daily papers said. "That tells you all you need to know, right there."

Professional people have done better, although not as well as might be expected in a black-run city. A few weeks after our first meeting, the mayor attended the dedication of a downtown building. The architects involved stood on the podium. One was a towering black man, well over six-five. After the ceremony, he was introduced, by a mutual friend, to the mayor. "I noticed you up there," Young said.

"It's kind of hard to miss me," said the architect. "I was the tallest one on the stage."

"Yeah, and the only nigger, too," snapped Young.

The mayor's critics say that his tough racial rhetoric has kept whites from moving back to the city, but he dismisses the notion. "White people find it extremely hard to live in an environment they don't control," he observed archly.

This is very likely true, but the mayor has done little to allay the fears of his neighbors. A few years ago, Detroit constructed a monument to Joe Louis. The statue—a giant black fist—stands at the foot of Woodward Avenue, off the Lodge Expressway, where white commuters can't miss it; it is not the sort of symbol calculated to calm jittery suburban nerves.

Nor is Coleman Young anybody's idea of a law-and-order mayor. In his first inaugural address he made his famous remark about crooks hitting Eight Mile Road, but if they did, others have taken their place. And the fact that Young, who has an abiding distrust of cops, took that opportunity to include racist policemen in his list of personae non grata, did not endear him to the department.

Occasionally the mayor, reacting to public outcries, has assumed a sterner stance. After a spate of shootings in schools, he called for metal detectors at schoolhouse entrances. In the wake of persistent reports that Detroit cops were using drugs, he advocated random testing in the department. Both decisions violated his own principles of civil rights, and he adopted them with obvious reluctance.

Despite these sporadic get-tough efforts, however, Coleman Young clings resolutely to his old image as a bad-ass rebel. The mayor has an extensive collection of firearms, and he talks about guns with fond expertise. Within minutes of assuring me that Detroit's violent image is a media exaggeration, he bragged about how dangerous the city is. "I always carried a gun when I knew it was necessary," he said of the years before he became mayor. "In the old days, in the barbershop, there was a guy named Sol—Solomon— who used to make regular gun runs to Ohio. We'd order any damn gun we wanted." Today, with two bodyguards, he no longer packs his own piece, but he leaves no doubt that he would know what to do with one.

Young's machismo makes him a dubious role model for the city's teenagers. Toward the end of the year, the mayor appeared before a group of two hundred high school students at a rally of Congressman George Crockett's Youth Caucus. The kids, all but one of whom were black, listened avidly but with a certain bemusement as the mayor lectured them about their civic duties.

"I know I have the responsibility to close down the crack houses and scoop up the guns," he said. But, he told them, they had to cooperate—by saying no to drugs, helping their friends to stay clean, and by calling the police to report crack dealers at school or in the neighborhood. The mayor used a mixture of mild profanity and occasional slang to make the point, and unlike most septuagenarians, he carried it off; Coleman Young's street talk is still impeccable.

"Now," he hollered to the kids, "are you tired of crime?"

"Yeah!" they chorused.

"Are you going to do something about it?"

"Yeah!" they answered.

"Are you prepared to point a finger and drop a dime on the sons of a bitch who're dealing?" he thundered.

"No!" yelled most of the audience, with a spontaneity that startled the mayor. He narrowed his eyes, but his shoulders began to work, suppressing laughter. He made them answer again, getting a halfhearted "Yeah" the second time, but it was clear that everybody knew where everybody else stood.

Later, when I asked him about the rally, his eyes crinkled up and he began to laugh. "Did you really expect that the kids would agree to turn in pushers?" I wondered.

"Shit no; I know about the code of silence," he said.

"Would you have turned in a drug dealer when you were their age?" I asked, and he looked at me as if I were softheaded.

"Me?" he said, in a tone of disbelief. "Hell no. But don't forget, it was a different city then. Cops used to shoot black kids for fun. They'd tell you to run, and call themselves shooting over your head, and shoot you in the back. I learned when I was ten or eleven not to turn my back on a cop." Although he could fire the chief of police with a phone call, there is still a lot of little Coleman in him, and the people of his city, the good guys and the bad guys, sense it.

One of the ways in which Coleman Young conveys his allegiance to his roots is through the use of profanity; when the mood is on him, he elevates cussing to a minor art form. Suburbanites and some prissy Detroiters complain about the mayor's foul language, and church leaders often grumble that, as a role model, the mayor shouldn't be saying "all kinds of bitches and motherfuckers." Young, for his part, genuinely savors the shock value of his rough talk.

The newspapers in Detroit often go into reportorial contortions to convey the mayor's language. Many interviews with him look as if they were written in Morse code, dots and dashes filling in for unprintable words. Local journalists take a certain pride in their inventiveness. During the mayor's 1983 visit to Japan, for example, the *Detroit Free Press* began an article this way:

"When you speak Japanese," the elderly interpreter explained, "there are many words that have different meanings by your tone of voice, your emphasis."

"Oh, yes," Mayor Young said. "We have words like that in English, too."

He then pronounced a 12-letter compound expletive that he uses frequently, in various contexts . . .

During that same visit, Young was the dinner guest of the mayor of Toyota, Detroit's sister city in Japan. After the meal, the Japanese host honored his colleague by donning a kimono and performing a warrior dance with a spear and fan. Then, in accordance with good manners, he asked Young to perform a dance of his own.

"I hate to disillusion you," said Young, "but I can't dance and I can't sing. And I don't like watermelon, either."

Young is, indeed, tone-deaf, but he had changed his mind on the watermelon issue by the time, in December, he visited Detroit's open-air Eastern Market. He was on one of his periodic forays around the city, and he stopped in to say hello to an Italian vegetable man, a crony from the old days.

After some vigorous hand-shaking, the vendor informed the mayor that a Chinese restaurant was about to open not far from his shop. Young, a connoisseur of Chinese cooking, nodded approvingly.

"What's the owner's name," he asked.

"Don Pollack, something like that," said the grocer.

"Pollack? What the hell kinda Chinaman is he?" demanded Mayor Young with mock outrage.

Trying to recoup, the Italian offered the mayor some poinsettias for his office.

"I don't need no got-damned poin-settas," said the mayor of Detroit. Pause. "How 'bout a watermelon?" The small crowd that had assembled laughed loudly. Coleman loves watermelon; we love watermelon; ergo . . .

On a state visit to Zimbabwe, Coleman Young approvingly called his host, President Robert Mugabe, "a mean sucker," and compared his own problems with the bureaucracy of Detroit to local practice. "He doesn't have a civil service, and he can shoot people if he wants to, I guess. I can't do that," Young said wistfully.

The mayor's international style is not the product of ill-mannered buffoonery, any more than calling the governor of Michigan a "motherfucker" in a meeting or his periodic references to Ronald

Reagan as "Old Pruneface" were slips on the tongue. Young's language is calculated to get heads nodding on the corner, to serve as proof that Coleman hasn't forgotten who he is and where he came from. A black businessman summed it up nicely. "I like Coleman because he's him, and he ain't gonna *change* him," he said.

Young, the Cadillac mayor, is prickly about his prerogatives as leader of the black polis. During his first administration, he went to Washington to meet with the secretary of HUD. Instead, he was greeted by a black undersecretary. "I didn't come here to see the house nigger," he told the official. "Get me the Man."

But the mayor is also capable of great charm and diplomacy when the occasion calls for it. This was in evidence one afternoon when, together with a representative of the governor's office and the leaders of Wayne, Oakland and Macomb counties, he unveiled a new joint marketing scheme for the tri-county area. The room at the Detroit Art Institute was crowded with businessmen in dark suits and a three-martini afterglow. On the dais, Young was the only black, a reminder of the true balance of power in the area.

The occasion was heralded as historic. "Never before has the tri-county region presented a common face to the nation and the world," said the governor's man. He explained that the idea was to launch a media blitz, showing the Detroit area as a center of world technology. This was to be accomplished through a series of glitzy promo films, set to a Motown sound track, which were screened for the assembled civic leaders.

Young sat watching the films with an amused look on his face, and from time to time he went into a private spasm of laughter. When he was introduced, his analysis of the program's goals was a bit less high-minded than the state official's.

"People from Japan, Mexico and, uh, Ohio been stealing us blind," he said, getting the chuckle he wanted. "We got to stop fighting among ourselves and go out and steal from Ohio." The assembled businessmen and officials, many of whom had been his targets in the past, laughed and applauded, happy to be on the mayor's good side for once.

Following the meeting, Young was surrounded by a group of reporters. There is a keen sense of grievance in the Young administration against the local media. The mayor believes that they sensationalize and exaggerate crime in order to titillate suburbanites and increase advertising.

As far as I could tell, reporting in Detroit is actually unusually tame. The mayor's tactic for keeping the media in check has been to holler racism at the first sign of criticism. The daily newspapers and television stations, run by white executives, are acutely conscious of the danger of having the charge stick.

After negative press coverage of several municipal scandals, Young's administration commissioned three professors from Ohio University to do a media study. The report, a mostly boring review of the coverage of the scandals, concludes with the following admonition: "The media have to recognize that as long as they continue to operate in an unequal society where that inequality is based on race and do not constantly try to change that inequality by taking affirmative action, they are racist." This is Mayor Young's view, as well; visiting reporters are given a copy of the report as a warning that they, too, can be labeled racists.

No one is immune. The mayor publicly referred to Chauncey Bailey, a talented black journalist who writes for the *Detroit News*, as an Uncle Tom. Gary Baumgarten, a radio reporter who once worked for the black-owned *Michigan Chronicle*, was smeared as a racist for extending professional courtesy to a visiting Japanese television crew that produced an unflattering documentary on the city. In Baumgarten's case, the mayor not only blasted his reporting, he gave him a push in the chest when the two met at a news conference.

The Young tactic of Mau-mauing the press has left reporters ambivalent toward him. His flamboyant style makes him a journalist's dream, but it is extremely hard to get any real news out of him or his employees.

"Detroit is an ideal place to train for covering the Kremlin," a *Free Press* reporter told me. "You can't get any information in this city, even about things that are in the public domain. No one will talk to you without permission, and the mayor is the only one who can give permission."

Unlike other cities, where politicians eagerly cultivate reporters, most of the journalists who cover the mayor have never had a personal conversation with him. A *Free Press* reporter, who has been on the city hall beat off and on for several years, refused to believe that I had been invited to Young's home. "He actually served you a glass of lemonade?" the reporter asked with evident incredulity. "Christ, he's never given me a glass of water."

At that first meeting, I mentioned to the mayor that I was having trouble making appointments with city officials. He reacted with a disingenuous astonishment, apparently unable to believe that public servants would withhold information from the press. "Bob will take care of it," he said, gesturing toward his press secretary.

Bob's help proved unnecessary. Within an hour of our meeting I was flooded with phone calls from bureaucrats who suddenly wanted to talk. I have no idea how they found out I had met with their boss, but they knew. It was a lesson in the power of Coleman Young, and the antipress attitude he has fostered among his officials.

That attitude was on display at the Art Institute as the mayor laid into the assembled reporters. "I'm tired of you printing allegations and unfounded rumors," he told them in a stern voice, and went on to accuse them of being tools of their editors.

Young's vehemence put the journalists on the defensive. "Mr. Mayor," protested one, "believe me, I rarely get any requests from my editors about what to write."

Young looked at him contemptuously. "Hell yeah, *rarely*, that's what I just said."

"You mean we shouldn't report when—" began a journalist, but the mayor cut him off. "Yeah, you should not report an unfounded allegation, goddamn it," he snapped. Having got their attention, he then announced that he planned to sue the local press—in toto—for libel.

"You mean you're going to sue *us*?" a young woman television correspondent asked plaintively, opening the way for a Colemanism. "Hell, no, I'm not gonna sue you," he said. "I'm gonna sue the got-damn owners. Reporters don't have any money."

Despite the battering, the reporters stayed clustered around him. No one really protested, no one walked away in anger. Young's indignation was finely calibrated. He hit just the right note, made his point, and kept his audience.

The mayor has the ability to captivate white people in face-to-face encounters, but he doesn't use it promiscuously. It is a tool in his arsenal, like the cursing, the suburb-baiting and the occasional outbursts of his incendiary temper. He is capable of cordial, even close relations with trusted whites, especially old comrades from the radical union days, and he has been able to build strong working relationships with a number of wealthy businessmen. But these are always based on mutual interest, never on sentiment. Coleman Young is the black mayor of a black city, a fact never far from his consciousness.

As Arthur Johnson observed, in no other place in the country have blacks succeeded in gathering so much political power into their own hands; specifically, the hands of the mayor. After four terms, he has cast the city government in his own image. Five of the nine members of the City Council are black. So were the chief of police, the fire chief, all four police commissioners, and the heads of most city departments (and, although Young does not appoint them, both congressmen, the superintendent of schools and a majority of the city's judges). The few whites on the mayor's personal staff were in positions that required liaison with the outside world. Spokesman Bob Berg's job was to maintain lines of communication with the mostly white press corps. Young's chief federal lobbyist, Dorothy Brody, was recruited to deal with the Washington establishment. June Roselle, a holdover from the Gribbs administration, was the mayor's main fund-raiser. Roselle, Berg, Brody and a handful of others were accepted because they were Young's people, but they exercised no independent power of their own.

In city departments, where they are a minority, whites often feel like outsiders. One senior official told me that she received bomb threats from colleagues because she was not part of the "black political mafia." Others complained about reverse racism, although not on the part of the mayor himself. But most people simply take the black complexion of the administration for granted. After all, Coleman Young is not exactly the first big-city mayor to provide patronage and power to his own supporters.

But Young has done more than broaden access to the pork barrel. Under him, Detroit has become not merely an American city that happens to have a black majority, but a black metropolis, the first major Third World city in the United States. The trappings are all there—showcase projects, black-fisted symbols, an external enemy and the cult of personality. Detroit has even developed a quasi-official ideology that regards the pre–Young era as a time of white colonialism, ended by the 1967 insurrection and its aftermath. An official city publication describes the police department as having been "a hostile white army, entrusted by white authorities with the job of keeping nonwhites penned up in ghettoes."

Not surprisingly, some of Coleman Young's closest associates identify readily with Africa and the Third World. One of them, Ron Hewitt, the city's planning director, is a disciple of Jaramogi Abebe Agyeman.

"Race is the element that makes Detroit completely different from other American cities," Hewitt told me. "We are seen as not just black, but aggressive and assertive. I told the mayor that the chief thing that enrages the suburbs is that he has the temerity to actually believe that he *is* the mayor. People in the suburbs want us to fail. The situation here is *very* similar to postcolonial situations in the Third World. People always say, 'The Africans can't govern themselves,' and that's what they say about us, too."

Hewitt, no less than Young himself, regards the relationship with the surrounding white communities as an ongoing war of liberation. "If you feel at the end of every day that you have struggled, that's liberating. That's probably the extent of the black man's liberation in America. Now, we may lose the struggle with the suburbs, but we will make it interesting. They better bring their lunch."

Hewitt is the planner for America's sixth largest city, once the symbol of the country's industrial power. But the old myths of the Arsenal of Democracy mean little to him. "As a people we have more soul, we are more spiritual than others," he said. "Our technology will be tempered by that soul. If white folks could leave us alone and give us the resources, we could solve our own problems."

Outsiders, especially white outsiders, tend to view this sort of talk with skepticism; Detroit is the place where blacks have been left on their own to sink or swim—and, by every conventional measure of prosperity, security and growth, they are sinking. Even senior officials and politicians cannot isolate themselves from the morass of poverty and violence—several years ago, Ron Hewitt's own son was shot to death in a street incident.

But most black Detroiters do not measure their lives, or their city, by the yardsticks of the American middle class. Young may not have provided them with the safest streets or most efficient services; nor has he been able to raise their standard of living. But he has given his constituents something even more valuable: a feeling of empowerment and personal worth. Detroit is one of the few places in the country where blacks can live in a sympathetic, black-oriented milieu.

"Detroit is an environment where you can forget about being

black," said Cassandra Smith-Gray, who heads the city's welfare department. "I don't think about being black, because everybody is. This is a very different place from the South Bronx, L.A. or Jackson, Mississippi. Here, our government is black. This is not the real world. Some of my anger has been knocked out, but it comes back if I cross Eight Mile Road."

Detroit's politics and government are now so monochromatic that it is hard to recall that in the not too distant past, America's sixth largest city was governed by men with names like Cobo, Miriani and Cavanaugh. Albert Cobo has since been memorialized in a downtown convention center. Louis B. Miriani, who ended his career in prison, is largely unsung. But Jerome Cavanaugh, once the wunderkind of American municipal politics, is still something of a presence in Detroit. Although the former mayor died more than a decade ago, he lives on in the memory of a coterie of loyalists, who recall his administration as the Motor City Camelot.

Once a month the Cavanaugh Clan gathers at the Irish Saloon on Trumbull Avenue, near Tiger Stadium. There, in the back room, they meet to recall old times, plot new strategies and keep the Cavanaugh machine together.

Of course they have no hope of regaining control of the city; demographics and the far more muscular Young machine have made that an impossibility. Unlike New York, Chicago or Los Angeles, white candidates are no longer taken seriously in Detroit. Cavanaugh's forces have retreated to the suburbs, where they have parlayed experience, solidarity and residual popularity into county office.

Many of them were there at the Irish Saloon one afternoon in late October: Cliff Sullivan, Cavanaugh's city assessor; Bobby Holmes of the Teamsters Union; Woody Youngblood, registrar of deeds in Wayne County; and a triumvirate of Irish judges—Tom Gallagher, Joe A. Sullivan and Joe B. Sullivan (presumably Cavanaugh left office before his machine could find a Joe C.). They were, for the most part, hale-looking men in late middle age, dressed in suburban leisurewear and sporting exemplary dentures.

At a table near the corner sat Bart Donlan, a spruce, handsome man of seventy-eight with glistening eyes and a dry sense of humor. Donlan, once the secretary of the Board of Health and district chairman of the Democratic Party, now lives in Warren, and he is one of the driving forces behind the monthly conclaves. When I asked if the supporters of any other former mayor, such as Louis Miriani, still held similar gatherings, he shook his head. "Miriani had the misfortune of going to jail," he explained philosophically.

In the old days the Cavanaugh machine was known as the Irish Mafia, although a number of its members were Jewish. Detroit has never had a dominant Irish population like those of some eastern cities, but, according to Donlan, people like to vote for the Irish. "When the Poles run out of Polish candidates to vote for, they always pick an Irishman," he said.

People stopped by Donlan's table to pay respects and josh with the old man, whom one described as "Jerry Cavanaugh's Dutch uncle." When Tyrus (named for Ty Cobb) Place, the group's lone Republican, came over to say hello, Donlan regarded his Bush for President button with amused contempt. "They named a whole league after your candidate," he said with a disarming smile.

From time to time Donlan scanned the crowded room, counting the present and noting the absent. Wayne County executive Ed MacNamara wasn't there that day, nor was Patty Knox, the state liquor commissioner, or Jim Killeen, the county clerk. Their absence was more than compensated for, however, by the presence of three of Cavanaugh's eight children.

Mark Cavanaugh, a studious-looking young man, was running for a seat on the court of appeals in Oakland County, and his campaign was very much on the agenda. The meeting opened with Donlan's wife announcing a hundred-dollar-a-plate fund-raiser for him at a suburban eatery. Mark, who needed no introduction, stood and waved.

More announcements followed. Ex-state senator Eddie Robinson reminded the group of the Monsignor Kern golf outing. Then Cliff Sullivan introduced a guest, a black police inspector. There were a few elderly black men in the room, obligatory officeholders from the time when tokenism was a liberal necessity, but the inspector clearly wasn't one of the old guard; Coleman Young speaks well of Cavanaugh, but his appointees don't come from the Irish Mafia. The inspector was a representative of the new order, a reminder that outside the congenial atmosphere of the Irish Saloon, Detroit is now in the hands of blacks. The officer stood up and took a bow, and there was an awkward silence until a lilting voice called out, "It's nice to have a fine Irishman like yourself on the force," and the tension in the room dissolved into laughter.

The old-time Cavanaugh people are nothing if not professionals, and they regard Coleman Young with a dispassionate admiration uncommon among white Detroiters. "Sure he cries racism all the time," said a lawyer. "But that's just politics. The man is brilliant."

The only amateurs present that day were Cavanaugh sons Chris and J.C., who were there to show solidarity with brother Mark's campaign. The Cavanaughs do not look like brothers; it's as if each was sired by a different aspect of their father's complex personality. Chris, in his late twenties, is a Notre Dame graduate who said he was "just basically taking it easy," although he hoped to go into sales. He is the nostalgic Cavanaugh, the custodian of his father's legacy, and he was far from complimentary about the new regime.

"We have a silent majority in Detroit," he said. "White people are neglected. They don't want to leave. There are so many people who think that the city is still what it was—Coleman Young to them is like a blackout."

Chris and his twenty-five-year-old brother J.C., a Wayne State student, share a house on Detroit's far east side, in one of the city's few remaining middle-class enclaves. J.C. is reserved and handsome, the inheritor of his father's sex appeal. He listened to his older brother, but said nothing.

"I'd love to get involved in Detroit politics," said Chris, "but I don't think it's realistic. I'd love to see the old-time politics come back, but the Kennedys and the Cavanaughs are gone. In this city, old neighborhoods are being destroyed, old schools are closing down. The Cavanaugh years were good, happy times."

Mark joined the conversation. He has his father's political ambitions, along with a strong measure of caution. He is also a realist. "Those were Camelot days," he said. "But the riot took the steam out of that."

The Cavanaugh boys lost their father when they were young; they speak about him warmly, but with a certain detachment. A good deal of what they know about him seems to come from history books or the recollections of former cronies.

"In 1963, dad marched with Martin Luther King," Chris said. J.C. nodded; he had heard that, too.

"If dad were alive today, Detroit would break his heart," said Chris. "I think that Coleman Young is awfully intimidating."

"Well, there's a certain amount of balancing the scales that had to be done," Mark said judiciously. "Coleman has gone to the school of hard knocks, like us. The Irish were the niggers of the world in the early 1900s." He thought about what he had said and began to explain it, when his younger brother broke in.

"Put *niggers* in quotes," Chris instructed. "And put in that he tried to cover up afterwards." He laughed, a full-throated laugh that had once belonged to a young liberal by the name of Jerome P. Cavanaugh.

Nobody bothers to put the word *nigger* in quotes at the City Residence Club. Whites in Detroit have learned to be circumspect in their language, but at the Residence Club, the storefront headquarters of Coleman Young's political machine, there are no whites, and *nigger* is a term of endearment.

The few white visitors to the clubhouse are quickly reminded of the realities of Coleman Young's Detroit. When I stopped by, accompanied by a member, we were greeted at the door by Chuck Bailey, a large man in a leather cap. "If you're with her you must be all right," he said, gesturing toward my host. "But down in Georgia, my daddy used to say that it ain't enough for a white man to be all right. You got to be *all* all right." He laughed, but there was a hard edge to it; at the City Residence Club, the white man's burden is the burden of proof.

It was a few days before the presidential election of 1988, and the Residence Club was serving as a headquarters for the Dukakis campaign in Detroit. Dukakis's people were counting on the city to off-set the expected Bush vote in the once Democratic, now basically Republican, suburbs. Handbills were stacked on tables and posters of the narrow-eyed Duke hung over the door and on the walls. In the front room, wholesome-looking young men in white shirts and dark ties, political apprentices, milled around stuffing envelopes and talking into telephones. An older man supervised the activity. When the phones rang, they answered "Dukakis headquarters," but the salutation somehow lacked conviction. As a Democrat, Dukakis would carry the city but, as elsewhere in black America, he was seen as not much more than the lesser of two evils.

Anybody can volunteer to work in the outer office of the Residence Club, but not everyone can pass into the inner sanctum, where the serious politicians gather. The room is dominated by a long wooden table, a television set and, in the corner, a card table. That night, several civic leaders were engaged in a card-slapping game of bridge. Others lounged around talking politics. A sense of urgency about the upcoming election was notably absent.

A retired, dapper-looking man named Mr. Holly sat at the long table and regarded me with interest. "How ya doin'?" he said, meaning, Who are you and what do you want?

"I'm a writer from Israel," I said. "Maybe I'll become an honorary out-of-town member. How do I sign up?"

The old man laughed. "All you gotta do is pay your dues," he said, and then paused, considering. "Hell, forget that. Don't nobody pay no dues around here anyway."

But there are all sorts of dues in Detroit politics, and the most important kind don't involve money. The members of the Residence Club are old friends and political allies of the mayor, men and women who remember the city before it was delivered into the hands of its black citizens. In the campaign of 1969, when a black candidate, Richard Austin, narrowly lost to a white, Roman Gribbs, they learned the value of organization. The Residence Club, for all its informal camaraderie, has been organizing ever since.

Its techniques are the tried-and-true commonplaces of urban politics—petition drives, telephone solicitation, door-to-door campaigning, and a little old-fashioned problem solving for the deserving citizen. Boss Tweed might not have understood the dialect, but he would have spoken their language.

The mayor's political power, however, does not rest entirely on the Residence Club machine. Young, who occasionally throws himself a fund-raiser, had a campaign war chest said to be in excess of four million dollars. "The mayor was raised during the Depression," Bob Berg told me. "He doesn't really *need* the money, but it makes him feel better having it around."

The issue of the mayor's finances intrigues the local press and political establishment. His administration has not been scandal-free—in the early 1980s, six people, including a top city official, were convicted of bribery, conspiracy and fraud in a multi-million-dollar sludge-removal scam known as the Vista case—but, although the FBI investigated him, there never has been any proof that Young was involved.

Despite the absence of evidence, Young's enemies believe that he *must* be a crook. The chief proponent of this theory is state senator Gil DeNello, who grew up in an Italian neighborhood called Cagalube, which, he says proudly, means "where the fox shits."

"My biggest criticism of Coleman Young is that he is using his political office, that the public has entrusted him with, for his own personal gain. Enriching himself in favors and money," DeNello said. "Do you think Coleman is above taking money under the table? They tapped his phone. The mere fact that the mayor of this town was involved in this shit [the Vista scandal]—there's a saying that the appearance of impropriety is worse than actuality. . . . He's got four million dollars and his people are starving. The government won't tackle him because he's black and they're afraid of another riot. But the man belongs in jail. He's let his own people down."

At the Residence Club, DeNello's unsubstantiated charges elicited little more than a yawn. Besides, nobody there seemed to think that the mayor had let them down. A businessman spoke for everybody. "I'll tell you the truth. I ain't doin' good, I'm doing got-*damned* good," he said. "Mind now, I got along before. I ain't never bought no shoes better than the other ones."

Young's critics have compared the mayor to another master of municipal machine politics, Richard C. Daley. Young himself has a high regard for the methods of the late Chicago mayor, and there are, indeed, some similarities of technique. Young, like Daley, has been in office a long time; and if, after sixteen years, some of his appointees want to help their boss by turning out for a political rally or fund-raiser, this seems to him to be nothing more than commendable loyalty.

In the summer of 1988, Young raised a proposal for casino gambling in Detroit. The proposal was opposed by what he calls the ABC (Anybody But Coleman) coalition, good government types and the churches, some of which objected on moral grounds, others because they feared it might cut into their bingo business. The antigambling forces staged a rally downtown early one Saturday morning, but their speakers were drowned out by hundreds of aroused procasino people who happened to drift by with posters, leaflets and bullhorns. Many also happened to be employed by the city of Detroit. The proposal failed to overcome the moral reservations of Detroiters, but it was an impressive show of force by the mayor, all the same.

At about the same time, Young suffered a far more serious defeat. In the Michigan primary he supported Michael Dukakis, largely because he hates Jesse Jackson. This animosity goes back to Young's first campaign, in 1973, when, his supporters claim, Jackson demanded payment for endorsing him. The mayor, who is proud of his own executive abilities, was also contemptuous of the preacher-politician's rhetorical flourishes. "The only thing Jesse ever ran was his mouth," he once said.

Despite the mayor's opposition, Jackson carried Detroit overwhelmingly; even many of Young's own loyalists voted for him. Ironically, people went for Jackson for much the same reason they supported the mayor—because they saw him as a defiant black man whose conventional credentials for office were beside the point.

These setbacks were not taken seriously at the Residence Club, however. "Coleman ain't the best candidate," a member told me happily. "He's the only candidate."

That fall, a year before the next mayoral campaign, Young was not worried about reelection. According to his spokesman, Bob Berg, his main concern was helping Michael Dukakis beat George Bush. "We can't afford another four years of Reaganism," Berg said, echoing his boss.

Under "Old Pruneface," Detroit, like other major cities, experienced lean times. The local mythology is that the city was singled out for special punishment, but this doesn't seem to be true. Young's own staff told me that under Reagan, Detroit got more federal money than any big city except New York. The problem was more structural than personal: Reagan's policy was to steer federal funds to state governments for disbursal to the cities, rather than to give them it directly, as Carter had.

In any event, Young was willing to help the Democrats. In the weeks before the election he stumped the city, turning up at events he would have normally skipped, sharing the dais with a number of visiting politicos. Still, it didn't seem like his heart was in it; political pros said he was sulking over Jackson's primary victory.

One morning about ten days before election day, Young joined another of Jackson's critics, Coretta Scott King, at a get-out-the-vote rally at the Veteran's Memorial Building. Nominally it was a non-partisan affair, but since there are more Eskimos than Republicans in Detroit, no one had any doubt who its beneficiary would be.

Like all public meetings, this one began with gospel singing, "One in the Father, One in the Son." Then Kim Weston sang black America's national anthem, "Lift Every Voice and Sing." This, too, is standard Detroit practice. On occasions when the presence of white dignitaries makes "The Star-Spangled Banner" necessary, the master of ceremonies invariably follows it by saying, "Now we will sing *our* anthem," and "Lift Every Voice" is performed.

An invocation followed. Mrs. King, for whom praying comes naturally, lowered her eyes reverently. Coleman Young, for whom it evidently does not, took the occasion to glance through some papers.

Young's lack of piety is impressive, especially for a politician in such a devout city. He was raised a Catholic, although he left the church early; typically, his memories of it revolve around its bias against blacks in general and him in particular. When he graduated from St. Mary's elementary school, Young was turned down for scholarships by three Catholic high schools, despite his A average. A teacher told him that he had only been considered because they thought he was Asian; blacks were ineligible.

Almost sixty years later that memory still rankles. A few days earlier, the Archdiocese of Detroit announced that it was closing 43 of the 114 churches in the city—the largest shutdown in the history of the American church. Young, who snarls at shopkeepers who move their stores to the suburbs, took the news with an uncharacteristic public shrug. Privately he made it clear that he was not sorry to see the churches close. "What Cardinal Shaka did is only good sense," he told me. "Catholics are mostly white, and they've left the city. And a lot of the churches that are still here have erected racial barriers. Why should the church subsidize prejudice?"

There was more than just the memory of a youthful insult behind this attitude. The ethnic whites who have remained in the city— mostly elderly, mostly Catholic—are a major faction in the ABC vote. The church itself has never been an active enemy of the mayor; but, funded and led independently, it is one of the few institutions he doesn't dominate.

The evangelical flavor of the get-out-the-vote meeting continued through the introductory remarks. The mayor of Highland Park began her speech with a ritual, "Giving praise unto God who is the head of my life," in much the same way that Iranian mullahs praise Allah before every public utterance.

In the back of the room, I spotted a group I had come to think of as "The Mayor's Men." They are the new political class of Detroit, ubiquitous young black men in power suits and gleaming glasses who congregate whenever Young is present. They stood in small clusters and exchanged the coin of municipal government—gossip about contracts, appointments, and what the mayor had said to them just the other day. From time to time they switched groups, like partners in a folk dance.

Not far away, all alone, stood Dick "Night Train" Lane, the legendary former defensive back of the Detroit Lions, and a crony of Young. Lane, who runs the Police Athletic Program, was dressed out of another era—purple suit draped over his now dining-car-sized frame, and tan shoes. He is an anachronism in an administration dominated by smooth, polished young men, but it was hard to imagine the mayor, smoother and more polished than any of them, sipping late-night brandies in the Manoogian mansion with the woolworsted yuppies.

When the time came, Coleman Young offered the crowd a few platitudes about good citizenship and then introduced Coretta King. They embraced, making an odd couple. Mrs. King is the living symbol of the civil rights movement, the custodian of her husband's legend, with all the moral fervor and idealism it implies. Young, who came out of the labor movement and the smoke-filled rooms of big-city politics, is closer in temperament, if not in ideology, to Boss Curly than to any southern preacher.

Mrs. King made a fine speech about the need for black people to elect candidates who support their interests. As she talked, Young grew visibly restless. He glanced more often at his official papers and looked around the room. The men in the suits tried to catch his eye. Occasionally he acknowledged them with a nod or a gesture. When the speech ended, the mayor seemed relieved. He gave Mrs. King an avuncular kiss on the cheek, gathered up his papers and headed back to his office, where there was real work to do. The men climbed into their city cars and followed.

They were there again, a day or two later, at a political breakfast at the Lomax church. The mayor's men were virtually indistinguishable from the hundred or so ministers in attendance, who were also dressed like investment bankers. The bureaucrats and divines sat at long tables as white-clad members of the ladies' auxilliary passed among them with plates of bacon and eggs, grits and biscuits. Occasionally the churchwomen collided with political aspirants who walked through the crowd passing out pamphlets and campaign buttons like waiters in a dim sum restaurant.

Coleman Young entered, accompanied by Congressman Fauntroy of Washington, D.C., and took his place at the head table. The ministers stood at respectful attention and applauded, and a line immediately formed a few feet from the dais. One by one they approached the mayor for brief whispered conversations, each of which ended in a whooping laugh. Men of God on Sunday, during the week they were Young's precinct captains, and he treated them each to a one-liner or anecdote they could dine out on in the days ahead.

Congressman Fauntroy rose to introduce the mayor. "People love Coleman Young," he told them, "because he always says the appropriate word—the *appropriate* word." A laugh went up; everybody knew what word Fauntroy was talking about. "And he says it the way you *like* to say it," Fauntroy added, getting an even bigger laugh.

Young's remarks were, once again, brief and dry. He is a good speaker, but not an inspired one. Probably twenty men in the room were better orators. Unlike Jesse Jackson, Andrew Young, or Fauntroy himself, all of whom are ordained ministers, Young lacks the intense, gospel-inspired cadences of the church. When he attacked the Reagan administration and called the members of its civil rights commission "Uncle Toms and Aunt Jemimahs," they hollered "Yessir!" and "That's right!" but these were courtesy calls. Fauntroy's compliment notwithstanding, the mayor is appreciated more for what he says than how he says it.

The congressman's speech was a different story. He is the pastor of one of the largest black churches in Washington, and he was in his element, quoting from the Bible, praising the preachers for their political power ("Black ministers are the umpires, and you can call this one for the Democrats") and carrying them away with a rolling litany of past heroes. "Somebody has to vote this year for Martin Luther King," he intoned. "Somebody has to vote for Medgar Evers. Somebody has to vote for Malcolm; somebody has to vote for Schwerner, Chaney and Goodman." As he called off the names, the ministers hollered "Vote, vote!" and the church basement filled with emotional energy. Fauntroy was doing more than whipping up the troops; he was providing his fellow clergymen with a model sermon for the following Sunday morning.

Suddenly, without warning, the congressman began to sing "The

Greatest Love of All." He sang in a high, professional voice, tore off his jacket to cheers, and swung the microphone by its cord like a nightclub crooner. The ministers stood and sang along with him, and only the tone-deaf mayor remained seated, his shoulders shaking with appreciative laughter.

I was sitting next to Jim Holley, who had greeted me with a collegial "Good morning, Reverend," when I came in. He cheered and clapped with the others, but I knew he wasn't applauding for the mayor. The two men have clashed often, particularly over Holley's support of Jesse Jackson. Young calls Holley "an Oreo" and the feeling is mutual.

As I watched the mayor leave, surrounded by his entourage, I recalled what Holley had told me about him a few weeks before. We had been sitting in his study when Young's name came up, and suddenly the black rabbi sounded like Brooks Patterson.

"We asked for control of this city," he said. "Well, now we're in control and everything is out of control. We don't build anything, not even a grocery store. The mayor has been in office fifteen years and only two blacks own anything downtown. Why? Because we don't hold Coleman accountable. What we have is a group of blacks running a black plantation."

I mentioned to Holley that the mayor seemed pretty popular for a plantation master.

"Maybe he's still popular, but there were slaves who loved their owners, too," he said. "If Coleman was white, he would have been gone a long time ago, and that's a fact. But black politicians think they can do any damn thing to black people and get away with it. White people aren't our problem. They don't control our schools. We got to stop blaming white people for everything.

"I'll tell you something else," he continued. "If Coleman gets in trouble, he'll get a white lawyer. A slave is a slave, whether he's in the house or the field. We call them rent-a-Toms today. Their job is to keep the black folks calm and quiet. Coleman feeds us emotions and gives the bread to the white folks. And you can't ride to freedom in Pharaoh's chariot. Maybe once he was good for this city, but it's time for him to move on—it's Joshua time."

Holley's was a minority opinion among black Detroiters that fall. Despite the city's manifest difficulties, he was still Big Daddy, leader of the revolution, first president of the republic, field marshal of the forces of retribution. If he had not solved all their problems, he had at least provided the people of Detroit some of the nation's best political theater. And, more important, he had given them a sense of control over some portion of their own lives. For this they forgave him his trespasses, as he condemned their trespassers.

Surrounded by reverent loyal appointees, sustained by a campaign fund that made a run at his job impractical at best, checked-and-balanced by a city council grown accustomed to his authoritarian rule, supported by a white industrial establishment indebted to him for keeping the lid on, covered by a press frequently charmed and bludgeoned into averting its gaze, in the fall of 1988, Coleman Young was perhaps the most powerful and independent black politician in the United States.

And yet, a year before the next election, even some of Young's strongest supporters were beginning to wonder how long he could go on. He was seventy years old and, some said, not in the best of health. Worse, it was whispered that the old lion was going soft. He had taken his casino gambling defeat almost philosophically, had gone out of his way to patch things up with Jesse Jackson; and it had been months since his last tirade against the hostile suburbs.

More and more he was given to reflection. One day, during a drive through the city in the mayoral limo, he unexpectedly mentioned the fact that Isiah Thomas and Magic Johnson exchange kisses in public.

"You know something?" he said. "I never even kissed my father when I was a kid. It was that macho thing we had. I don't think I hugged him more than a couple of times. It's only in the last few years that I feel comfortable embracing another man, and I'm past seventy." Young looked into the distance, and suddenly he seemed strangely vulnerable. He wondered aloud how long he could continue. Sometimes, he said, he dreams of a quiet old age, far removed from his battles with the suburbs and the challenges of his job. He talked of the joys of peace and solitude, a well-earned rest. It was a moving, convincing meditation, and his spokesman, Bob Berg, listened to it with growing concern.

"So, am I ready to bow out gracefully?" Coleman Young asked in what seemed to be a rhetorical tone. "Am I ready?" Suddenly the mayor of Detroit crinkled his eyes and his shoulders began to work up and down. "Hell no, I ain't ready," he said. "They'll have to carry me out on my fucking shield."

Chapter Seven

THE FAT LADY SINGS

Early in 1989, election year, Coleman Young got some unexpected news—he was a father.

The stork arrived in the form of a paternity suit filed by a thirty-five-year-old former city employee, Annivory Calvert. Calvert, now living in California, charged that Young was the father of her six-year-old son, Joel. Through her lawyers she demanded that the mayor acknowledge the boy and pay child support.

At first, the heretofore childless seventy-one-year-old Young seemed nonplussed. "If it weren't so serious, it would be flattering or funny," he told the press, and then refused further comment. But it was too good a story to go away. The papers had a field day with the news that Big Daddy had become a dad. Political opponent Tom

Barrow tut-tutted that the mayor was a poor role model for the city's youth. Women's groups demanded that Young meet his obligations. Here and there, church leaders raised their voices in moral indignation.

Worse than the indignation were the jokes; Young became the butt of disrespectful humor. In an act of lesse majeste, a local disc jockey changed the words of David Bowie's "Space Odyssey" from "Earth control to Major Tom" to "Birth control to Mayor Young," and played it on the radio. For the first time in years, people were laughing at him, and Young didn't like it at all.

The election was eight months away and the mayor had no intention of running with a paternity suit on his back. When a blood test revealed that the odds were 270 billion to one that he was, indeed, the father of Annivory Calvert's son, Young instructed his lawyer to work out a deal.

It proved expensive—close to $1,000 a month in child support and the establishment of a $150,000 trust fund—but it was money well spent. One of the mayor's reelection slogans was "Do the Right Thing," and he could hardly face the electorate, many of whom were, themselves, victims of indifferent fathers, as a coldhearted skinflint.

I was in Israel when the scandal broke, and when I returned, a month or so before the November election, I asked a reporter if it had affected the mayor's chances. "It was bad for a while," he said. "Some church people were offended. But it's blown over. The truth is, a lot of folks are proud of the old man. Now there's an heir to the crown."

There were also pretenders to the throne that year. Since Young first came to power, in 1973, by narrowly defeating White Hope candidate John Nichols, he had won a string of easy reelection victories over second-rate-opponents. In 1977, he beat Ernest Browne, a bland, black city councilman, by some twenty points. Four years later, he whipped an unknown white accountant, Perry Koslowski,

63 percent to 37 percent. His last time out, in 1985, Young walked through a contest against another anonymous accountant, thirty-five-year-old Tom Barrow, 61 percent to 39 percent.

The mediocre quality of the opposition was not accidental; no serious politician wanted to take Young on. He had all the advantages of incumbency, including a multi-million-dollar campaign fund, an army of city workers, the support of organized labor and financial aid from the white surburban business establishment, which, whatever it thought of Young personally, counted on him to keep the city under control. Most important, he had the unshakable loyalty of the city's black voters. To challenge him was to call into question the legitimacy of their revolution, and no ambitious black politician wanted to be accused of that.

All that was left was the ABC coalition—a steady 35 percent of the vote composed mostly of elderly white ethnics who lived on the city's fringes, and a smattering of disgruntled blacks. To beat the mayor, somebody would have to find a way of holding the dissidents and, at the same time, making inroads into his core of black admirers.

In 1989, for the first time in sixteen years, it suddenly seemed possible. Young was on a losing streak—the casino gambling issue, the humiliating Jackson landslide in the 1988 Michigan presidential primary, the paternity suit—and he seemed old and vulnerable. The city's problems were not getting any better, but Young appeared curiously detached, rarely venturing out of his office and mansion. Most important, a new generation of voters had grown up under black rule. According to the conventional wisdom, they regarded Coleman Young as a politician, not a savior. That was the feeling in the city: The old man could be taken.

In Detroit's two-stage electoral system, a September primary free-for-all would be followed, in November, by a runoff between the two leading candidates. No one doubted that Young would be one of them, but there was stiff competition for the second slot. Four con-

tenders eventually came forward—Tom Barrow, on a roll after having led the antigambling crusade in the summer of 1988; Erma
Henderson, the septuagenarian president of the Common Council;
Charles Costa, a Maltese immigrant businessman; and, most dra-
matically, thirteen-term U.S. Congressman John Conyers.

The first to declare was Costa, who cast himself as the great
almost-white hope. On a morning in the late fall of 1988, he invited
me to his downtown paint store–campaign headquarters for a brief-
ing on his electoral strategy, which could best be described as flexible.

"I'm a chameleon," he confided. "I'm a conservative, I'm a liberal;
I can be both. Greeks, Italians, Mexicans, they all think I'm one of
them. And with blacks, well, I'm dark complected. They think I'm
part black. I tell them that Malta is an island off the coast of Africa."

Costa is a small, compelling man in his fifties, with white hair and
piercing brown eyes, who came to America at age sixteen, started
out as an announcer at the Stone Burlesque, mastered the essentials
of business ("I can play that Jewish piano, you know, the cash register") and eventually became a major inner-city landlord. At his
peak, he had some five thousand tenants, but he went bankrupt in
1971. Undaunted, he commissioned a biography, which he called
Slumlord, and set himself up in the paint business, where he has
flourished.

"I'm capable of thinkin' in the fourth dimension," he said in a
voice ringing with conviction. "What other candidate can say that?
In my life I've done things that are incredible. I'm calculative and
from a PR point of view, ain't nobody who can beat me. I shall climb
my mountain."

There is a certain fourth-dimensional aspect to Costa's surround-
ings. He has five talking parrots in his office, a Pac-man machine,
four life-sized teddy bears seated around a card table, and hundreds
of antique clocks, blunderbusses, electric trains, stuffed animals, fig-
urines, wagon wheels, model ships in bottles and other such collec-
tor's items. His floors are covered with carpets of all nationalities,

the walls adorned with uncountable pictures—mostly of Costa himself, including one taken with Ronald Reagan—busts of American
presidents, a lifetime membership plaque from the NAACP and, dis-
played prominently, a photograph of Coleman Young.

"Coleman is going to be history. His own people are going to put
me in office," said the Maltese challenger. "Blacks want a change.
They know their own can't cut it. I'm white but I'm not too white.
I'm just right for the transition. And I talk their language. I've got
soul."

To demonstrate, Costa called over a customer, a thin black man
in a painter's hat. He advised the man on the best kind of paint to
buy. "And don't forget to make a profit on the deal; that's how you
grow," he said in a fatherly tone.

"Hey, man, I been doin' this for eight years," said the painter.

Costa shrugged. Okay, okay, just trying to help," he said.

Despite his chameleon-based appeal to blacks, Costa was counting
mainly on substantial white support. "Thirty-five percent of the vote
in Detroit is white, and historically whites vote five to one for a
white candidate against a black," he explained. "Last time two
thirds of the whites didn't vote. But this time, I'll bring them out."

Costa was careful to point out that this strategy was not antiblack. "Most white people perceive all blacks as bad," said the candidate, displaying his liberal side. "In fact, only seventy-five
thousand to a hundred thousand are undesirables. The rest are fine.

"I know there might be some opposition who would like to keep
Coleman in," he continued. "They might try to stop me. I still could
be assassinated. They could drive by right now and throw a firebomb
through the window. I'm not afraid, but that don't prevail me from
thinkin' about it."

Morbidity does not come naturally to the ebullient Costa, however; he is a positive thinker who likes to get out on the campaign
trail and mingle with the voters. That morning he loaded a batch of
"Costa for Mayor" posters and leaflets into his car and headed off

to press the flesh. His destination was a downtown residential hotel, its check-in counter protected by bulletproof glass. "A guy got shot here by a guy with no legs," he said, laughing, amused by the endless vagaries of Detroit's human comedy.

In the airless lobby, Costa passed out literature and made small talk with the elderly white men who make up the hotel's main clientele. A toothless fellow dressed in a dirty flannel work shirt and jeans approached, and Costa handed him a campaign leaflet. "I'm running for mayor, and I'd like your support," he said.

The man looked at him in disbelief. "Forget it, buddy," he said. "You're the wrong color. In this city, white people are toilet paper."

After a few more handshakes, we took the rickety elevator upstairs to meet with the hotel manager, an old friend whom Costa wanted to enlist in the campaign. The manager greeted him cordially, but he was less interested in politics than in battlefield stories.

"Hey, I went to see a building that's in receivership," he said. "I get there and as soon as I come up to the door, a guy with his hands tied behind him comes flying out the window. How about that?"

This precipitated a whole series of guys-falling-out-of-windows anecdotes, each gruesome, each told with the special relish that white Detroiters use when they deplore their city's violence. "You know, the place looks worse to me than ever," said the manager. "I personally think that anyone who stays in Detroit willingly is a real asshole."

"I'm gonna turn things around," said Costa.

His friend regarded him with good-natured skepticism. "They've been saying that it's gonna turn around for twenty years, Chuck," he said. "No offense, but if God performed a miracle, could you think of anything He could do to save this city?

The Young camp was not particularly disturbed by the Costa challenge (when I mentioned Costa to Bob Berg, he looked at me blankly and said, "Chuck who?"); to make the primary, he would have to get a majority of the white vote—and that was going to Tom Barrow.

Barrow is a handsome, open-faced accountant of forty, with a neat mustache, an Ivy League wardrobe and a manner to match. In 1985, running as a complete unknown, he got about two thirds of the white vote. Whites liked him for two reasons: first, he wasn't Coleman Young; and second, he was a modest, businesslike coalition builder who made it a point to reach out to them.

Unfortunately for Barrow, these same qualities were interpreted by blacks as a lack of ethnic authenticity. In a city where blackness is equated with street-smart militance, he didn't seem like the real thing. Over and over, Barrow, the cousin of folk hero Joe Louis, was reduced to claiming, "I'm just as black as the rest of 'em," but no one believed him. "Coleman is hot black coffee," a woman told me. "Barrow is decaffeinated." In the election of 1985, Barrow got less than one third of the black vote.

"He doesn't even curse," a reporter said of the challenger. "He thinks it's a bad example for kids. He says he's going to beat the heck out of Coleman. I'll bet Big Daddy is just shaking in his boots."

In 1985, Young's method of dealing with Barrow had been to ignore him; the mayor barely bothered to campaign. This time, however, Barrow seemed more formidable, coming off his success in leading the fight against casino gambling. Polls showed him trailing the mayor by a relatively small margin. The 1985 run had given him name recognition and experience. He was also better organized, thanks to Geoffrey Garfield, a pudgy, bespectacled, black political consultant from New York who once worked with David Dinkins.

Barrow's 1989 strategy was simple. He would keep his white base and concentrate on making inroads in the black community. Barrow could not hope to compete with Young's civil rights credentials or signifying street style, but he thought he could attract support from young black professionals and tap into the dissatisfactions of other middle-class voters who cared more about safe streets, good schools and clean neighborhoods than about the ideology of liberation.

Nobody knew quite what Erma Henderson's stategy was, and it didn't matter much. Henderson, an ordained minister, was the president of the Detroit Common Council, a body with about as much influence as the Albanian parliament. Her power base was among elderly churchwomen, not enough to make her a serious threat. Henderson's main contribution to the campaign was an uncharacteristically shrill attack on the mayor's strategy, which she said was "the way Hitler came to power." "Erma's a fine lady," a Young aide told me afterward. "She just got a little carried away." After the primary, to show there were no hard feelings, the mayor named a city park after her.

As the September contest neared, the smart money in Detroit was on Barrow to finish second—and second, again, in November. But then, in the end of July, John Conyers suddenly announced that he was in the running, and it was a whole new race.

Conyers was just what the ABC people had been waiting for—a real contender. He had been in Congress since 1964, and his name was almost as well known as Young's. He had solid civil rights credentials and a reputation for militance that matched the mayor's. He also had a solid base of support in his west side district and access to money: his brother, Nathan, owns a Ford dealership that grossed $21 million in 1987.

For sixteen years, Coleman Young had been fighting lightweights, opponents who came out for the opening bell, sparred tentatively and went down for the count, pleased to have lasted a round or two with the champ. But Conyers was a heavyweight; Young finally would be fighting in his class. Even people who did not like the congressman were excited at the prospect of a brawl.

Conyers came out swinging. "It's all over, Big Daddy," he warned at his first press conference, sounding like the young Cassius Clay hollering at Sonny Liston. No one could recall another opponent talking so brashly to the mayor.

On Labor Day, the unions staged their annual parade down Woodward Avenue. Conyers marched the 1.2 miles to the podium; Young walked a block, then got in his official limo and rode the rest of the way. A reporter asked the congressman if this was a sign that the mayor was old and burned out.

"Don't make me answer that question," Conyers said. "I might have to apologize."

Conyers kept jabbing away. He called the chief of police, William Hart, "the dumbest cop on the force." He also challenged Young's hostile suburb remark by coming out for regional disarmament. "As long as we tell all the suburbs that we're not giving up our guns, I don't know how we expect them to give up their guns," he said.

The loser in the early stages of Conyers's campaign was Tom Barrow. A poll taken a few days after the congressman announced his candidacy showed him fourteen points ahead of Barrow, and within shouting distance of Young. Conyers's smooth, elegant style and Washington credentials were cutting into the black middle-class support that Barrow needed to finish in the running. A Young-Conyers face-off appeared to be a certainty.

But then, Conyers's campaign began to unravel. An aide, Sam Riddle, resigned, claiming that people around the congressman were using drugs. Conyers himself refused on principle to take a drug test, stirring up inevitable speculation. When he finally bowed to public pressure and took the test, he came up "clean as the Board of Health," but the affair made him look indecisive and a bit suspicious.

There were other problems. Conyers, a bachelor, became the focus of a nasty whispering campaign about his personal life. There were also snide comments about his less than distinguished legislative record. "The only thing John did this term was get a resolution creating National Tap Dance Day," a Young supporter said.

Conyers told reporters that Jesse Jackson was coming to the city to campaign for him, but Jackson never made it, and waited until three days before the primary to release a letter endorsing him. He began missing meetings, or showing up hours late, and it became apparent that he couldn't even run his own schedule. John Conyers might once have been a heavyweight, but after twenty-five years of running almost unopposed in a safe district, he was in no shape for a championship fight. On primary night, Tom Barrow held his white vote and got enough black support to beat Conyers, 24 percent to 17 percent. Henderson and Costa, the Maltese chameleon, each got about 4 percent. Coleman A. Young came in first with just over half the votes.

Five days after the primary, the *Free Press* published a poll on the issues that most interested voters. It showed their most pressing concerns to be crime (21 percent); drugs (16 percent); conditions in the neighborhoods (16 percent); and schools (14 percent). The same survey revealed that, if the election were held the next day, 45 percent would vote for Young and 36 percent for Barrow; 19 percent were undecided. The *Free Press* concluded that the poll "lends credence to the notion that Young may have slipped to his most vulnerable point in four terms as mayor."

Barrow, adrenaline pumping from his primary showing, was encouraged by the numbers. He intended to campaign on two basic issues—quality of life and competent management—and to charge the mayor with responsibility for the disastrous shape of the city after sixteen years of inept government.

The Barrow approach elicited support where he least needed it— in the white community. A week after the primary, Chuck Moss, a columnist for the conservative *Detroit News*, compared the Young era with the pre-*glasnost* U.S.S.R., and heralded Barrow as an example of the new generation of black leaders that would bring about a change:

... old Detroit, where a monolithic black community supported a monolithic power structure, is crumbling. Much is due to a natural changing of the generational guard, much to the specific discrediting of Mayor Coleman Young and a lot is due to the failure of the current black leadership's general outlook and policies.

... the first generation black leaders, whose stuggles brought political power, are being crowded by a new generation that is more interested in results than oratory. The Youngs ... are being slowly supplanted ... by snappy, savvy brokers who realize black America must move beyond its ethnic hearth to progress.

Moss saw Barrow—and Barrow saw himself—as one of the new, savvy brokers, who could reach out to white people, talk their language and aspire to mainstream American values. " ... we as black people are going to have to stop blaming and pointing the finger at the white folks," Barrow said in a *News* interview. "We are running the police department, the fire department ... We have a black City Council, a black mayor, a black school board, a black superintendent. But look at our quality of life. We are not demanding from them what we would demand from a white person doing the same job. ..."

Barrow was doing something daring: He was running in the black polis as an American politician who happened to be black. He was a liberal yuppie, a product, not of the civil rights movement or the unions, but of higher education, affirmative action and his own hard work. It was difficult to imagine him unemployed, "driving a little taxi, handling a little beef," as Young had; harder still to picture him defiantly facing down the suburbs. Cooperation and accountability were his issues; he was offering the city American-style good government.

Young had no intention of going along. This was Detroit, not America, and in the black polis, all politics are ultimately about race. The mayor did not object to competence (a good case could be made that he is a far better manager than Barrow), but it was beside the point. To him, the issue was, as always, protecting Detroit's black integrity and independence from the suburbs.

In previous campaigns, the mayor had received unwitting help in this strategy from his angry neighbors on the other side of Eight Mile Road. But by 1989, the white abandonment of Detroit—emotional as well as physical—was so complete that the suburbanites barely noticed that an election was taking place. Young's favorite nemesis, Brooks Patterson, was practicing law and keeping quiet. The other Coleman-bashers held their peace. There was an eerie silence from across the border.

The mayor had to create his own targets, and he chose two: Tom Barrow himself and the news media. He portrayed his opponent as a stalking horse for suburban interests, and cast the press, especially the two daily newspapers, as Trojan horses within the gates of the city.

Young made a policy of not mentioning his opponent by name, but the accusation against Barrow was plain enough. During an interview with the editorial board of the *Detroit News*, he called the challenger a fifth columnist.

Q: You have sided with those of your supporters who have charged your opponent, Tom Barrow, as representing the interests of white suburbanites who want to reclaim control of the city . . .

A: You are putting words in my mouth now, but okay."

Q: But you did not refute . . .

A: It's up to me to refute it? I think that the words speak for themselves and the numbers speak for themselves.

The numbers that Young refered to were dollars—52 percent of the $211,000 that Barrow had raised for his primary came from suburban donors or from other, presumably white, outsiders. This was meant to constitute proof that the challenger was actually a tool of the hostile foreign power beyond Eight Mile Road.

Coming from Young, this was a bold accusation. The mayor went into the campaign with a multi-million dollar war chest, and he kept raising money up to election day. Some of these funds came from celebrity admirers such as the Four Tops, who gave him $300 in 1987 ($75 per Top), but most was donated by less disinterested sources. In 1988, for example, 22 percent was given by city employees, such as Police Chief Hart ($1,200), who did the right thing; and 37 percent more came from people or companies who had done business with the city in the previous three years.

Interestingly, almost 45 percent of the mayor's cash flowed in from out of town, most of it from the suburbs. This irony did not escape the *News* editorial board.

Q: The fact is, you have accepted five times as much money [as Barrow] from people who live outside the city.

A: That's because I have raised five times as much money.

Q: Does that suggest that you also have . . .

A: It means I'm five times as effective, that's what it suggests.

Young had no ready explanation for why so many hostile white suburbanites gave him money. Cynics said that it might have something to do with the fact that many of them did business with the city, but June Roselle, the mayor's chief fund-raiser, had a different theory. "People know that the mayor enjoys getting contributions," she told me one night at a donor's affair. "And they like to make him happy."

During Young's session at the *News*, he exchanged heated words with a young black reporter, Yolanda Woodlee, who, the mayor thought, was questioning him too aggressively about a report that his ally, Councilman Nicholas Hood, had been guilty of financial improprieties. "I know what you're trying to do," snapped Young. He turned angrily to Woodlee's boss, editor-in-chief Robert Giles. "You ought to give her a raise," he said with heavy sarcasm.

A few days later, in an interview with the black-owned *Michigan Chronicle*, the mayor publicly labeled Woodlee an Aunt Jemimah, the female equivalent of an Uncle Tom. His implication was clear: the reporter had sold out to her white, anti-Detroit bosses. The slur, which hurt Woodlee deeply, wasn't personal, however; it was simply part of the broad Young strategy to paint the press as a subversive enemy of the black polis.

The antimedia theme emerged early in the campaign. Before the primary, the Black Slate, political arm of the Shrine of the Black Madonna, published a warning to black voters: "The powerful white news media is [sic] fighting to reestablish white control of Detroit. Only the reelection of Coleman Young and incumbent black councilmen will enable us to save our city!"

The Young camp heartily seconded the warning. "I think there's an element of self-determination [in the Slate's statement], and I think that self-determination is a legitimate factor of American politics," said David Lewis, the mayor's reelection chairman.

In the primary, the *News* endorsed Barrow, and the *Free Press*, a traditional Young supporter, went for Conyers. During the general election, both papers came out for Barrow. This played right into the mayor's hands. He offered the endorsements as proof that the white-owned-and-operated press was trying to brainwash Detroiters into voting against their own interests.

"They can't see for us, they can't think for us," he told a black audience at a fund-raiser at Steve's Soul Food Restaurant. "They don't tell it like it is, they tell it the way they would like it to be. It's too late in my life to start dancing—I don't dance. And I ain't got no rhythm anyhow." The crowd laughed and cheered, and Young grinned, shoulders shaking. "This election should be a declaration of independence," he said. "We took our freedom in 1973, and they're trying to take it back from us in 1989."

The mayor repeated this message in every stump speech and interview throughout the campaign. Indeed, it often appeared that he was running for reelection against the *Free Press* and the *News*. When the papers counterattacked by condemning Young's antipress message as reverse racism, he was ready for them. "I've always fought for unity between black and white," he told J. P. McCarthy, a popular radio talk show host. "I think my record on that is a little better than the *Detroit News.* Fifty percent of my appointees are white. I don't think the *News* can say that."

The antipress fever of the Young campaign ran so high that it even infected the Barrow camp. One Saturday morning in mid-October I dropped in at his headquarters, a large storefront next to the towering General Motors Building on Grand Boulevard. The large main room was decorated like a child's birthday party, with balloons and streamers. Donuts and coffee were set out on a long table. The walls were plastered with pictures of the candidate, district voting charts and handmade homilies, such as GOD DON'T CARE IF YOU'RE BLACK OR WHITE; THERE'S SOMEBODY TRYING TO PULL US APART.

Campaign workers, about half of them white, sat on folding chairs and waited for Geoffrey Garfield, Barrow's consultant, to call the assembly to order. As usual, the meeting began with a gospel song—"The things I used to do, I don't do no more, since Jesus came into my life"—and a benediction. Most of the ministers in town were supporting Young, but Barrow had a few clerical dissidents, and one of them offered a long, special anti–Coleman prayer.

After the last amen, Garfield opened the session to general discussion. Several people reported progress in their districts and were rewarded with applause. Then, without warning, a man arose and turned toward the back of the room, in the direction of a young black reporter named Dori Maynard.

"There's a woman back there, works for the *Free Press,*" he said, pointing her out. "Last week, Coleman called her 'a stupid fool,' and she didn't report it. Now she turns around and blasts us, yes she does!" An angry murmur rose from the crowd. Maynard, uncomfortable at having become the center of attention, shifted her weight from foot to foot.

Another man stood up smiling, and for a moment I thought he was going to defend the reporter. "We welcome you," he said in a gracious voice. There were protests from the crowd, but he held up his hand for silence. "Yes we do, we welcome you. But we pray for your soul."

The question of black control not only dominated the race for mayor, it became an issue in the Common Council election as well. In the primary, a white incumbent with impeccable liberal credentials named Maryanne Mahaffey led the field. A similar showing in the general election would make her president of council. In Detroit's strong mayor system, the body is little more than a debating society, but there was symbolic importance in keeping the office in black hands, and Young came out for Reverend Nicholas Hood.

The mayor didn't want to expressly say that he favored a black candidate, but he didn't need to. Shortly after the primary, Reverend Jim Holley, now officially neutral despite his Joshua-time rhetoric of the previous year, reminded voters that if Mahaffey were elected president of the council, she would automatically be next in line in case something happened to Young. He called on black Detroiters to prevent such an eventuality by supporting Hood.

Holley was strongly criticized by many black journalists and politicians, who saw voting for a qualified white as an opportunity to display noblesse oblige. Young, however, refused to disassociate himself from the remark. Late in the campaign, when it appeared that Mahaffey would, indeed, come in first, he went further, telling audiences that Holley had raised "a legitimate issue."

Yet, for all the emotions that the Mahaffey affair engendered, it was a secondary issue. The real race was for mayor, and in late October, Young staged a coup that staggered the Barrow camp.

For weeks, the challenger had been dickering with his defeated primary opponents for their support. Conyers had publicly promised to come out for him; Costa was supposedly brokering the deal. There were also rumors that Jesse Jackson, who had endorsed Conyers in the primary, and whose hatred for Young was well known, would come to Detroit to stump for Barrow. Conyers's and Jackson's support would go a long way toward defusing charges that Barrow was a tool of the white interests.

In late October, Jackson did come to town—but not to campaign for Barrow. On an overcast Friday afternoon, just as the shift at the Chrysler plant was about to change, a long convoy of large black cars, led by the mayor's Cadillac, rolled up Jefferson Avenue to the factory gate. Uniformed policemen opened the rear doors and the mayor emerged—followed by Jesse Jackson.

The two men stood side by side and shook hands with a stream of workers. Young wore a statesmanlike gray homburg, a pearl gray overcoat, and the delighted expression of a magician who has just pulled an especially elusive rabbit out of the hat. Jackson, bareheaded and coatless, looked like his son. The men smiled and joked with the crowd while a handful of Barrow protesters circled, shouting "Why, Jesse, why?" in denunciation of the sellout.

It was fine political theater, and it was only the first act. From the factory, Young and Jackson drove to the mayor's mansion on the Detroit River, where a group of reporters was assembled in the basement rumpus room. Jackson and Young disappeared upstairs, leaving the journalists to cool their heels, gaze longingly at the well-stocked white leather bar in the corner and make ribald remarks about the mayor's love life.

A television reporter picked up a red-and-gray booklet from a coffee table and began to thumb through it. Entitled *Hit the Road*, in honor of Young's famous challenge to the city's hoodlums, it was written by someone called "King George" Cunningham, Jr., and published in 1974. Several of the journalists gathered around and guffawed at Cunningham's overblown prose. "Look at this," one said, turning to page 19, and read aloud: "Thank you, Jesus. We've got a new god, Coleman."

"That's enough to turn you into an atheist, right there," a cameraman said.

On page 16, Cunningham had listed "Some Good Things About Detroit":

Detroit is one of the few cities in the world where a worker can earn $1,000 a month—or learn a shop trade and earn $1,500 and more a month—buy a new home, two or three cars, a boat, a Saturday Night Special, a camping trailer, dabble in the stock market, play the numbers daily and the lottery weekly.

"Well, you can still get a Saturday Night Special and play the numbers," a white reporter said, laughing. A black radio newsman, who overheard the remark, scowled but said nothing.

A few minutes later, Young and Jackson came in, accompanied by Conyers, Costa and a Henderson aide. They were there, Jackson said, to formally endorse the mayor. Conyers seemed uncomfortable with his about-face, and embarrassment played hell with his normal eloquence. "Any previous promises to support anyone are abrogated," he said, "and any other assumptions, implied or otherwise, that I endorse him, of course, don't exist." Costa beamed, pleased that his fourth-dimensional powers had elevated him to such lofty company. Henderson's man, asked if his presence meant that Henderson also supported Young, confined himself to a laconic "It does." Most of the talking was done by Jackson, who said that endorsing the mayor "will regroup our family."

There was no doubt which family he meant, or who wasn't in it. Jackson, the favorite son of the black political clan, was telling Detroit that Big Daddy was still pater familias. Tom Barrow was, at best, a stepson.

Barrow's people tried to put the best face on things. They charged that Jackson's endorsement had been bought, and that Conyers was trying to protect his congressional seat from the wrath of the Young machine. "They brought the big guns out on me, and that means we got the big boys upset," Barrow said.

In fact, Barrow had a point. The mayor, who had barely cam-
paigned in previous elections, was, by his standards, running hard.
Bringing in Jackson was an indication that he was taking the challenger seriously; in past years, he wouldn't have bothered.

A few days later I bumped into Young at the City County Building. He was in a good mood, but cautious about his chances.
"Things look pretty good right now," he conceded, "but you can
never be too sure of anything in politics. It ain't over until the fat
lady sings."

The mayor's caution was based on arithmetic. "We've got eighty-
five percent of the white vote," Barrow's advisor, Geoffrey Garfield
told me. "To beat us, Coleman needs eighty percent of the black
vote, and with the city in the shape it's in, there's no way he's gonna
get it." Young, who was counting ballots when Garfield was still
learning addition and subtraction, knew that he would need a large
black turnout. He also knew where to find his voters—in church.

Throughout the campaign, the mayor refused to attend Candidate
Nights or to press flesh in the neighborhoods. He spent his weekdays
acting mayoral, cutting ribbons on new projects and issuing state-
ments about municipal affairs. But every Sunday morning, the normally irreverent Young donned a double-breasted silk suit and, at
the head of a ten-car motorcade, made the rounds of the city's
churches.

One Sunday toward the end of the campaign I joined the caval-
cade, which commenced at Sacred Heart, a downtown Catholic
church with a decidedly Baptist flavor. Its choir is accompanied by
drums, an organ and a saxophone, and the worshipers clap and sing
along in fine down-home style. A song was just ending when Young
swept in, accompanied by Barbara Rose Collins, who was running
for reelection to the Common Council.

Things had not gone well for Collins since her near defeat of
George Crockett the year before. In the spring, her son, Tony, had
been shot in a street altercation. A few months later, he was caught

holding up a suburban sporting-goods store, and was awaiting sentencing. Her son's problems had distracted Collins, and she had not run her usual strenuous campaign; now, she was counting on Young's coattails to carry her to victory.

Young and Collins were seated on the pulpit. A priest read from Second Timothy: "You, for your part, must remain faithful to what you have learned, because you know who your teachers are." Young nodded, appreciating the sentiment, and he took up the text to remind the congregation of what they had learned in Detroit. He talked about the achievements of his administration and blasted the press. "There are people who don't admit the progress that we have made," he said. "They have eyes, but they will not see. They have ears, but they will not hear. They have mouths, but they will not speak the truth. And," he snapped, "on top of that, they're liars," The crowd cheered, Young thanked the priest for allowing him to deliver his message, waved to the congregation and left. The whole thing had taken fifteen minutes.

The mayor repeated his speech in four more churches that morning. Everywhere he was greeted as an old friend. Some of the ministers seemed to take a special pleasure in welcoming the profane, "not too moral" mayor of Motown.

"Several years ago, Coleman came to a group of us preachers and asked us to pray for him," a Baptist pastor told his flock. "He asked us to pray that he stop smoking and stop cussing. We told him, 'Mayor, we'll pray for you to quit smoking, but not to quit cussing—'cause there's some folks need to be cussed out." The congregation laughed, and Young chuckled, eyes crinkled shut and shoulders working.

On the way out of the St. Stephen's African Methodist Episcopal Church, the mayor spotted me in the crowd of reporters and stopped for a minute.

"What the hell you doin' out here?" he asked with mock surprise.

"Working, same as you," I told him. Young laughed. "Well, if you're the same as me, this ought to last you for the next four years," he said, and climbed into his limo.

That morning, Barrow was also hitting the churches. Since I already knew Young's "eyes and will not see, mouths and will not speak the truth" routine by heart, a *Free Press* reporter and I left the mayor and went to the Dexter Avenue Baptist Church, a subdued, middle-class institution, where the challenger was scheduled to appear. We were seated in the corner of a small balcony that enabled us to see the pulpit without, apparently, being seen.

Barrow received a polite reception when he was introduced to the congregation, and he began his remarks by bowing his head slightly and saying, "I want to give honor to God, who is the head of my life." Several old women sitting nearby nodded their heads emphatically; Barrow is the kind of young man that devout old ladies appreciate.

The challenger launched into his usual "time for a change" message, emphasizing the need for city services and sound fiscal management that would concentrate on improving the quality of life. But then, unexpectedly, he veered off into a defense of his own racial authenticity. He mentioned the fact that he had been born in Black Bottom and raised on the east side, in a black neighborhood, and he recalled boyhood trips to the segregated South. "I remember having to drink out of the colored water fountain," he said, his flat Michigan inflection taking on a southern tone. "The water pressure was so bad that we had to put a Popsicle stick under the button to get a drink." The story reminded me of Helen Livingstone Bogle's struggle to get a telephone at the Art Institute; some people just don't make convincing victims.

"They say I'm gonna turn this city back to white folks," he thundered. "Well, that's ridiculous. We don't need anyone from outside the city to tell us how to run our own lives. Y'all know that it's easy to sit out there and tell us what to do!" The *Free Press* man raised his eyebrows; Barrow, the apostle of cooperation and harmony, was trying to out-Coleman Coleman.

After services, Barrow stood around outside shaking hands. When he saw the *Free Press* man he smiled broadly and waved him over. "Things are going just great," he beamed, speaking in his normal Michigan tone. "You should have been in church this morning; I got a wonderful reception."

"I was in there," the reporter said. "You couldn't see me, but I saw you."

A troubled look came over Barrow's open face, but he recovered quickly. "Hey, let me show you the latest computer printouts on our telephone surveys," he said, opening a loose-leaf folder. "All our numbers show us running much stronger than anticipated among Coleman's constituency." Barrow went over the list of figures, an accountant safely in his element once again.

"When you say Coleman's constituency, you're talking about black voters, right?" I asked.

"That's right," he said, and then the troubled look returned. "Hey, we're not writing off anyone," he said. "I've got a whole lot of black folks supporting me."

A horn blew and a black man stopped at a traffic light and called Barrow's name. "Hey, man, how you doin'?" Barrow shouted back. The driver smiled and yelled, "Good luck, Tom."

"See what I mean?" said Barrow. "Things are really coming together. We're going to win, man, we're definitely going to win."

As the race came into the homestretch, polls continued to show Young leading by a substantial, but not decisive, margin. However, there was one more hurdle for the mayor to cross—Devil's Night, which fell only eight days before the election.

Both Young and Barrow were keenly aware of the potential importance of Devil's Night. In recent years there had been a steady annual decline in the number of fires. A further drop would underscore the mayor's contention that things were turning around and that he had the city under control. On the other hand, serious arson couldn't help but strengthen Barrow's quality-of-life message. For the challenger, there was nothing to do but wait; but Young had an army at his disposal, and he deployed it to ensure tranquility.

The mayor declared the customary three-day dawn-to-dusk curfew for kids under eighteen. He also ordered the mobilization of every city vehicle, including garbage trucks, for street patrol duties. A volunteer force estimated by City Hall to number thirty thousand citizens was raised to keep watch over the neighborhoods, and a special command center was set up to enable motorists with car phones to dial WATCH and report fires. As an incentive for kids to stay at home, a local cable television station agreed to unscramble its signal so that the Pistons–76ers' game would be available to nonsubscribers.

On the eve of Devil's Night, Martin Luther King Jr. High School hosted a citywide youth rally under the slogan "Celebrate Halloween Right." Homemade posters decorated the lobby. One pictured Batman holding a burning figure: "This may be you as a result of an arsonal fire," it said. Another, showing Lucifer with pitchfork in hand, was captioned, "Stop the Devil from Destroying Our City." Teachers and parents mingled with senior city officials, including the newly appointed fire chief, Harold Watkins, a tall, mocca-skinned man in a navy blue uniform and braided cap that made him look like the admiral of an African fleet.

In the large, modernistic auditorium, hundreds of kids listened to a performance by the police r&b band, the Blue Pigs ("We have an arresting sound"), who performed hits such as "That's My Prerogative," substituting anti–Devil's Night lyrics for the original. Then, winners of a citywide essay competition took the stage to read their compositions. "Many Detroiters have left our city because of Devil's Night and its consequences," trilled a grammar school girl in a starched red dress and pigtails. "Let's turn back the hands of time to when there was no guns, gangs or cocaine," implored a junior high school coed. "Do the right thing, that's where it's at/Don't kill kids with baseball bats," declaimed a high school rapper.

The mayor was introduced to enthusiastic applause. "Devil's Night is becoming more like any other night," he said. "This year we should cooperate to see that there are less fires on Devil's Night than any other night of the year. Now, will you help me to prove that those who say Detroit is dead are wrong?" Children and parents cheered and Young began to hand out prizes to the winners. "This is pathetic," said a radio reporter. "In what other American city do kids get awards for writing about not burning down their own town?"

Young's short speech struck me as an amazing gamble. I had expected him to lower public expectations, so that he could claim a post–Halloween success. Instead, he had belittled Devil's Night and called for fewer fires than usual—a demand that would inevitably become the standard by which this year would be judged. "You think he knows something we don't?" I asked the reporter, who shrugged. "He's God," he said. "Maybe he's planning to make it rain."

It didn't. Devil's Night was crisp and clear, and there was a feeling of expectation in the air as a group of fire buffs gathered for their traditional preholiday dinner at a McDonald's on the far east side. There were eight of them, including two firemen from nearby Farmington, members of an informal Devil's Night society that has been meeting for years. Over Big Macs and milk shakes they plotted their evening's activity. The plan was to fan out to various parts of the city and to inform each other of good blazes by car phone.

I was invited to ride with Harvey and Si, two ex–Detroiters in their early fifties who now live in the suburbs. Like the others, they were equipped with a shortwave radio, street maps and a cellular phone. The didn't intend to miss a thing. "If we catch one good house fire, the night will have been worthwhile," Si said.

We hadn't been cruising for more than fifteen minutes when a fire was reported on the west side. Harvey expertly navigated the freeways and pulled up in front of a flaming wood house several minutes before the fire trucks arrived. The street was filled with neighborhood people who greeted the suburban voyeurs without apparent resentment.

Next to the burning building a thin, youthful black man stood on his lawn and sprayed the side of his white-shingled house with a garden hose. The wind was blowing the other way, but the fire was close enough to cast him in dramatic outline, and press photographers crowded around. He ignored them as he sprayed, a look of intense, fearful concentration on his face.

In the street, in front of the house, I spotted John Aboud, the owner of the Tailwind. He had a minicamera on his shoulder, and he was bent on one knee, filming the scene. He looked up and waved in recognition. It had been almost a year since our last meeting.

"How's it going, John?" I asked.

"My cousin was killed six weeks ago in a video store," he said, giving me an update on his family body count. "That makes seven. And he had four kids, too." He stared briefly at the flames leaping from the roof of the house to the telephone wires, sighed and then put the Minicam back on his shoulder.

A few minutes later the fire trucks began to arrive, and we watched for a while as they battled the blaze. The man with the garden hose ignored the engines and continued to spray his house. I felt a tap on my shoulder and saw Harvey. "Come on," he said impatiently. "They've got this one under control. There's supposed to be four houses going up on the east side."

"Four?" asked his partner, Si. "That's music to my ears."

The report was only half true; when we reached our destination, a narrow residential street, there were two houses ablaze. One, reputedly a crack house, had already burned to the ground, leaving only a chimney. The other, which belonged to a family, was going fast.

Its residents had already been taken to a shelter by emergency workers.

A television crew stood in the street, recording the scene while a blond reporter in a trenchcoat went from neighbor to neighbor, trying to get someone to say that the crack house had been torched. No one knew anything. "Coleman says we don't have an arson problem here," he said to a group of onlookers in a bitter tone. "Tell that to the lady whose house got burned down."

"What you care, man?" asked a woman in a bathrobe and house shoes. "You don't live 'round here noway."

"Coleman gonna win, and if you think I'm lying, my mother is a bitch," said a teenager, and a laugh went up. A look of disgust passed over the reporter's face, and he walked away shaking his head.

"The only people who support Coleman are his constituents," Si observed as we drove toward the next fire.

"The intelligence level of these people is so low that they don't know they need a change," agreed Harvey. He dialed a number on the car phone. "Hey," he said into the receiver, "we had a good one over here, you got anything good over there?"

For the next few hours we hopped from fire to fire. A commercial building ("Probably for the insurance," said Harvey), a few abandoned houses, several dumpsters. Harvey and Si were still waiting for the big one, and they were getting restless.

Finally a call came over the radio—an apartment building was ablaze in Highland Park. "Bingo," said Si happily. "I know just where that is. We used to live around there."

The apartment building was deserted, but flames shot out of its windows, and fire fighters clambered along the roof. Across the street, an old lady sat on the steps of the Greater Emmanuel Church of God in Christ. "I heard my church was on fire so I came right down here," she said in a determined voice. "I'm on the Mothers Board, and I'm not letting anything hurt my church. I intend to sit here until the last fire truck leaves."

Several people had gathered around the lady. One of them was a cop from New Jersey who had come to Detroit especially to observe Devil's Night. "I have an M.A. in public safety," he said, "but tonight I'm getting a Ph.D. in reality."

Si and Harvey smiled at the compliment. "You picked a good year to come," Harvey said. "This is much better than last year. But what the heck, good year, bad year, there'll always be a Devil's Night."

The next day Bill Bonds, an outspoken anchorman on ABC-TV affiliate WXYT, delivered a furious commentary on the fires of Devil's Night. "It was like a vision from hell," he told viewers. "Well, people say, those yo-yos burn down their city every year, don't they? But this year is different; this year, I've heard the words 'who cares?'"

That more or less summed up the suburban attitude. But in the city, with a week to go before the election, Devil's Night flared into a raging political controversy.

Tom Barrow struck first. Accompanied by reporters and press photographers, he toured the burned ruins, had his picture taken with victims and blasted the mayor. For months he had been talking about the declining quality of life and attacking Young for concentrating on grandiose buildings in the business district at the expense of the neighborhoods. Now he hammered home his point. "Just look at downtown," he said in an I-told-you-so tone. "Everything's fine down there. Nothing burned down there."

For three days, city officials declined to publish Devil's Night statistics; they wanted to wait until after Halloween and the end of what they called "the seventy-two-hour Devil's Night period." Young's only comment was that the number of fires had been "about normal." Off the record, the mayor's people admitted that it might have risen slightly from the previous year's 104.

That estimate was loudly disputed by the Firefighters Union, which also happened to be Barrow's biggest financial supporter.

Union officials claimed their men had fought 285 Devil's Night fires—far more than in any of the previous four years, and almost as many as 1984's all-time record of 297.

On the day after Halloween, Young finally called a news conference at the City-County Building. Dressed in a blue blazer and pink shirt, the mayor gave his version of what had happened. There had been 115 fires on Devil's Night itself, he said—up slightly from the year before. But, for the overall three-day period, the number had declined. He pointed to a red-white-and-blue chart, which showed constant decreases for the "Devil's Night period" since 1984. The mayor praised the community spirit of the thirty thousand patrol volunteers, saluted the city's "outstanding effort" and then offered to answer questions.

The reporters sitting around the conference table seemed momentarily speechless. None of them knew exactly how many fires there had been, but they had been on the street on Devil's Night, and they knew that it had been bad, certainly worse than the year before. They had come to the press conference expecting to hear a chastened mayor explain his failure; instead, he had declared victory.

The months of media bashing and personal attacks on journalists suddenly hung heavy over the crowded room. Young glowered at them, daring them to dispute his version of reality. Finally a reporter broke the silence. "Mr. Mayor, I don't want to be critical, but . . ."

"Yeah, sure you don't," interrupted the mayor with heavy sarcasm. "None of you wants to be critical."

For the next half hour, the mayor snapped and raged at the reporters. He answered their gentle queries with harsh denunciations, demanding to know if they dared to dispute his official figures, and then waiting for their docile "no sirs" before moving on. Despite the fact that at least twenty journalists were present, the silences between questions grew longer and longer.

Finally a TV correspondent in the back of the room spoke up.

"Mr. Mayor, what we really want to know is, well, did the number of fires actually go down this year or what?"

Young fixed him with an imperious stare. "What do you think?" he demanded. "You can see the chart."

"Yes sir," said the reporter. "But you're the mayor, I want to know what you think."

Young refused to be appeased. "You got a big opinion," he said. "I hear it on television every night. Let's hear what *you* think." The reporter reddened like a schoolboy and said nothing. "Next question," snapped the mayor.

At the end of the press conference, the journalists filed quietly out of the room. They had been intimidated and they knew it. I was standing in the hall with Bill McGraw of the *Free Press* when a young black radio reporter came over and introduced himself. "That was a good question you asked in there," McGraw told him in an encouraging tone.

"I had another question," said the radio man. "I wanted more sound. But when I talk to the Man, I walk on coals. Maybe when I get bigger, y'know?"

Young's performance had won him a partial victory. The next day the press would report two sets of figures—his and the Firefighters Union's—without being able to say which was correct. Now he had to find a way to make voters give him the benefit of the doubt.

That evening, Young attended a fund-raiser sponsored by the Black Firefighters organization. The affair was held in an elegant nightclub just inside the Eight Mile border. Soul Muzak played softly in the background and civil servants in their Sunday clothes lined up for a free buffet supper. These were the mayor's people, beneficiaries of his affirmative action policies, and they were in a receptive mood.

Young began his remarks with a general overview of his accomplishments, among which he included the construction of town houses on the Detroit River. "You can drive into your garage, walk through the house and out the back door, get into your boat and float over to the marina," he said. He was reminding them of their prosperity—and its source. Before Coleman Young, blacks in Detroit didn't have boats—or jobs as fire fighters.

Then the mayor turned to the main business of the night, an attack on the lily-white leadership" of the Firefighters Union. "They oppose affirmative action," he said, "and so does my opponent. My opponent supports that damn union. Now, that's some kind of an uncle. . . . And he's got the right first name for it, too." The room burst into laughter and applause. Young joined them, shoulders shaking. "Back home they call that signifyin'," he said.

And so, Devil's Night was Colemanized. It had taken one day for him to turn the "vision from hell" into a racial confrontation, with the bigoted white fire fighters and Uncle Tom Barrow on one side and the signifying leader of the black polis on the other. Barrow didn't even mention the conflagration during the last week of the campaign.

On the Sunday before the election, Coleman Young staged his final rally, at the New St. Paul's Tabernacle. The street outside the large church was festooned with triangular red-and-white Young '89 signs. Dozens of city employees loitered in front of the building, talking politics and sniffing the aroma of fried chicken that wafted over from the Kentucky Fried Chicken on the corner. From time to time a Barrow car cruised by, and the Colemanites hooted good-naturedly.

When I arrived, notebook in hand, some of them mistook me for a local newsman. "Quit tellin' people what to think," they shouted. "We're gonna have the last laugh!" They weren't able to put any real hostility in it though; they could parrot their boss's phrases, but not his rage.

Inside, a large crowd filled the pews of the blue-carpeted sanctuary. As usual, virtually everyone was black; throughout the campaign, the mayor almost never appeared before a predominantly white audience. Special roped-off areas were reserved for "Clergy" and "Elected Officials." There was no press section. I took a seat in the rear of the church, next to a *Free Press* reporter.

There was none of the rowdy energy normally associated with a political rally. Men and women sat in dignified silence, waiting for the mayor and Jesse Jackson, who was also scheduled to speak. Church ushers escorted latecomers to seats. An organ played quietly in the background.

A group of dignitaries, led by Pastor Charles Butler, came to the pulpit, and began to warm up the crowd. UAW vice-president Ernie Lofton delivered an impassioned attack on the press: "We have two papers in this town that can't tell fact from fiction," he hollered. "We remember what Detroit was like prior to Coleman Young and we didn't like what we saw." When he finished, the crowd gave the union official a warm hand. "Seems like Brother Lofton came here to preach today," said Reverend Butler, getting an appreciative chuckle.

More brief remarks followed. An activitist from Operation Get-Down seconded the attack on the press. "We don't listen to any local media and we don't listen to any national media, either," he said. Tom Turner of the AFL-CIO was the only speaker to even allude to Barrow. "I don't recall Coleman's opponent ever paying any dues," he told them. The attack on Barrow got much less applause than the press-bashing.

The choir sang "Victory Shall Be Mine," and the crowd, more like a congregation, swayed and clapped. Then Young and Jackson took the pulpit, accompanied by Aretha Franklin, dressed for church in a modest black brocade suit and white pearls. There was an excited buzzing in the audience—they hadn't known that she was on the show.

Reverend Butler introduced the mayor in three words: "Behold the man." The crowd rose and cheered as Young, dressed as usual in an elegant double-breasted suit, came to the rostrum. His remarks were short and surprisingly low-key. He talked briefly about his accomplishments, praised the church as a pillar of the community and called for racial harmony. "There are some who have mistaken African-American unity as antiwhite," he said. "Nothing could be further from the truth." The proverbial visitor from Mars, landing at New St. Paul's Tabernacle that afternoon, would have thought Coleman A. Young a conciliatory, statesmanlike old man with a very good tailor.

Then Aretha Franklin sang "Precious Lord," the same song she sang at Martin Luther King's funeral. She was a little hoarse in the beginning, but her voice returned as she went along, and as she soared to the end, the *Free Press* man turned to me. Like the other reporters on the campaign trail, he had come in for a fair share of personal abuse. Now he had a beatific smile on his face. "Covering politics in Detroit has its compensations," he said.

Jesse Jackson delivered the finale. He is to black political oratory what Franklin is to gospel music—an inspired, inspiring virtuoso—and he was at the top of his form that afternoon. "I'm here today for an emancipation rally," he intoned. "The blood of Malcolm and Martin brings us to an emancipation rally. When they were needed, they were there. And when the roll was called, Coleman Young was there. He answered 'Present.'"

Skillfully, Jackson contrasted the mayor's long, distinguished civil rights record with that of his yuppie opponent. He talked about Young's defiance of Jim Crow regulations in the army, of his battle with the House Un-American Activities Committee, of his dedication to black causes. "The most effective affirmative action policy for jobs and contracts in America is right here in Detroit, Michigan," he said.

Then Jackson turned his rhetorical guns on Barrow. "They say he knows how to get along with white folks," he thundered contemptuously. "Well, that's no great accomplishment. That's no special skill. African-Americans have always known how to get along with white people. We learned how to get along with white people during slavery. The time has come for white people to learn to get along with us." The church rocked with applause and cheers.

Finally Jackson and the others held hands and led the audience in "We Shall Overcome." For a moment it was 1963, and Aretha's father, C. L. Franklin, was leading Martin Luther King up Woodward Avenue at the head of a giant crowd. Back then, no one could have imagined the Detroit of today. In that sense, they *had* overcome; self-determination was a fact of life. But there were other facts, too. Dr. King had been murdered by a racist, and Reverend Franklin by a criminal—victims of the polarities of black suffering. In 1989, no one was certain anymore who the real enemy was—them, or us.

No one, that is, but Coleman Young. He had built a black city-state in the heart of the American middle west, given his people a government that spoke their language, streets and parks named for their heroes, city jobs and contracts and more political control than blacks have ever had, anywhere, in North America. He had, more than any politician in the country, created a city in his own image.

The irony was that he, better than anyone, knew the terrible limitations of his achievement. The price of black control had been abandonment and antipathy. White people had taken their businesses and factories and fled; the motherfuckers had stolen the city's boots along with its bootstraps. It was this certainty—that the hostility of the white press, the white suburbs and, by extension, white America was ultimately responsible for the plight of his city and his people—that enabled the most powerful man in Detroit to hold Aretha Franklin's hand and, in a wobbly, off-key voice, to sing, with sincere defiance, "We Shall Overcome."

They sang "We Shall Overcome" at Tom Barrow's final rally, too, but with a different accent and a different meaning.

The rally, held on the eve of the election, began at Barrow's headquarters. Clusters of black-and-white balloons hung from the ceiling, and clusters of black-and-white supporters waited for the candidate's towering brother, Shorty, to form them into a line for the candlelight march up Woodward Avenue. One wall was dominated by a large placard: "God Bless America, Land of Opportunity."

Shorty, who bears a remarkable resemblance to Joe Louis, called "Hey-yo, hey-yo" and began herding the marchers to the door, where each was given a lit candle. Barrow, dressed in an open-collared striped shirt, blue blazer and gray slacks, led the procession. At his side was Reverend William Quick, the white pastor of the largely white Metropolitan United Methodist Church, where the rally was to take place.

Quick and Barrow marched four blocks up Woodward Avenue to the church, past vacant lots and boarded-up pawnshops. They sang as they went, "This little light of mine, I'm gonna make it shine," but there was no one to hear them; at 6:30 P.M., the sidewalks of Detroit's main street were deserted, and only a trickle of cars drove past.

The procession wound past the apartment building of the black grandmother who had been propositioned by Floyd at my cocktail party, almost a year before. Once, driving by Metropolitan United, she had pointed out the church, an imposing building that dominates a city block. "Every Sunday I see those white folks coming in from the suburbs to go to church," she said. "They come to thank God— they thank Him that they don't have to live next to niggers."

The Barrow crowd was thin enough to fit into the church's small sanctuary without filling up the balcony. Naturally, the rally began with a prayer, and then a middle-aged white woman in a white dress and thick glasses sang "Be Not Afraid" in a Joan Baez-like soprano, accompanied by an elderly white woman on the organ.

Reverend Quick kicked off the speeches with a rousing denunciation of Coleman Young and all his works. The litany of sins included buying off Quick's fellow divines. "Millions of dollars have gone to the churches," he declaimed. "Whatever happened to the separation of church and state?" The whites applauded but many of the blacks looked quizzical; they were mad at Coleman, after all, not at Jesus.

Quick was followed by another white minister, and then a black woman. "When the wicked are removed, the people rejoice," she quoted, bursting into tears. A collective "Aw" rose from the pews, and Barrow, on his way to the podium, hugged her.

Barrow's text that night was his usual message of responsibility and racial cooperation. "We're sick of crime, crack, hate and racism," he told the audience. "We're not going to blame the white folks. Nobody is going to save us from us but us . . ."

As he talked, several reporters in the balcony began to compare notes on the campaign. Judging by the rally, it seemed to me that Barrow had failed to galvanize much black support—the key to his strategy. But the others dissented. "Barrow says that he's only three points back," said a usually well-informed journalist. "He's got a poll, and I believe it. There's a hell of a lot of dissatisfaction out there." He took out a piece of paper and wrote "Coleman 51%, Barrow 49%." "And it could go the other way," he said.

" . . . In order for Detroit to come back, we've got to bring the community back together," yelled Barrow, coming to a close. "It's time to stop thinking about black and white, city and suburbs. We've got to work together. United, we can make this a great city again."

Reverend Quick came forward and held the candidate's hand high in the air. The two men began to sing "We Shall Overcome" in a flat tone. The Barrow partisans joined in—"Black and white together, black and white to-ge-he-ther," they sang, swaying gently in the pews. "Deep in my heart, I do believe, we shall overcome some day."

There was little doubt what the crowd had in mind; they intended to overcome Coleman Young, to liberate his liberated city, seize it from the forces of black self-determination and return it to America. Dr. King's heir, Jesse Jackson, had been with Young at New St. Paul's but his disciples, believers in assimilation and integration, were with the yuppie accountant at Metropolitan United Methodist.

Thus did the campaign of 1989 come to a close. Nominally it was a race for mayor of America's sixth largest city, but there was much more at stake than who would occupy the Manoogian mansion for the next four years. There had been talk about housing and education, crime and clean streets, but despite Barrow's best efforts, the city's quality of life was never the main issue. The election was really about the black state of mind in a place where blacks are free to express themselves without worrying about white people.

The campaign posed serious ideological questions that went far beyond the specifics of Detroit. What is the root cause of the desperate condition of African-America—black irresponsibility or white racism? What is the best way for African-Americans to progress—self-rule or a junior partnership with whites? Is defiant struggle merely an evolutionary step toward inclusion in the broader American polity—or is it, in the words of Ronald Hewitt, the best that blacks can hope for in the United States? In a very real sense, the election in Detroit was a referendum on the contemporary black interpretation of reality.

On election day, the voters of America's African-American capital returned their verdict, and it wasn't even close. Coleman Young was reelected by a margin of 56 percent to 44 percent, with almost 70 percent of the black vote (and only 13 percent of the whites). Detroit, the city with the country's highest rate of teenage murder, unemployment and depopulation, twelve thousand abandoned homes, a Third World infant mortality rate and an epidemic drug problem, had spoken: Four More Years.

That night, the citizens of the black polis came together to celebrate the fifth consecutive victory of Coleman Alexander Young.

Several thousand people packed Cobo Hall, the convention center on the river—executives with gleaming, gold-rimmed glasses and thousand-dollar suits and street people in jeans and torn sweaters; churchwomen wearing crosses large enough to frighten vampires and stylish ladies in ball gowns and glittering jewelry; aging auto workers sporting UAW jackets and young Muslims dressed in white robes and skullcaps. The mayor's rainbow coalition ranged from coal black to light tan—there weren't more than a couple of dozen whites at the celebration.

The Muslims and church ladies munched sedately on catered fried chicken while the others bellied up to the bar for drinks at $3.50 a shot. Giant speakers poured out r&b and several hundred young people did the electric boogie, moving together in coordinated lines like Fred Busby dancers. A young black reporter from the *News*, attending her first election night bash, surveyed the room with wonder. "The mayor sure knows how to throw a party," she said.

Close to midnight, "Respect" came blaring over the loudspeakers and Coleman Young took the stage, accompanied by an entourage that included a rotund black woman in a red dress. The crowd screamed "Four more years!" and the mayor smiled and waved. Then the woman, whose name was Gloria McKee, took the microphone and sang—"You're the best thing that ever happened to me." She finished to loud applause, and the mayor seized the microphone. "The lady has sung," he announced, and the room burst into appreciative laughter.

Suddenly Young turned serious and statesmanlike. "We should join in the spirit of democracy here by extending the hand of unity, brotherhood and friendship," he told his followers. "Let us all come forward together now and move this city forward. Let us join hands across Eight Mile Road. We can't make it without the suburbs, and they can't make it without us."

"He sounds like Tom Barrow tonight," I remarked to the *News* reporter. "He wants harmony with the white folks."

"There's only one difference," she said. "Coleman wants it on his terms."

That, indeed, was the difference, not only between Young and Barrow, but between him and the other two black candidates who won major victories that night. Young congratulated David Dinkins, for being elected mayor of New York, and L. Douglas Wilder, for winning the governorship of Virginia. Television pundits were already heralding them as harbingers of the new black politician— moderate, mainstream liberals, successful because they eschewed racial rhetoric. But in Detroit, they wouldn't have had a chance. In the city that has so often been the true bellwether of black America, Dinkins and Wilder were yesterday, not tomorrow.

A few days after the election, *News* columnist Chauncey Bailey, a thoughtful man whom Coleman Young once branded an Uncle Tom, explained why.

> Observers miss the point when they suggest that Young is less of a historical figure because he does not come across as "moderate" as do other African-American leaders now making inroads in less black cities, and is therefore out of step with a "new generation" of leadership.
>
> Only New York City and Chicago have more African-American residents than Detroit. New York is 25 percent African-American and has just elected its "first black" mayor. Chicago is 40 percent African-American but lost power when African-Americans showed disunity. Due to their racial makeups, leaders in those cities must be more moderate to win. But Detroit is where more big cities will be in coming decades. Young's legend will be the model, not a myth, that many will turn to.

Bailey's prediction reminded me of something I had heard more than a year earlier from Father William Cunningham, a very savvy white priest who has worked in the inner city for twenty years. "Detroit is the center of an American revolution," he had told me. "We're twenty years ahead of Chicago, forty years ahead of New

York City. God knows where we are in comparison to San Diego. In terms of civil rights, this is Broadway. There's no place else where black power has spoken like it has in this city. And what happens here will eventually happen in the rest of the country."

After his acceptance speech, Coleman Young met with the press in a small room off the main hall. He sat in an upholstered wing chair and the reporters gathered around him like eager children before a grumpy uncle. They had been through a long, bitter campaign, in which he had turned them into targets. Now they were clearly hoping that Young's conciliatory mood would lead to an armistice.

The old man seemed to be in a mellow mood. He told them that this was the happiest night of his life; every victory, he explained, is sweeter than the ones before. He smiled and they smiled back, glad to be sharing a pleasant moment.

"But aren't you a little bit disappointed by the results?" asked a young black newsman. Suddenly, the mayor bristled.

"What the hell you talkin' about?" he demanded. "I won, didn't I?"

The reporter was taken aback by his tone, but he persisted. "Yes, but, I mean, you didn't do quite as well this time as you did in the past . . ."

"Do you know what I got in the past?" Young demanded.

"Yes sir," said the reporter, assuming the question to be rhetorical. "And I wanted to know—"

"Well, what did I get?" Young demanded. "How many votes did I get in previous elections?"

The reporter stood in embarrassed silence and his colleagues regarded him nervously. They were sympathetic, but they didn't want to get into this particular confrontation. Finally he spoke. "Ah, last time I believe you got, ah, seventy percent or so."

"Man, I didn't get any seventy percent," snapped the mayor.

"You don't know what the hell I got, do you? Do you?" The report-er's silence infuriated Young. "Well, do you?" he almost shouted. The reporter shrugged.

"You don't," said Young. No matter how much he won, "they" were always trying to take it away. "The press tried to brainwash us in this election, and we refused to be brainwashed," he snapped.

The assembled journalists stood there looking glum and confused. Coleman wasn't their grumpy uncle; he was no kind of uncle at all. Even on the happiest night of his life, he was an angry black man and they were the paid representatives of the enemy. It would be a long four years.

A white television reporter gave it one more try. "Come on, Mr. Mayor," she cajoled with a bright, girlish smile. "You know you really love us."

Young regarded her in stony silence. "Well, kinda love us?" she pleaded in an uncertain voice.

The mayor stared for a long moment at the white lady begging for absolution. There was a lifetime in that pause, seventy-one years of humiliations, army stockades, unemployment, government harassment . . . and victory. Finally, in spite of himself, he laughed. "Kinda," he said. "Yeah, kinda."

Epilogue

CHARLES

I was almost ready to go home, but there was one more thing I wanted to do. I wanted to find Charles.

Throughout my stay in Detroit, he had been on my mind. The kids I met reminded me of him as he had been, the middle-aged men made me wonder what he would be like now. I couldn't walk past the ramshackle houses of the east side without thinking of his mother's old place in the projects, crowded with crying children and smelling of wet walls, fatback and beans. Old songs on the radio brought back dances we had gone to, girls we had liked. I had spent a year on America's Corner, and I had missed Charles out there.

Still, something had kept me from looking for him. The last time we met, in that miserable flophouse on Twelfth street, he had been a scared kid on the run from the law, and I was afraid to find out what had happened to him. I had seen too many black men our age, beaten down and defeated, to be optimistic. There was another thing, too. Over the years, Charles had loomed large in my imagination; he had become almost a legendary figure, so much so that I sometimes wondered if I had invented him. I wasn't sure he would remember me, or want to remember.

One day I told Kim Weston about Charles. "I wish I could find him, but I have no idea where he is," I said. "He's not in the phone book. I don't even know if he's alive."

"I'll find him for you," she said, and she did.

From an old friend at the Pontiac City Hall she learned that Charles was still living in town. He had an unlisted number, which she wouldn't give out without permission, but she promised to call him and ask if it would be all right. A few minutes later the phone rang. "Here's the number," said the lady from City Hall. "He's waiting for your call."

I took a long time before dialing, phrasing in my own mind what I wanted to say. At our last meeting I had confronted Charles as an indignant victim and treated him like a common thief. I could still recall the cold, righteous fury with which I took back my pawn tickets, and the secret relief I felt at being given a reason to turn my back on him and his poor black problems.

But the years since then—especially the last one, in Detroit—had taught me about the pressures and terrors of living without a margin of error. In principle, I had been right to confront Charles; but I had learned that being right isn't always the most important thing. I wanted, across a gap of almost a quarter century, to apologize to him for the cruel, callous teenager I had been.

I finally dialed the number and he picked it up on the first ring. "Charles?" I asked. I didn't know what to say. I felt as if I were talking to a ghost. "Do you remember me?"

"Oh man," he said in his familiar, high-pitched voice. "Oh man, it's you. I've been waiting twenty-three years to tell you how sorry

I am." His voice broke. "I've been praying that I'd get a chance to do that."

Charles gave me his address in a part of town I didn't know, near the Silverdome. On the way out there I played our phone conversation over in my mind. I had been ready for almost anything—anger, disdain, indifference—but not remorse. It made me uneasy. Life must have been very hard on him, I thought. As I approached his neighborhood I steeled myself, expecting the worst.

Charles's home was a neat, white, two-story frame house on a quiet, gently rolling street—not at all what I had expected. A late-model Ford van was parked in the driveway. I rang the bell for a long time but no one answered and I wondered if I had come to the wrong place. Then an elderly white man who was raking leaves across the street called out: "If you're looking for Charles, he's around back."

I walked down the narrow driveway past the house. A basketball rim was attached to the garage, and it reminded me of our first meeting, Charles leaping in the air and stuffing the ball. I wonder if he can still dunk, I thought incongruously, and tucked in my gut.

I saw Charles before he saw me. He was sitting on a picnic bench in his large, freshly mowed backyard, drinking a cup of coffee. Under a Detroit Tigers cap his face was rounder than I remembered it, but otherwise he looked the same. On the table next to him, a radio played Ruby and the Romantics' "Our Day Will Come."

"Hey, Charles," I called. He turned, grinned, rose with an effort and began walking toward me with a pronounced limp. The sentimental greeting I had prepared vanished. Suddenly I was fifteen again.

"Charles," I said, "you got fat."

"Yeah, so did you," he said. "Oglier, too." He was twenty feet away.

"You walk like Chester from *Gunsmoke*," I said, playing the dozens the way we used to. "You couldn't dunk a donut."

"Man, you all gray," he replied with mock anger. "Look at your beard, you look like a damn rabbi." We met in the driveway and he grabbed me around the shoulders, lifting me off the ground. "Got-damn, man, it's really you," he said. When he picked me up his hat fell off, exposing a bald head.

"You lost all your hair!" I said, laughing. "You're an old man."

"That's cool," he said, laughing too. "Ain't no woman ever asked me for no hair. And Bill," he said, using my American name, suddenly serious, "I'm a grandfather now."

Charles's flight from the law ended with capture; he had spent thirty months in a federal prison in Milan, Michigan. When he got out he married the girl who had been with him that night in Detroit. They were still married, with five children. Charles took their pictures out of his wallet.

"They're my pride and joy," he said. "This is my oldest boy, the one that Kathy was carrying that night. These are my son and daughter, they're both in high school. This little girl is in junior high, and this is my baby, he's in the sixth grade." Charles beamed as he handed me the photos. I searched their faces for the wild, fierce young man Charles had been, but there was no trace of him there; these were pictures of secure, happy children.

"They look like great kids," I said. "They must take after their mother."

Charles smiled. "They do take after her. She's a real fine woman. But they know they got a father, too," he said in a quiet, serious voice.

"Did any of them inherit your athletic ability?" I said.

"My youngest boy is a football player," Charles said, "but I don't care nothin' about football. I tell these kids that sports don't mean a damn thing. I want to see grades. They all A and B students, Bill, all my kids. My daughter's going to Spellman next year. They not gonna need no athletic scholarships. Their dad got money saved up to put all those kids through college."

When he got out of jail, Charles went to work in an auto plant, and later took a job as an orderly in a mental hospital. He had been there fifteen years. "It can get rough out there—I got this limp when a patient kicked me in the hip," he said. "But he couldn't help it, he was sick. Some of these patients don't have anyone to visit them. They don't have any money. Sometimes I buy them a hamburger, or some cigarettes. Someday I'm going to have to meet God, and I want to be able to say I did somebody some good down here, that I did my best."

"Don't tell me you've got religion in your old age," I joked.

Charles shook his head. "My wife does most of the churchgoing," he said. "She takes the kids, every Sunday. But I believe in God, and I know right from wrong. And so do my children." He looked at me with brown, serious eyes. It was as close as we got that day to discussing what had happened between us. Charles, my old mentor from The Corner, was giving me one last lesson about black people: not to expect too little.

"You got any kids, Bill?" he asked.

"Two," I said. "I'm divorced now."

"You take care of those kids, Bill," he said in the tone he once used to tell me to do my homework. "You take care of them, be a father. That's the most important thing."

"Come on, Charles," I said. "I don't need you to tell me that."

He grinned, the old Charles. "I'm still older than you, and badder than you," he said. "I can still tell you what to do, and I can still beat your bootie to make you do it, too. I don't care how many gray rabbi-ass beards you got."

Charles and I sat for a couple of hours on the picnic bench, drinking bourbon out of tall glasses and talking about old times. A lot of the kids we had gone to school with were dead; others were in trouble with drugs or in jail. He shook his head at their folly, and at his own good fortune. We both knew that he could have been them.

"I wouldn't be twenty years old again for anything," he said. "I was so confused all the time, it was pitiful. I didn't have nobody to turn to for help, you know? I needed a father. I only saw mine twice, once when I was seven years old, and again just before he died. I always envied you for having a father," he said.

"How did you know how to be a father?" I asked.

"Instinct," he said. "I knew what I wanted and what I needed, and that's what I've tried to be for my children. When you don't have a model, you just got to make things up as you go along."

One of Charles's sons came back to visit us. He wore steel-rimmed glasses that gave him a mild, scholarly look and a black-and-orange high school jacket. "Say hello to Mr. Chafets, son," Charles said. "He's an old, old friend."

"Hello, Mr. Chafets," the boy said, shaking hands self-consciously. "I know who you are. You live in Israel. Dad has an article about you from one of the newspapers. He keeps it upstairs in his bedroom. He said that someday you'd come to visit." He turned to Charles. "Dad, what's for dinner?"

"I'll fix you something when I get home, son," he said. "First, I got to pick up your brother from football practice."

The sun was going down when we got back from picking up Charles's son. The two of us sat in the backyard, drinking the last of the bourbon. "Charles," I asked, "did you ever wonder what your life would have been like if you weren't black?"

"Sure I wonder," he said. "You wonder about all kinds of things. It's a disadvantage, no doubt about that. There's still a hell of a lot of discrimination in the world. My children got opportunities I never dreamed about, but opportunities don't mean nothing if you can't take advantage of them. And everybody, black or white, needs some help to do that."

Charles gazed at the large vacant lot just beyond his chain link fence. "Someday I'm going to buy that property," he said, "and the first thing I'm going to do is have a family reunion. I dream of that, right back there."

He gestured with his eyes to a large black metal smoker next to the garage. "I'll be over here cooking bar-be-cue—and you know I can cook some bar-be-cue—and my children and grandchildren will be gathered all around. They'll even come up here from Georgia. Then at night, everybody will be sleeping in the house, and we'll all be together. Won't that be a motherfucker, though; won't that be a stone motherfucker?"

"You've done fine, haven't you, Charles?" I said. I was feeling the bourbon, and the long, happy day we had spent together.

"Yes I have, Bill," he said, looking in the direction of his cozy house, where his kids were doing their homework. "It took me some time, and it hasn't been easy, but yeah, got-dammit, thank God, I've made it over."

ABOUT THE AUTHOR

ZE'EV CHAFETS was born in Pontiac, Michigan, and moved to Israel at the age of twenty in 1967. He is the author of *Double Vision, Heroes and Hustlers, Hard Hats and Holy Men,* and *Members of the Tribe.* He lives in Tel Aviv, Israel.